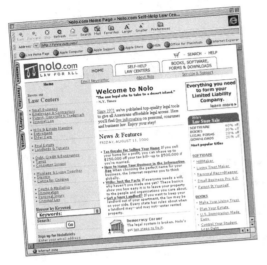

Read This First

The information in this book is as up to date and accurate as we can make it. But it's important to realize that the law changes frequently, as do fees, forms and procedures. If you handle your own legal matters, it's up to you to be sure that all information you use—including the information in this book—is accurate. Here are some suggestions to help you:

First, make sure you've got the most recent edition of this book. To learn whether a later edition is available, check the edition number on the book's spine and then go to Nolo's online Law Store at www.nolo.com or call Nolo's Customer Service Department at 800-728-3555.

Next, even if you have a current edition, you need to be sure it's fully up to date. The law can change overnight. At www.nolo.com, we post notices of major legal and practical changes that affect the latest edition of a book. To check for updates, find your book in the Law Store on Nolo's website (you can use the "A to Z Product List" and click the book's title). If you see an "Updates" link on the left side of the page, click it. If you don't see a link, that means we haven't posted any updates. (But check back regularly.)

Finally, we believe accurate and current legal information should help you solve many of your own legal problems on a cost-efficient basis. But this text is not a substitute for personalized advice from a knowledgeable lawyer. If you want the help of a trained professional, consult an attorney licensed to practice in your state.

6th edition

The Partnership Book

How to Write a Partnership Agreement

by Attorneys Denis Clifford & Ralph Warner

SIXTH EDITION

Third Printing	July 2003
COVER DESIGN	Toni Ihara
EDITOR	Diana Fitzpatrick
BOOK DESIGN	Terri Hearsh
PRODUCTION	Sarah Hinman
CD-ROM PREPARATION	André Zivkovich
ILLUSTRATOR	Linda Allison
INDEX	Thérèse Shere
PROOFREADING	Sheryl Rose
PRINTING	Consolidated Printers, Inc.

Clifford, Denis.
    The partnership book : how to write a partnership agreement / by Denis Clifford &
Ralph Warner. -- 6th ed.
        p.   cm.
    Includes index.
    ISBN 0-87337-560-2
    1. Partnership--United States--Popular works. 2. Articles of partnership--United
States--Popular works.   I. Title II. Warner, Ralph E.

KF1375.Z9 C55   2000
346.73'0682 21--dc21   99-046091

For information on bulk purchases or corporate premium sales, please contact the Special Sales Department. For academic sales or textbook adoptions, ask for Academic Sales. Call 800-955-4775 or write to Nolo, 950 Parker Street, Berkeley, CA 94710.

Acknowledgments

Putting together this Sixth Edition of *The Partnership Book* was a surprisingly big, and humbling, job. Without the help of many people, we would have produced a less thorough and less readable book, and had much less fun preparing it. So our gratitude and thanks to the following friends:

First, to our current editor, Diana Fitzpatrick, for her thorough editing of this printing, and to André Zivkovich, for his work with the forms on disk.

Second, we want to express our deep appreciation to all those who've helped in many editions of this book, all our previous editors, and Terri Hearsh, who laid out the manuscript with professional skill and a keen editor's eye. Next, to Kit Duane, an excellent editor, superb writer and great friend. Moving on, several lawyer friends and partnership experts who graciously gave us considerable time to discuss what they (and we) have learned about partnerships: Lawrence A. Baskin, San Rafael, California; Dick Duane, of Duane, Lyman & Seltzer, Berkeley, California; Hayden Curry, Oakland, California; Marvin Cherrin, Oakland, California; Tom Fike, Oakland, California; and Steve Antler, Fort Bragg, California. And several business friends who also greatly aided us in updating our understanding of partnerships: Ray Castor, Carla Jupiter, Steve Clifford and Carol Kizziah. Also of great help have been the many thoughtful readers who've written us of their experiences forming partnerships. We've used many of these readers' suggestions to expand and deepen our coverage of partnership concerns in this edition.

Next, we want to thank our wonderful gang at Nolo, a truly unique place to work. Even though we've grown too large to acknowledge the names of each of Nolo's over eighty employees, each one is part of the Nolo family and contributes to making Nolo work. Collectively, they make it possible for us to bring you this book. In addition, we want to specifically thank a few Noloids who personally assisted with the editing and preparation of previous editions of the manuscript: Stephanie Harolde, Tony Mancuso, Barbara Hodovon and Ann Heron.

Finally, we want to express our continued appreciation to others who helped us on previous editions: Bill Petrocelli, Marilyn Putnam, Brad Bunin, Patti Unterman, Chris Cunningham, Christie Rigg, Walter Warner, John Larimore and two partnership experts for suggestions for improvements to the second edition—Roger Pritchard, a Berkeley, California small business advisor, and Attorney Elisse Brown of Oakland. And maniacal thanks to our favorite sharp-penciled accountants: Margo Miller, of San Francisco, tax expert for small business owners; Bernard "Bear" Kamoroff, author of *Small Time Operator*; and Malcolm Roberts, Berkeley, another tax wiz.

About the Authors

Denis Clifford is a lawyer who has worked with many partnerships and was a law partner in Clifford, Curry & Cherrin. He is the author of several other Nolo books, including *Plan Your Estate* and *Make Your Own Living Trust*. A graduate of Columbia Law School, where he was an editor of *The Law Review*, he has practiced law in various ways and became convinced that people can do much of the legal work they need themselves.

Ralph Warner is one of the pioneers of the modern American self-help law movement. He has a license to practice law but doesn't use it. Instead, through books, lectures and workshops, he teaches non-lawyers to handle everyday legal problems. He has been involved in two partnerships, has successfully started several small businesses and has talked with a number of small business people about the legal intricacies of getting their enterprise started.

Table of Contents

3 Partnership Name, Contributions, Profits and Management

4 Changes and Growth of Your Partnership

5 Changes: Departure of a Partner, Buy-Outs and Business Continuation

6 Partnership Disputes: Mediation and Arbitration

11 Drafting Your Own Partnership Agreement

Appendix 1

Resources

Appendix 2

How to Use the CD-ROM

Appendix 3

Partnership Agreements

Index

Introduction

A. Partnership: Dream and Reality

If you're considering going into business with a friend or several friends, you're joining in a basic American dream—running your own show, being your own boss and hopefully gaining some control over your economic destiny. Shared ownership of a business has many benefits. The chemistry and spirit of two, three or more minds working together can often produce exciting results. There's more energy and enthusiasm, and—at least as important—more cash, skills and resources. And it's a lot easier to arrange for time off if you have partners than if you're trying to run a business all by yourself.

But for all of those who dream of doing their own thing—and who hasn't?—only a relatively small number will be committed (or nutty) enough to invest the love and labor necessary to get a small business off the ground. Those who do will almost inevitably go through periods of stress, and their survival will depend on their ability to quickly and competently master all sorts of unfamiliar skills and tasks. In a partnership business, there are also the stresses and risks that can come with shared ownership. Money can be incendiary stuff, and when you share making money with business partners, you need to make sure you're willing and able to become involved that intimately with each other.

B. If You're Planning to Start a Partnership, Or Even Considering One, This Book Is for You

To understand how a partnership works, you need to understand its legal nature. In this book we'll answer many of your questions about the basic choices for a shared-ownership business, including other legal forms you might consider, such as corporations and limited liability companies. Once you understand these basics, and assuming you decide to go ahead with your partnership, we'll show you how to create a written partnership agreement that fits your needs.

Of course, we can't advise you on the most fundamental aspects of your business—the product or service that you'll sell, and who to pick for partners (except to caution you to be as sure as you can that they're people you trust), but if you've come up with the brilliant idea for your business and the people who share that dream, this book can help you translate that dream into a reality.

C. Do You Really Need a Partnership Agreement?

Idealistic friends have asked, "Do we really need a formal partnership agreement? Why bother with the paperwork if honesty, good faith and trust are what really matter? Can't we just work on a handshake?" Our answer is that while we'd all like life to be so utopian that nothing ever needs to be written down, we've learned that effective, harmonious business relationships depend in large measure on good planning and attention to detail. Writing a commonsense partnership agreement is an important part of this process; it's much more prudent to create a written record of an understanding than to rely on all-too-fallible human memory.

Also, despite the fact that even the most astute businesspeople won't be able to foresee what will happen to the business, it makes sense to draft a partnership agreement to anticipate and plan for all the future possibilities you can sensibly consider now, such as what will happen if a partner leaves. Finally, and often most importantly, getting down to specifics about what each potential partner expects and will agree to can help you and your future partners evaluate whether you'll actually be able to share running a business. If you can work together to create a solid agreement, you're off to a fine start. If you can't work it out, at least you can stop the process now, before you've all become enmeshed.

Keep in mind as you prepare your partnership agreement that in your business future, many problems can arise: You may need more capital to expand or pay debts; you may consider adding new partners; one partner may quit or wish to sell her share; a partner may become disabled or die, leaving her interest to a spouse and children. Putting together a partnership agreement allows you to discuss your plans for these sorts of possibilities; at the same time it gives you a chance to test whether you're all comfortable working with each other around questions of power and money. If you aren't, you'll save yourself immense future pain and trouble by bailing out now.

D. Creating a Partnership Agreement

The purpose of this book is to enable you to create your own partnership agreement. We include many sample clauses and detailed instructions on how to use them. If you have a computer with a word processor, use the CD-ROM that comes with this book to draft your agreement. (See Chapter 11 and Appendix 2 for more information on putting your agreement together.) Both authors have been members of partnerships, and we've learned that the clauses used to create a partnership can't (or shouldn't) be viewed in isolation from real life. So, along with explanations of these sample clauses, we discuss how partnerships work in the actual business world.

This book has been available for 20 years. In this 6th edition, we've brought the book up-to-date with the latest legal developments affecting partnerships and with current issues that may come up when forming a partnership. In doing this, we have been greatly aided by the many perceptive comments and helpful suggestions from readers of earlier editions. Also, friends of ours who run small businesses have learned valuable (and sometimes painful) lessons and have passed along their suggestions. Other friends who advise small businesses, as

either lawyers or other experts, have also lent a hand. And since in our own writing and business relationship at Nolo, we function as a kind of partnership, we've learned first hand a few of the practical, day-to-day lessons that only experience can teach. We've drawn from all these resources to include the best and most helpful illustrations of how partnerships function in the real world, where you'll have to meet payroll, pay your taxes and the shiny new coffee machine is useless unless someone remembers to buy the coffee.

Although we are confident that this book will be an invaluable tool in helping you prepare a sound partnership agreement, we have to caution you about a few things. We can't tell you precisely what you should put in your partnership agreement; you, and you alone, must resolve how you want to structure and operate your business. Instead, our role is to inform you of the legal and practical issues generally covered in partnership agreements and to present various methods for handling each. It's vital that all would-be partners understand and discuss these basic issues, air their own views, resolve any conflicts and reach an understanding. In some circumstances, this will necessarily involve getting help, beyond what we provide in this book, from an accountant, lawyer or other expert. Once you've resolved what you want your partnership to accomplish, writing up your formal agreement won't be difficult.

E. How to Use This Book

This is a workbook. It covers each major aspect of preparing a partnership agreement, from deciding if the partnership form is best for your business to basic issues we believe should be resolved in every partnership agreement. Throughout the text, we present and explain various clauses you can include in your agreement to handle these issues. Finally, we take you step-by-step through the process of putting your own partnership agreement together.

One practical suggestion: As you read through the book, expect minor attacks of bewilderment. A partnership agreement is not something you throw together in a day. You don't have to grasp every detail the first time through. Start by reading the entire book to get a rough understanding of what's involved, making a few notes as to clauses or provisions that seem particularly applicable to you. Allow plenty of time for discussions with your partners. Then go back, focus on the areas of most concern and begin to pin down exactly what you want in your agreement.

Icons Used in This Book

Throughout this book, these icons alert you to certain information.

 Tip. A legal or commonsense tip to help you understand or comply with legal requirements.

 Warning. A caution to slow down and consider potential problems.

 See an Expert. A suggestion to seek the advice of an attorney or tax expert.

 Recommended Reading. A suggestion to consult another legal or tax resource.

 Cross-Reference. This icon refers you to a further discussion of the topic elsewhere in the book.

 Form on CD-ROM. The form discussed in the text is on the Forms CD included with this book and a tear-out copy is in Appendix 3.

Companion CD-ROM

Included at the back of this book is a CD-ROM containing files with word processing (rich text format) versions of the clauses contained in the tear-out partnership agreement in Appendix 3. For specific instructions on using the CD-ROM, see Appendix 2.

Macintosh Users: Most new Macintosh computers can also read the enclosed CD-ROM.

F. A Personal Note

Before we get into the nitty-gritty of starting and operating a partnership and drafting a partnership agreement, we want to include a few personal words. Both of the authors of this book grew up on the East Coast, went off to college and emerged, like so many others, unsure about "what we wanted to do." We considered lots of choices; both of us drifted to law school with the vague hope that the law would give us some skills useful in making the world a better place. How we each became disillusioned with that dream is another story; the point here is that through all of our dreaming and planning, neither of us ever imagined that we'd wind up as proprietors of small businesses, full-fledged members of the "free enterprise system." But that's what happened. We've experienced both great satisfaction and some very real pain in running our own shops. We've been through our complete beginner stage and have made most of the routine mistakes, as well as pioneering some lulus. Somehow, we've survived it all to realize that doing our own thing at Nolo gives us a sense of freedom and self-worth, and at the same time we make a good living—a combination that's hard to match in this increasingly bureaucratized world.

We know we are not alone in finding a measure of satisfaction in jointly participating in a small business. In the process of putting this book together, we talked to many people who have successfully created their own small business partnerships. We've been told time and again about the satisfaction, and even joy, derived from providing a product or service that genuinely interests the provider and benefits the consumer. We've also learned a lot about how people relate to—and may even gain some satisfaction from—the tough competition that's so much a part of the world of small business, where survival depends on your offering something that people really want and need. And most of all, we've been reminded constantly that although money is important, it's not usually the primary reason people organize their own businesses. It's gratifying to talk with partners more concerned with the quality of work and a sensible life than the top dollar. Happily, we've found that integrity and creativity—even altruism—are alive and well in small business America. ■

Getting Started— Choosing a Business Structure

You're ready to get serious. Whatever your great idea—a store, a product, a service—you want to get your business going. Or, if you've already started in a small way, you've realized it's time to pin things down and formally establish your business. One of your first decisions is what the business structure of your enterprise will be. What legal form is best for you? To decide this sensibly, you need to understand the consequences of choosing one structure rather than another.

A. Your Choices

There are five common legal forms of business ownership:

- partnership
- sole proprietorship
- corporation
- limited liability company, and
- limited partnership.

(Some states have distinct subcategories of these five, especially partnerships. For example, there's a creature called a "mining partnership" used for mining and oil ventures in some states. In this chapter, we'll just concern ourselves with the basic forms.)

To help you choose the business structure that best suits your needs, in this chapter we discuss the legal and practical realities of each one. Of course, our emphasis is on the partnership form, but don't assume that it must be the right one for you without exploring your alternatives. We've received cards from readers of earlier editions telling us that after reading these materials, they decided to form a small corporation or a sole proprietorship. That's great; the time to consider your options is here at the start. Once you've created your legal form, it takes a fair amount of time and trouble to change it.

Common Sense, Competence and Trust

Before considering the details of business structures, we want to note that if you decide on shared ownership, the most important assets of any shared business are the co-owners' competence, determination to work hard and the trust they have in one another, not matters having to do with legal forms. No written agreement will help if the people you plan to work with are not honorable and hardworking. Second, these key realities, so important to whether a shared ownership business will prosper, remain the same whether you choose a partnership, a small corporation, a limited liability company or even a sole proprietorship with a profit-sharing agreement for key employees.

B. Partnerships

In this section, we give you a quick look at the nature of partnerships, so that you can compare them to corporations and sole proprietorships. Then, later in this chapter, we'll explore the partnership legal form in more depth.

Here are five key points about partnerships:

1. A partnership is a business owned by two or more people.

2. Each partner can perform all acts that are necessary to operate the business, including hiring employees and spending or borrowing money. (However, there may be some limitations on a partner's authority; see Section H3 of this chapter.) Each partner is personally liable for all debts incurred by the business. This is one vital reason why your partners must be trustworthy. If a creditor has a claim against your partnership and the partnership

assets are insufficient to satisfy that claim, the personal assets of any partner can be taken to pay the business debts.

3. Partners share in profits or losses, in whatever proportion they've agreed on. Partnerships themselves don't pay taxes (although they do file an annual tax form). The partners report their share of (partnership) profits or losses on their individual tax returns, as part of their regular income.

4. Partnerships begin when two or more people form a business. Although technically a partnership ends if one partner leaves, you can agree at the beginning that the partnership business will continue, to be run by the remaining partners, if there are any. If you want the business to continue if a partner leaves—and almost all partnerships work this way—you'll need to work out what will happen to the interest of the departing partner. Who can, or must, buy that interest? How will you determine a fair price for that interest? (See Chapter 5.)

History Lesson # 1

Partnerships date to the beginning of recorded history. References are made to partnerships in the Babylonian Code of Hammurabi, approximately 2300 B.C. The Jews, around 2000 B.C., a pastoral (not a commercial) people, evolved a form of landsharing or grazing partnership called a "shutolin." Later, commercial Jewish partnerships evolved from trading caravans.

---

5. The owners normally have a written partnership agreement specifying their respective rights and responsibilities. The purpose of this agreement is to cover all major issues that may affect the partnership, from the manner of dividing profits and losses to management

of the business to buy-out provisions in case a partner leaves or dies. This agreement does not have to be filed with any government agency, and no official approval is required to start the partnership. (There are different rules for limited partnerships. See Section G of this chapter, and Chapter 9.)

C. The Sole Proprietorship

A sole proprietor means, as the words say, that there's one single owner of the business. This owner may hire (and fire) employees. She may also even arrange for employees to receive a percentage of the business profits as part of their wages, but she remains the sole owner. The owner—and the owner alone—is personally liable for all the debts, taxes and liabilities of the business, including claims made against employees acting in the course and scope of their employment. The business does not pay taxes as an entity; instead, the owner reports and pays taxes on the profits of the business on her own individual income tax returns.

A good source of information on how to start and operate a small sole proprietorship is Small Time Operator, *by Bernard Kamoroff (Bell Springs). Also helpful are* The Small Business Start-Up Kit, *by Peri Pakroo,* Legal Guide for Starting and Running a Small Business, *by Fred Steingold, and* Quicken Legal Business Pro *(software), all by Nolo.*

1. Personality Traits and the Sole Proprietorship

Quite simply, the main advantage of a sole proprietorship is that there is only one boss (you), so potential managerial conflicts are eliminated, except for your inner ones. The disadvantages stem from the same reality as the advantages—there is only you as owner and boss. If you get sick, want time off or simply want to share the responsibility of decision-making with someone else, you won't have a lot of flexibility.

Deciding to be the only boss is often a question of temperament. Some people like, and need, to run the whole show and always chafe in a shared ownership situation, while others want, need or at least appreciate the resources and strengths, from cash to camaraderie, that co-owners can bring. The best advice we can give you here is that old axiom—know thyself.

2. Sole Proprietorship Compared With Shared Ownership

In deciding whether to operate a business as a sole proprietorship or adopt a form of shared ownership such as a partnership, a business organizer may be inclined to choose shared ownership because she wants to involve key employees in the future of the business. While it may make great sense to allow important employees to become co-owners, either as partners or stockholders, this is not the only way to reward dedicated and talented employees. A profit-sharing agreement within the framework of the sole proprietorship may be a good alternative approach, at least until you see if you and the key employees are compatible over the long term.

> **EXAMPLE 1:** Eric is a self-employed architect. He gets a big job and advertises for help, soon hiring Frank and Samantha to assist with the drafting. Halfway through the new job, things are working so well that Eric decides to bid on an even larger job. He knows that to complete this new job successfully, he'll have to depend a great deal on his two assistants. Eric first considers making Frank and Samantha junior partners. However, because he has only known them for a few months, and because Samantha is pondering moving to the other side of the country, Eric decides that it makes more sense to put off the partnership decision and offer each 15% of his profit on the deal, over and above their regular salary.

> **EXAMPLE 2:** Susan decides to open a sandwich shop near a busy college campus. She wants her friend Ellen to work with real enthusiasm but, because money is short, can only pay her a modest salary to start. To insure Ellen's continued dedication, Susan offers her a bonus of a profit-sharing agreement under which Ellen gets 25% of all net profits.

3. Terminating a Sole Proprietorship

When the owner dies, a sole proprietorship ends. By contrast, in theory at least, a partnership, a small corporation or a limited liability company can continue under the direction of the surviving owners. Practically, however, a sole proprietor who wants his business to continue beyond his death can leave the remaining assets (after paying off its debts, of course) to whomever he chooses.

⚠️ **Sole proprietors need to plan for probate.**
If the owner of a sole proprietorship leaves business assets through the owner's will, the probate process can take up to a year and can make it difficult for the inheritors either to operate or sell the business (or any of its assets). To avoid this, small business owners should consider transferring the business into a living trust, a legal device which avoids probate and allows the assets to be transferred to the inheritors promptly. (For more information on creating a living trust for a business, see Plan Your Estate, *by Denis Clifford and Cora Jordan (Nolo).)*

D. Corporations

A corporation is a legal entity separate from its owners, who are its shareholders. Traditionally, the chief attraction of running a small business as a cor-

poration is that the shareholder owners enjoy limited personal liability for business debts or obligations. This means that normally the most each shareholder can be liable for, or lose, is the amount of her investment in the corporation. Other assets, such as the owners' houses and investments, can't be grabbed to pay business debts.

Because of the recent development of what is called a "limited liability company" (LLC), discussed in the next section, the corporate form of ownership has lost much of its appeal for shared owners of a small business. This is because limited liability companies also offer owners limited personal liability at the same time that, for many small businesses, they avoid some of the drawbacks of organizing either as a partnership or a corporation. We examine those drawbacks in Section F, below. Here we'll take a brief closer look at how the corporate form works.

In theory, a corporation involves three groups: those who direct the business (directors), those who run the business (officers) and those who invest in it (shareholders). In the case of a small business corporation, these three groups are often one and the same person. Indeed, one-person corporations are legal and common in many states.

A corporation is created by filing articles of incorporation with the appropriate state agency, usu-ally the Secretary or Department of State. Once this is done, the corporation comes into legal existence. The directors are responsible for the overall supervision of the business. The officers (president or chief executive officer (CEO), vice president, treasurer and secretary) are in charge of the day-to-day operation of the business. The shareholders are the owners, who have invested in the business by buying stock.

The directors normally adopt bylaws of the corporation, which cover the basic rules of how the business will actually operate. Practically speaking, for a small business, corporate bylaws can serve the same purpose as a partnership agreement. However, many shareholders of small corporations also enter into a shareholders' agreement, which usually spells out the circumstances under which a shareholder may sell his or her stock and describes what happens to a shareholder's shares if he or she dies, becomes disabled, gets divorced or retires.

Unlike partnerships, sole proprietorships and LLCs, corporations must also hold formal director and shareholder meetings and document major corporate decisions in corporate minutes. If corporations don't hold these meetings or prepare records of these corporate decisions, the owners risk losing their limited liability.

Corporations are taxed first at the business entity level and, then again, when corporate owners pay personal income tax on corporate profits distributed to them. But as discussed in Section F, below, this double taxation can be minimized or avoided if the owners pay out profits to themselves as tax deductible salaries and benefits.

Corporations, as we know them, have evolved in the last 150 years as the major organizational form through which large-scale international capitalism does business. Because corporations seem to be such a grown-up, big-time way of doing business, some people starting a small business are convinced that they, too, need a corporation—or at least that there must be great advantages to doing business in corporate form.

As we discuss in depth in Section F, below, for many new owners of small businesses, immediately forming a corporation isn't necessary; usually the corporate form of doing business provides no real advantage over a partnership or limited liability company and sometimes can be disadvantageous. And remember, whichever legal ownership form you decide upon, you'll have to resolve the same basic issues regarding power between the owners.

E. The Limited Liability Company

There's a relatively new legal animal in the business world, called a "limited liability company," commonly abbreviated "LLC." This business entity is now available in every state. And in every state except Massachusetts, an LLC only needs one member, so even sole proprietors now have the option of structuring their businesses as LLCs.

This new form attempts to blend many of the benefits of a partnership and a corporation. The business can choose to be treated as a partnership, taxwise, which means all profits are taxed at the individual level rather than the business level. But LLCs also permit owners to obtain a key attraction of a corporation—limited liability. An LLC owner's personal assets cannot be taken to pay business debts. However, LLCs are generally not required to observe the same formalities as a corporation—they don't have to elect directors, hold annual shareholders meetings or even prepare formal minutes of meetings or business decisions, unless they agree to do so in writing.

To form an LLC, the owners prepare articles of organization, a document quite similar in form and content to corporate articles of incorporation. Articles of organization typically cover basic facts, such as the LLC name, principal office address, agent and office for receiving legal papers, and the names of the initial owners.

An LLC's articles of organization must be filed with the appropriate state agency, usually the Department or Secretary of State's office. In a few states, you must also pay a fee, which can range from about $200 to as much as $800, depending on the state. Most states also require an LLC to file an annual form or report. (This is in addition to state required LLC income tax returns, discussed below.) Further, a number of states impose annual fees on LLCs and a few impose annual franchise taxes.

Like a partnership, an LLC also should have a written agreement (called an "operating agreement"), which defines the basic rights and responsibilities of the LLC owners. To prepare a sound operating agreement, LLC owners must deal with the same issues as partners preparing a partnership agreement, including how much capital each member will contribute to get the business going, how much each person will work for the business, to whom departing members can sell their share of the business and how that share is to be valued.

 All the forms and information you need to create an LLC are contained in Form Your Own Limited Liability Company, *by Anthony Mancuso (Nolo). Nolo also publishes* LLC Maker, *by Anthony Mancuso, a computer program that automates the process of creating a limited liability company in all 50 states.*

Like shareholders of a corporation, the owners of an LLC generally are not liable for company debts beyond the amount each has invested in the company. However, unlike a corporation, an LLC is not subject to income tax as a business entity unless its owners choose to be taxed this way. Usually, owners choose to be treated like a partnership for tax purposes with LLC profits "flowing through" to the owners, meaning that any profits the business earns are subject to federal income tax only on the owner's personal tax return.

For most small businesses organized as an LLC, the owners are normally also the managers of the business. However, an LLC can also be used as a type of investment device. Here, typically many or even most owners do not take an active role in business management but instead are passive investors. The business is run by a small group of the owners, called a "management group" or "board of managers." This use of the LLC form is similar to a limited partnership, discussed below in Section G. Using an LLC for investment goals means that the (active) owners must comply with federal and state securities laws when selling interests in the LLC to passive investors. To be sure you know how to comply with the securities laws, you must do careful legal research yourself or see a securities lawyer.

Business Structures for Professionals

Some professions are regulated by state law and cannot use simple, ordinary partnerships. For example, under almost all states' laws, doctors cannot form a general partnership. Other health care professionals—dentists, nurses, opticians, optometrists, pharmacists, physical therapists—are similarly regulated. So are some other professions, normally including: psychologists, accountants, engineers and veterinarians. The scope and details of regulation vary from state to state.

However, laws in every state permit shared ownership by regulated professionals using different business structures. They can form a "professional corporation," or a "professional service corporation," and, in some states, a "professional limited liability company." Also, in some states, certain specific types of partnerships are allowed, sometimes called "limited liability partnerships." If you are in a regulated profession, see a lawyer.

Whatever legal form a shared professional business takes, the owners must resolve the same basic questions as are involved in setting up a partnership: who contributes what, how is work allocated, how profits are shared and what happens if an owner leaves. Though you'll eventually need a lawyer to prepare the formal ownership documents, you'll benefit by working through these issues yourselves, before seeking legal help.

Converting a Partnership to an LLC

It's fully legal to change the structure of a business from a partnership to an LLC at any time. Essentially, the type of LLC articles of organization that you must create and file to convert a partnership are the same as those required to create an LLC from scratch. The partnership agreement, perhaps with minor technical modifications, can be renamed the LLC operating agreement. Once a partnership has been converted into an LLC, the owners have limited liability for all future business debts and obligations. The creation of the LLC does not, however, wipe out the owners' (the former partners') responsibility for any *previous* partnership debts or obligations.

F. Partnerships vs. Limited Liability Companies or Small Corporations

Let's look at the realities of partnership versus LLC or corporate ownership for small businesses. Right off, we want to stress again that no matter which of these three legal forms you and your co-owners choose, you must confront and resolve the same day-to-day problems. This includes matters such as allocating shares of ownership, operating the business, paying salaries and profits and resolving disputes, among others. Because there are fewer legal formalities to comply with, business owners who form partnerships have more time to focus on questions of their relationship with each other. By contrast, when creating an LLC or a corporation, the vital issues surrounding the owners' own personal decision-making and ways to resolve disputes can sometimes be diminished by a sense that the formalistic documents filed with state agencies are more important than the owners' relationship to

each other. And once the LLC or corporation is legally formed, some owners may try to operate using an "off the shelf" or canned agreement that isn't tailored to their situation instead of confronting the many key issues covered in this book.

One obvious advantage of a partnership is that the paperwork needed doesn't require costly filing and other fees, as a corporation does. But, overall, we suspect you'll probably conclude, as we have, that the advantages and disadvantages of these three ways to organize your business are not as significant as many advocates of one or the other approach would have you believe.

For example, suppose you and two friends are co-owners of a computer repair business. It's clearly prudent to make provisions to cover what happens if one person unexpectedly quits or dies. A common method of handling this is to create a "buy-out" clause, enabling the remaining owners to purchase (usually over time) the interest of the departing owner. If the business is owned as a partnership, the buy-out clause you devise will normally be included in the partnership agreement. If the business is an LLC, the clause will be in the owners' operating agreement. In a corporation, this clause is normally put in the bylaws or in a shareholders' agreement. But the practical reality will be the same.

Below we look in depth at key issues concerning the form of ownership of a shared business. We'll start here by summarizing the most important points:

- The partnership form is the simplest and least expensive of the three forms to create and maintain.
- For some types of small, shared ownership businesses, which face risks of major money lawsuits, the LLC is usually the best initial choice.
- For most other types of small shared ownership businesses, the partnership form is normally the best choice. If business growth makes one of those forms more desirable, the partners can easily convert to an LLC or a corporation.

- Occasionally, the corporate form makes sense for a new business. For instance, a corporation may be desirable if the owners want to raise large sums of money from a number of investors.

In this book about partnerships the discussion of other ways to organize your business is necessarily limited. For a more in-depth discussion of the pros and cons of sole proprietorships, LLCs and corporations, see Legal Guide for Starting & Running a Small Business, *by Fred S. Steingold (Nolo).*

1. Limited Liability

Shareholders of an LLC or corporation are not normally personally liable for corporate debts or liability stemming from lawsuits if the LLC or corporation is adequately capitalized (has sufficient cash or other assets invested). This is called "limited liability." In partnerships, all partners have open-ended personal liability for all partnership debts. But before you rush to form an LLC or incorporate, understand that, for many small businesses, the difference between limited and unlimited liability is less significant than many people believe.

Why? Well, there are two important forms of liability almost any business must deal with: lawsuits and business debts. To deal with the first possibility, most small business people with common sense, whether incorporated or not, purchase insurance to protect them from the most obvious sorts of liability claims (such as insurance protecting restaurant owners from claims filed by customers who become ill or fall down in the premises). An LLC or a corporation's limited liability is obviously no substitute for business liability insurance, since limited liability doesn't protect the assets of the LLC or corporation from being wiped out by a successful claim. However, limited liability can be a valuable protection if a small business is engaged in a high risk activity that may generate many damage claims

and lawsuits, and where insurance coverage is unavailable or too expensive.

Many—perhaps millions—of American businesses, including many retailers and small service providers, do not normally face serious risk of liability for acts caused in the course of business (aside from matters like vehicle accidents, which obviously can and should be covered by insurance). For instance, businesses as varied as a shoe store, a graphic design outfit, a small religious publishing company or an ice-cream parlor are very unlikely to face a lawsuit for large sums of money. By contrast, other types of business—for instance, manufacturers or businesses that handle toxic materials—have a much higher risk of liability claims. And because they do, it's often prohibitive for the owners of these types of businesses to purchase insurance to cover potential lawsuit judgments. Some other types of high-risk businesses include:

- **Accountants.** There have been some huge, successful claims against accounting firms for negligence. In some of these situations, accountants were found to be liable when they helped businesses conceal large losses or other damaging financial facts, thus costing investors and suppliers millions.
- **Lawyers.** Law firms can also face immense financial exposure for negligent, or worse, conduct. This conduct can range from actively participating in, or at least negligently abetting, fraudulent behavior by a client to causing financial injury to the law firm's own client.
- **Architects and Construction Companies.** In the day of multimillion dollar judgments for injured persons and frequent problems with cost overruns, everyone in the construction field is vulnerable to suit for all sorts of reasons.
- **Real Estate.** Increasingly, buyers of property who later discover undisclosed defects—everything from termites, water in the basement or land shifting to a nasty next door neighbor—sue both the seller and the real estate people who represent the seller.

This list is intended to be instructive, not exhaustive. We can't give you definitive advice about the liability/lawsuit risks of the type of business you plan to engage in. We trust that you can make your own judgment of how serious these risks are and what kinds of steps you can sensibly take to eliminate or at least minimize them. The higher the risk, the more desirable an LLC or corporation. And, obviously, the lower the risks, the more a partnership agreement, combined with basic liability insurance (such as, for "slip and fall" accidents on the business premises) and vehicle insurance should safely protect you.

But what about debts? If the business loses money, as lots of new ventures do, doesn't limited liability protect individual owners from having personal assets taken as part of an LLC or corporate bankruptcy or liquidation? Again, while the answer is "yes" in theory, in reality limited liability protection is likely to be immaterial. Why? Because lenders and major creditors are well aware of the rules of limited owner liability. Banks, landlords and other savvy businesspeople routinely require the owners of a new small business (whether an LLC or corporation) to personally guarantee any loan or significant extension of credit made to the business. By doing this, the LLC or corporate owners put themselves on much the same legal footing with their creditors as if they ran their business as a partnership. However, we should note that because many providers of routine business supplies and services do not require a personal guarantee from LLC or corporation owners, these owners can escape personal liability for these types of debts if the business becomes insolvent.

Here's another important restriction on the limited liability of corporate owners: A corporation must start with a minimally reasonable amount of cash ("capital") to function in the business world. If the corporation is only a shell, without any reasonable amount of cash to function, a legal doctrine called "piercing the corporate veil" permits a court to hold individual shareholders personally responsible for all corporate debts, whether they personally guaranteed them or not. While it is fairly rare for a court to determine that a corporation was undercapitalized, it's surely been known to occur, particularly if fraud is involved.

Limited liability companies are too new a legal form for there to be many court rulings on whether the doctrine of "piercing the veil" will also apply to undercapitalized LLCs. Logically, though, the doctrine should apply. Why should people be able to defraud creditors through use of one (new) legal form when courts have long held that they cannot achieve the same nefarious goal using a more traditional legal form? Some states' LLC laws provide that an LLC owner has the same protection from personal liability for business debts as a corporate shareholder, which increases the likelihood that this doctrine will also apply to LLCs. This means that an LLC owner is unlikely to be protected when a shareholder in the same situation would be held personally liable.

2. Business Continuity

Corporations have "eternal life." This means that if one (or even all) of the principal owners of a small corporation dies, the corporate entity continues to exist. Partnerships, on the other hand, can theoretically dissolve when any partner withdraws or dies; however, this difference is also immaterial in real life. It's easy, and fully legal, to insert a standard clause in your partnership agreement that provides that the partnership entity continues after one owner leaves or dies.

LLCs are often functionally similar to partnerships regarding business continuity. As noted, a partnership can technically dissolve when one partner retires, dies or withdraws. Similarly, some state statutes require members of an LLC to vote to continue the LLC within a specified period of time after a member withdraws or dies; if they do not, the LLC is technically dissolved. However, the dissolution of an LLC, like the dissolution of a partnership, can have unintended tax consequences for its members.

Many LLC operating agreements therefore mirror these statutory requirements and provide (without causing any IRS trouble) that an owner's departure triggers a vote by the remaining owners on whether to continue the LLC. The effect is that, if the owners wish it, the LLC will continue in business without legal interruption.

Additionally, a few states require LLCs to establish termination dates in their articles of organization. Even in those states, however, the owners can easily keep the business going by filing an amendment to the LLC's articles of organization extending the date on which the LLC is scheduled to dissolve. Partnership owners do not have to face this hassle, because no state has laws requiring a termination date for a partnership.

However, if one of the two co-owners of an LLC or small corporation quits or dies, the survivor of the business is in no better position than if he were a partner who had withdrawn or died. That's because no matter what business structure you choose, you'll want to compensate a departing owner (or her inheritors) fairly for her interest, but you'll also want to preserve the business for the remaining owners. How is the value of that departing interest to be calculated? How can the remaining owners be assured they'll have adequate cash to buy out a departing owner? We discuss methods of resolving these problems in Chapter 5. Our point now is simply that you don't avoid any of them by choosing a partnership, an LLC or a corporation.

⚠️ **General partnerships aren't the right business structure if you want to raise money from people who won't participate in the business.** *For larger businesses, which need to raise money from outside investors and will comply with complicated federal and state securities registration and sales laws to do so, it can sometimes be psychologically easier to raise capital by selling stock than by trying to sell participation in a partnership (which will constitute a limited partnership—see Chapter 9) to passive investors. However, businesses of this size are far beyond the scope of this book.*

3. Transfer of Ownership

Corporate ownership comes in the form of shares that can theoretically be transferred to new owners. By contrast, a partner's interest cannot be transferred without the consent of all partners unless, as is rarely the case, the partnership agreement expressly allows for free transferability. Similarly, an owner of an LLC is usually restricted by state law or the members' operating agreement, or both, from transferring her ownership interest in the business without the consent of all other owners. But does this legal difference really add up to a practical difference?

The answer is clearly no, for two reasons. First, when it comes to small, closely held corporations, state law often restricts the right of a shareholder to freely transfer shares no matter what the shareholders want. Second, and more importantly, the stock of most small corporations is extremely difficult or even impossible to sell. This is because there is no regular, public market for small business interests. Shares of small corporations are not listed on stock exchanges, and outsiders are rarely interested in working closely with total strangers, particularly if they can't purchase a majority, controlling interest. Even if the business is doing well, a potential buyer will probably be more interested in purchasing the entire business or profitable business assets (for example, a building, patent invention, inventory, etc.) than one owner's shares.

Finally, even if the shares or one person's LLC interest or partnership interest in a small business could be sold to an outside buyer, there are likely to be drawbacks. The success of almost any small business depends on the efforts and skills of a few people. If one of a corporation's owners can summarily transfer her interest to an outsider, the business and the other owners are obviously vulnerable if the new owner has no ability to help the corporation or is unacceptable for any other of a number of reasons. To protect against this happening, the bylaws or a shareholders' agreement of many small corporations—just like the partnership agreements of most partnerships and the operating agreements of LLCs—restrict the right of any owner to sell her interest to a third person and provide that the remaining owners have the option to buy out the interest of any departing owner. So again, the realities of running a small business dictate that the owners take certain similar steps regarding sales to outside buyers, no matter what the legal form of the business.

4. Business Formalities

No state or federal law or agency requires a partnership to file its original agreement or maintain any ongoing paperwork. By contrast, government paperwork and costs are required to start up an LLC or a corporation. An LLC must, as we've said, prepare articles of organization and file them with the Secretary or Department of State. The costs for the initial filing range from close to $1,000 in California to less than $100 in some other states. In addition, some states impose yearly fees or "franchise taxes." Further, as mentioned, some states require publication in a local paper of "intent to form" an LLC when the business starts.

Once it's operational, an LLC generally does not have to observe the same formalities as a corporation but can mostly function with the informality of a partnership. Specifically, most state LLC laws do not require members to hold annual meetings. Perhaps a better way to put this is that an LLC, like a partnership, can function with exactly the amount of formality—formal meetings, quorum requirements, keeping minutes of meetings, and so on—that the owners agree on. Most states do, however, require LLCs to file a brief annual report, in addition to any fees or taxes imposed. This annual form usually requires basic business information, such as the name and addresses of the current owners, and of the business agent for service of process (legal papers).

Creating and maintaining a corporation is usually more expensive than creating an LLC. Filing incorporation papers costs $300–$1,000 and up in some

states. (For example, in California, the cost is a $100 filing fee and, after the corporation's first two tax years, payment of a minimum franchise tax of $800. You must continue to pay at least this $800 tax every year, or more if the corporation's annual earnings go over a certain level.) If you hire a lawyer to set up your corporation, the total costs can easily approach $3,000–$5,000, or more. Moreover, a corporation requires more continuing paperwork, such as organizing and calling annual shareholders and directors meetings, preparing minutes of major decisions and issuing share certificates. In many states, it is possible to provide provisions in a corporation's bylaws that the corporation can legally skip many of these rules and operate relatively informally. (Banks and other financial institutions, however, have the discouraging practice of demanding a properly prepared corporation resolution before approving a loan or other transaction.) However, it remains accurate to say that partnerships normally can be created and operated with much less formality.

How to Form Your Own Corporation in California, *by Anthony Mancuso (Nolo), contains excellent information and forms on computer disk for creating a corporation in California. And for all states, you can use* Incorporate Your Business: A 50-State Legal Guide to Forming a Corporation, *by Anthony Mancuso (Nolo). Further,* The Corporate Minutes Book: The Legal Guide to Taking Care of Corporate Business, *by Anthony Mancuso (Nolo), provides all the forms and information corporations in any state need to properly document ongoing business matters. Using these books can significantly reduce the cost of creating and maintaining a corporation.*

The perceived formality of corporate existence is sometimes said to encourage some people to maintain better records and to engage in more organized management practices. There may be some truth in this, especially when a sole proprietorship is incorporated. But there is no logical reason why a partnership can't install excellent business controls and practices, and in our experience most successful ones do.

5. Taxation

A partnership is not taxed. Partnership net income (profits) is only reported by, and taxed on, the individual partners' income tax returns. An LLC can choose to be taxed in the same way as a partnership (to repeat, this means that LLC profits are not taxed at the business level but instead flow through to the individual owners) or as a small corporation. Most LLCs choose to be taxed in the same way as partnerships.

You may wonder if partnerships or LLCs enjoy a real advantage over corporations since corporate profits are taxed twice (first at the corporate level and then at the shareholder level), while partnership or LLC income is only taxed once. For small businesses, this distinction usually is immaterial. Small corporations can avoid double taxation in two ways. First, they can pay out to owners most of what would otherwise be corporate profits in the form of salaries, bonuses and other fringe benefits (rather than in dividends). This is usually easy to do because the principal corporate employees are normally also the owners. As long as the owners actually work in the business and the salaries aren't outrageously unreasonable, paying the owners salaries as employees is acceptable to the IRS. Because monies paid in salaries, bonuses, social security, health plans and other fringe benefits are deductible business expenses for the corporation, these expenses are not subject to corporate tax. In this way, many small corporations reduce their corporate income to zero, and corporate income is taxed only at the individual level.

In some situations, the corporate form or electing to have an LLC taxed as a corporation allows small business people who work for, as well as own, the corporation to pay less tax. This occurs in situations when a portion of corporate or LLC profits are retained in the corporation from one year to the next. The individual shareholder owner is taxed only on income she receives, whether paid to her in the form of corporate salary or as profits. The profits retained by the corporation or LLC are also taxed, but at a generally lower rate (15% for the first $50,000 and 25% on the next $25,000) than individual income. In a partnership or an LLC which has chosen to be taxed like a partnership, these retained profits would be taxed as income to the partners at their marginal rate, which will probably be much higher, whether or not cash was in fact distributed to them. For businesses which will pay all profits to owner-employees in the form of salaries and benefits, these initial low rates of corporate taxation offer no advantage. However, if your business will need to retain substantial earnings for future operations, incorporating or forming an LLC and choosing to be taxed like a corporation is likely to make economic sense if you plan to retain significant profits in the business. Corporations can retain profits of up to $250,000 for future needs without question by the IRS (except certain personal service corporations owned by professionals, such as doctors and lawyers, which are limited to $150,000) and take advantage of these lower corporate income tax rates. If the corporation has any type of valid business reason, it can with little difficulty retain much more than $250,000.

Small corporate businesses can also avoid double taxation by electing something called federal "S corporation" status. An S corporation functions like a partnership for income tax purposes. Thus, an S corporation doesn't pay income taxes on profits; only the shareholders do. You may ask, "Why form an S corporation if you can attain the same tax results with a partnership or LLC?" Good question.

The S corporation is rapidly being superseded by the LLC, which offers both principal attractions of an S corporation—limited liability and flow-through taxation. Further, LLCs are far more flexible than S corporations, which have to comply with complicated IRS rules.

Finally, it's true that a corporation or an LLC can establish a tax-deductible pension and/or profit-sharing plan for all its workers, including working shareholders and/or managing owners, while a partnership pension plan is only tax deductible for employees, not for partners themselves. However, this difference, too, is often more apparent than real, since partners are eligible for individual profit-sharing retirement plans, which tend to equalize tax treatment.

6. Termination

When a corporation is dissolved and distributes appreciated property to shareholders, the gain (increase) in value is taxed both to the corporation and to the shareholders. This means that it can potentially be more expensive from a tax point of view to close down a profitable corporation than a partnership or an LLC that has elected to be taxed like a partnership.

7. Summing Up

We come back to where we started: For many, perhaps most people who are planning a shared ownership business, there are few real-world advantages to forming an LLC or a corporation over a partnership. However, as noted, choosing an LLC or corporation can be preferable for owners of small businesses in fields where there's a plausible risk of lawsuits against the business for large amounts of money. A partnership agreement focuses on the basic issues which must be resolved to establish a shared-ownership business with a minimum of red

tape and cost. Therefore, we generally recommend the partnership form when starting many shared-ownership small businesses which are unlikely to face large debts or the threat of scary lawsuits. We recognize the possible advantages of becoming an LLC or a corporation later on, for limited liability reasons and possibly for tax purposes as well, if the business becomes successful. Fortunately, as we've discussed, you can legally transform your partnership into an LLC or a corporation at any time all partners agree to.

We suspect that the real reason why some people starting a business choose the corporate or LLC form has more to do with style than substance. Somehow they feel their business is more likely to prosper with that weighty INC. or trendy LLC decorating the stationery. This seems a bit silly but is harmless enough as long as the business owners don't get delusions of grandeur and remember that the form they've chosen will have little effect on how they operate the business day-to-day.

EXAMPLE: Polly, Maura and Linda, all librarians, want to open an electronic information search business with emphasis on information of special interest to women. At a meeting discussing what computer equipment they should buy, Polly veers off to announce that she wants the business run as professionally as possible, which to her means creating a corporation or an LLC. After a lengthy, confusing and frustrating discussion, they try to return to computer equipment, but their focus is gone.

Linda suggests that they all consider what really matters right now before they meet again. Polly consults a friend who's a business advisor. The friends suggests that they put their efforts into getting the business started and keep the legal structure as simple as possible—form a partnership.

At their next meeting, to the relief of Maura and Linda, Polly proposes that they run the business as a partnership and prepare a partnership agreement. If the business prospers and expands, they will then consider incorporating or forming an LLC. But for the present, they all agree that what their business needs is income, not energy consumed in creating sophisticated legal structures.

G. Limited Partnerships

A limited partnership is a special kind of legal animal that, in some circumstances, combines the best attributes of a partnership and a corporation. Its advantage as a business structure is that it provides a way for business owners to raise money without having to give up managerial control or engage in the intricacies of creating a corporation and issuing stock.

A limited partnership must have at least one entity or person called the "general partner," who really runs things. This general partner can be another partnership, an LLC, a corporation or a single human being. There can also be more than one general partner. However many there are, each general partner has the rights and potential liabilities normally involved in any partnership—such as management powers for the business and personal liability for business losses or debts. Limited partners, on the other hand, have no management powers, but neither are they personally liable for the debts of the partnership.

Limited partners are basically investors. The return they receive for their investment is defined in the partnership agreement. If the business fails, the most that the limited partners can lose is their investment (the amount of money or the property they contributed for their interest in the business).

In Chapter 9 we discuss limited partnerships in more detail, including the applicability of securities laws to limited partnership interests. Here, we just want to alert you to the existence of limited partnerships and their basic use.

EXAMPLE: Anthony and Janice plan to purchase rundown houses, renovate them, then (hopefully) sell them at a good profit. All they lack is the cash to make the initial purchases. To solve this minor difficulty, they first create a general partnership between themselves. Then they establish a limited partnership (with their own partnership as the general partner) and seek others who are willing to put up money for a defined interest in the venture. Janice and Anthony decide that they need $100,000 to get started, and they manage to sell ten limited partnership interests, each for $10,000.

As we've said, the return the general partners offer the limited partners is defined in the limited partnership agreement. Sometimes, limited partners receive a fixed return on their investment. For instance, they might receive "10% interest annually, with principal, to be repaid in three installments over seven years." Investing in a limited partnership is similar to making a loan, except it doesn't remain an obligation if the partnership business fails. That means that while limited partners aren't liable for the business's debts they also risk losing their entire investment if the partnership goes belly up.

More commonly, instead of a fixed return, limited partners receive a percentage of the profits (assuming the venture makes money) for a specific period of months or years, or even forever.

Limited partnerships can also be a useful means for expanding an existing business to raise money, especially at times when other sources of cash are tight and interest rates are high.

EXAMPLE: Judith and Aretha have a small picture frame shop that has just begun to prosper after a couple of years on short rations. Believing that the time is now right to expand, the two women spot a much larger store in a much better location, which will allow them to stock a large selection of fine art prints as well as frames. Unfortunately, they don't have the money they need to finance the move and the larger inventory that it will entail. To solve this problem, they create a limited partnership, offering a $20,000 investor an 8% interest in the total net profits of the store for the next three years as well as the return of the invested capital at the end of that period. They sell four of their limited partnerships, raising $80,000. (As Judith and Aretha's original partnership agreement didn't provide for limited partners, they must rewrite it, as well as create a separate limited partnership agreement.)

⚠ **Limited partnership interests are securities.** *Offering and selling limited partnership interests involves the sale of what's called a "security." The most common example of a security is a corporate stock or bond. You must check and comply with all federal and state securities laws before you offer any limited partnership interest for sale.*

1. Legal Formalities of Limited Partnerships

Limited partnerships involve many more legal formalities than general partnerships. In addition to securities laws, limited partnerships are generally subject to other state controls. Setting up and operating a limited partnership is similar in many ways to the process of organizing and operating a small corporation. State law usually requires that a registration certificate be filed with a government agency. The information required on this document varies, depending on state law. Often, partnership and limited partnership agreements must be disclosed, and the names and addresses of all partners and limited partners listed. Failure to comply with state registration requirements can subject the partnership to serious penalties and cause would-be limited partners to lose their limited liability status.

Fortunately, it's not difficult to comply with the registration requirements; thousands and thousands of limited partnerships are formed each year, and

the forms for registration are routine. Also, every state except Louisiana has adopted the Uniform Limited Partnership Act, which standardizes both substantial law and the registration procedures. Many states have adopted the Revised Uniform Limited Partnership Act, which further streamlines the law in this area.

2. Restrictions on Limited Partnerships

State law normally imposes restrictions on the availability and use of limited partnership names. ("Limited" or "Ltd." at the end of a business or partnership name does not automatically mean the entity is a limited partnership—these terms are simply the British equivalent of "incorporated" and "Inc." Some U.S. companies include these British terms in their name because they believe it sounds aristocratic.) In addition, these laws contain statutory requirements governing the manner of calling and holding meetings, and many other corporation-like legal requirements which apply to the operation of the limited partnership, unless alternative rules are clearly spelled out in the partnership agreement.

History Lesson # 2

In Europe, as in England, partnership law evolved from the customs of the merchants— so European civil law regarding partnerships is similar to ours. Civil law recognizes a "societas," the equivalent of our general partnership, and a "societe en common dite," the equivalent of our limited partnership.

H. A Closer Look at Partnerships

Since most readers of this book will decide on the partnership form, we are now going to take a deeper look at what a partnership involves legally.

Most people have a commonsense understanding of what partnership is—the partners are in it together, all-for-one and one-for-all. In a rough way, this is true, but it's obviously desirable to have a much clearer understanding of what is really involved—what you're committing yourself to when you decide to establish a partnership.

A partnership is an intimate relationship. "It's the business equivalent of a marriage," one friend aptly stated. Certainly, you'll be deeply enmeshed with your partners, learn much about them and develop close relationships after years of shared experience. But partners will also inevitably encounter periods of conflict and problems demanding resolution. As with any intimate relationship, you'll need to be able to speak openly and candidly with each other (and as members of partnerships ourselves, we can confirm that this is far easier said than done).

Partners and Spouses

Increasingly, couples are running businesses together. IRS statistics indicate that there are over 800,000 businesses in the U.S. with ownership shared between a man and woman. Indeed, there's a new name for a business co-run by mates: "co-preneurship."

There is no special IRS category for couple or husband–wife businesses. Unless another legal form is used, a business co-owned by a couple is simply a partnership.

Managing both living together and working together is certainly an art. The fact that so many couples are doing this or attempting it, is romantic, as well, probably, as grist for some good novels.

The legal definition of a partnership is "an association of two or more persons to carry on as co-owners of a business for profit." (Uniform Partnership Act (UPA) Section 6(1).) This concept of a partnership is very broad. For example, the IRS definition of a partnership includes: "…a syndicate, pool, joint venture or other unincorporated organization through which…any business is carried on…and is not…a corporation or trust or an estate [or sole ownership]…." (Internal Revenue Code Section 761(a).) Legal scholars have expended considerable energy trying to determine whether a partnership is an aggregate or an entity—that is, is it a legal thing separate and distinct from the partners or is it simply a continuation of the partners? Well, like light, which is a wave or a particle depending on how you view it, a partnership is sometimes a separate thing, and sometimes it isn't. We'll explain this a bit more throughout this section, but frankly, as an abstract question, it doesn't make any difference to you which it really is.

1. Partnership Basics

You don't have to use the words "partners" or "partnership" to become a legal partnership. If you simply join with other persons and run a shared business, you've created a partnership. Use of those words will, however, insure that you're involved in a partnership. For example, if there is a question whether a person is an employee of a sole proprietorship, or a partner, calling her a partner will make her one.

Some other partnership basics:

The Uniform Partnership Act: The UPA was adopted (often with some slight modifications) in all states except Louisiana. The act provides rules governing partnerships. A few rules cannot be varied, such as: "Each partner is responsible for all debts of the partnership." The second type of UPA rule, by far the most common, applies to partnerships which haven't provided their own rules in their partnership agreement for the situation. However, you're not stuck with the UPA rules; you can vary them. It's wiser to create your own rules in your own agreement. The purpose of a partnership agreement is to be tailor-made by you, for your needs, not to be stuck with general rules you may not want. In Appendix 1, we list the legal citation to each state's UPA—where you can find it in your state's law books.

The Revised Uniform Partnership Act (1994): A revised version of the Uniform Partnership Act (Revised UPA) was promulgated in 1994. Because about half of the states have not yet adopted the Revised UPA, and because the main provisions of the UPA and the Revised UPA are so similar, we continue to refer to the "old" UPA in this book when citing a provision to partnership laws.

However, the Revised UPA contains the few mandatory rules of the old UPA and introduces a few new mandatory rules as well. If you live in a state that has adopted the new act, all these rules are part of your agreement as a matter of law. Fortunately, these mandatory Revised UPA rules should prove to be no problem when preparing your partnership agreement because they don't require you to do or prevent you from doing anything that is not within the boundaries of minimum common sense. Put another way, you can safely draft your own partnership agreement with this book whether or not you live in a state that's adopted the Revised UPA.

The bulk of the rules in the Revised UPA are, like the rules in the "old" UPA, designed to take effect if you don't include a specific provision in your agreement covering an issue. (Lawyers often refer to these as "fallback" rules.) For readers of this book, fallback rules, whether included in the UPA or Revised UPA, should be immaterial; if you follow our recommendations, all major partnership issues should be covered in your agreement. Second, we hope that, with a sound agreement, none of you will ever wind up in court fighting over your partnership. After all, greatly reducing the possibility

that this will occur is a basic reason for preparing a detailed partnership agreement in the first place. As you'll see, we strongly urge you to have arbitration and mediation clauses in your agreement. That way, even if you can't resolve a dispute, you can still avoid court proceedings.

Following are the significant specific Revised UPA sections that cannot be varied or waived by partnership agreement. We use the term "significant" because some binding sections cover optional matters. (For example, if you file a partnership "Statement" with the Secretary or Department of State's office, mandatory sections apply. However, there is no requirement that you file any Statement, and, in reality, no reason to bother.) Under the Revised UPA, you cannot:

* Eliminate a partner's duties of loyalty (Sections 404(b) & (d) and (603(b)(3)). These loyalty sections are really common sense summaries of the minimum legal and practical duty of trust partners can expect of each other. Anyone who wants to lower or waive these sections should seriously question why they're forming a partnership.

* Vary the power of a court to expel a partner (Section 601(5)). This section sets forth a number of reasons a court may terminate a partnership, on application of a partner, including such reasons as a "partner engaged in wrongful conduct that adversely and materially affected the partnership business," or a partner's bankruptcy. All the grounds for which a court may terminate a partnership are so clearly reasonable that no sensible person would want to vary this section.

* Use your partnership agreement to try to restrict the rights of "third parties" (creditors) of the partnership (Section 103(b)(9)). Again, this is a restatement of what the law has always been, since you never legally could design a partnership agreement enabling the partners to evade legitimate partnership creditors.

In sum, the Revised UPA must have been fun for legal scholars to prepare (they do love that sort of stuff) and may be vital if partners don't draft an agreement in the first place or have a sloppy agreement that doesn't cover key issues. It should, however, have no impact on users of this book. (For a list of state partnership statutes, see Appendix 1.)

Oral Partnership Agreements: As a practical matter, partnerships should always have a written partnership agreement. You should know, however, that oral or handshake partnerships are often legal, although highly inadvisable. If there's even a minor disagreement between the partners, it will probably be very hard to prove what the agreement was—or even that the partnership existed.

Equal Versus Unequal Ownership: Partners don't have to share ownership equally. You can agree on any percentage of individual ownership or distribution of the profits that you want. Thus, one partner could own 80% of the partnership and four more could own 5% each.

Professional Partnerships: Partnerships can be organized for all sorts of purposes. They can sell products or services just as they can manufacture, mine or operate as agents. Professional partnerships, however, such as those of lawyers or doctors, are subject to special rules set down by the state, because of the special licensing and regulation of these professions. Usually the most important rule is that everyone in the partnership be a member of the profession.

Compensation of Partners: Partners don't normally receive salaries per se; usually, they get a percentage of the profits. However, partners often take an agreed-upon amount from the business—commonly called a draw—at regular intervals (for example, monthly, bi-weekly) against their yearly partnership shares.

Liability: As we've said, partners, as well as the partnership itself, are personally and individually liable for all the legal obligations of the partnership.

History Lesson # 3

Partnerships were permitted in Roman law (for instance, the Code of Justinian) by provisions that were very similar to our contemporary law. The Romans also evolved the rules of agency, which are the foundation of much of modern partnership law. As the Romans put it, *Qui facit per alium facit per se*—he who acts through another acts for himself.

Roman law considered voluntary choice of associates the essence of partnership, and *delectus personas*—choice of persons—remains a central element of partnerships.

Okay, so much for a quick sketch of what a partnership is. Now let's fill in the picture with a detailed look at several areas that will be important to you.

2. Intention to Be Partners

An area of possible confusion—whether or not a true legal partnership exists—involves the intentions of the people doing business together. To create a valid partnership, each person must volunteer to be a partner. They can't be drafted against their will. However, the law allows one's intention to be a partner to be implied from the circumstances of a business operation. For example, if three people who have no other business relationship each inherit one-third of some real estate or a business, they don't automatically become partners because they've never agreed to do business together. But if they then proceed to run the business or develop the land together, they've become partners even if there is no written partnership agreement.

Not every active joining of interests makes people partners, either for tax purposes or legally. Here are two examples taken from regulations of the Internal Revenue Service (Treasury Regs., Sections 1.761-1(a)(1); 301.7701-3(a)):

- Mere co-owners of property are not partners, even if they lease the property and share rents, provided they don't actively carry on a business on or with the property.
- The mere sharing of the expense of a project does not automatically create a partnership or joint venture. For example, if two adjoining landowners construct a ditch merely to drain surface waters from their property, there is no partnership for tax purposes.

In general, if a person receives a share of the profits of an (unincorporated) business, it's an indication that the person is a partner in the business. The complexities of business relationships, however, can make application of this rule murky.

> **EXAMPLE:** Al loans money to Jane and Joan's partnership business. That alone clearly doesn't make him a partner—unless the loan is really a disguised ownership investment in the business. A key factor here is if a definite time is established when the loan is due. If not, the loan looks like an investment. But suppose Al is worried about Jane and Joan's business sense, so he imposes some controls along with his loan (for example, he requires some new inventory controls or the installation of a time clock for employees). Does this render Al actively involved in the management of the business, and hence a partner? The answer is—it might. The IRS takes the position that when a lender imposes "excessive controls" on a loan, he or she becomes a partner. Just what are excessive controls isn't generally defined—so be wary.

Joint Ventures (Partnerships for a Single Purpose)

A joint venture (from "joint (ad)venture," a concept often used in the days of sailing vessels) is simply a partnership for a limited or specified purpose. If you and Jose go into the construction business together, that's a partnership. If you and Jose agree to build one house together, that's normally a joint venture. Common examples of joint ventures are natural resource projects—drilling for oil, or a cooperative mining venture.

Joint ventures are governed by partnership law. The relations of the joint venturers should be defined in a written agreement, just like any partnership. Indeed, except for the fact that the agreement should state that the venture is a specifically defined one limited to a specified project, the same issues and problems must be resolved when creating a joint venture agreement as in a partnership agreement.

3. The Rights and Responsibilities of Partners—Or, One Partner Can Bind Another

Each partner has full power to represent and bind the partnership within the normal course of business. (UPA Section 9.) This is one obvious reason trust is so vital in a partnership. One partner can obligate the other partners, even if they never authorized him to do so. Indeed, in many circumstances, a partner can bind a partnership even when the other partners told him not to.

EXAMPLE: Al, Fred and Mike are partners in a printing business. They discuss buying an expensive new press and vote two-to-one against it. Fred, the disgruntled loser, goes out and signs a contract for the press with a company that has no knowledge of Al's and Mike's vehement opposition. Since this is within the normal course of business, Fred's act binds the partnership.

It is legal to limit the powers of any partner in the partnership agreement. (UPA Section 18(3).) However, those limits are unlikely to be binding on people outside the partnership who have no actual knowledge of them. Legally, outsiders are entitled to rely on the apparent authority of a partner, as determined by the customs of the particular trade or business involved or the normal course of (that particular) business. When Fred bought the printing press, the salesman—as long as he had no actual knowledge of the partnership's limits on Fred—relied on Fred's apparent authority (a partner of a printing business can reasonably be expected to have the authority to buy a press). However, if Fred wanted to bind the printing partnership in a deal to open a chain of massage parlors, an outsider probably wouldn't be able to rely on his signature alone as binding on the partnership, because this would be outside the normal course of the partnership's business. (For more on a partner's authority to bind the partnership, see Chapter 3, Section D.)

4. Personal Liability for Partnership Debts

Another crucial partnership legal principle is that each partner is personally liable for all partnership debts and obligations that the partnership cannot pay. This is not a rule that the partners can change as far as debts to third parties go. Partners are not, however, liable for the personal, non-partnership debts and obligations of another partner. However, if one partner is having financial problems outside the partnership, her creditors can seek to get at her share of the partnership business, and this can severely disrupt the business. In addition to business debts, partners are also personally liable for any money damages that result from the negligence of another partner, as well as damages that result from any frauds or other intentional acts a partner commits in the ordinary course of partnership business.

EXAMPLE: Jane and Alfonso are partners in a retail flower business. Jane has no money; Alfonso is rich. The partnership just opened, and the partners haven't gotten around to buying insurance yet. While Jane is driving the flower delivery van to pick up flowers on partnership business, she hits and severely injures a pedestrian, who then sues and gets a substantial judgment. Alfonso is personally liable for any amount unpaid by the business—that is, what's left unpaid after all partnership assets have been used. If he doesn't have sufficient cash, or liquid assets, to cover the judgment, his other property, from real estate to cars—with the exception of whatever is protected by state debtors' exemption laws—can be seized to satisfy it.

Incidentally, a silent partner—one whose membership in the partnership is not revealed to the public—is every bit as liable for partnership debts as any other partner. However, a sub-partner (sometimes called an assignee) is not. A sub-partner or assignee is a person who agrees with one member of a partnership to share in that partner's profits. Although the assignee or sub-partner has the right to receive a portion of the partner's profits, he or she does not have any rights or responsibilities as a partner. This is a separate agreement between the partner and the sub-partner and does not, legally, involve the sub-partner in the partnership. Creating this kind of arrangement can get complicated, so see a lawyer if you're interested in doing this.

Some Words of Encouragement

We recite these rules of partnership responsibility not to discourage you from entering into a partnership, but to alert you to the fact that, like any human endeavor, you must acknowledge and deal with certain risks. As we've mentioned, while limited liability does give stockholders of a small corporation some, usually theoretical, protection, similar risks are also typically present if you elect to form a small corporation. With insurance (see Chapter 8, Section E) and other common sense business practices, many of the potential partnership risks can be minimized. The fact that there are so many functioning partnerships in the United States is probably the best evidence that the risks needn't be prohibitive.

5. Partnerships and Taxes

Partnerships do not pay federal or state income taxes. However, every partnership must file an informational partnership tax return (Form 1065) once a year. Any profits or losses from the partnership flow through the partnership to the individual partners. Thus, only the individual partners pay taxes on partnership profits. (See Chapter 7.)

This means that, unlike corporations, there cannot be double taxation of partnership profits, once at the partnership level and then a second time when partnership profits are distributed to the individual partners. Under the 1986 Tax Reform Act, partners' incomes or losses may be, for IRS purposes, either earned, investment or passive. Briefly, if all partners materially participate in the operations of the business—which is certainly the rule for most small business partnerships—partners' incomes will be considered earned. As we explain in Chapter 7, Section I, it's generally desirable from a tax point of view to have earned income rather than passive or investment income.

6. Partners' Legal Relation to One Another

Partners are fiduciaries vis-a-vis one another. This bit of legal jargon means that they owe complete loyalty to the partnership and cannot engage in any activity that conflicts with the partnership's business. As one court put it, "The rule of undivided loyalty is relentless and supreme." Another wrote, "Many forms of conduct permissible in a work-a-day world for those acting at arm's length are forbidden to those bound by fiduciary ties…Not honesty alone, but the punctilio of an honor the most sensitive, is thus the standard of behavior." (*Meinhard v. Salmon*, 164 N.E. 545 (1928).)

EXAMPLE: Fred and Tom agree to be partners in a real estate purchase. In the course of conducting negotiations for that purchase, Fred learns of another real estate buy, a real bargain. Legally, Fred cannot simply wait until the partnership expires and purchase the second property himself. He has a fiduciary duty to tell Tom any valuable information he learns while acting on partnership business. Similarly, if Fred proposes to buy Tom out of the partnership, he can't legally do so without telling Tom about the bargain he's found. The rule of caveat emptor (let the buyer beware) doesn't apply to a partner. Fred must act in complete good faith, including volunteering any significant information about the partnership, its worth and business possibilities, which he is aware Tom doesn't know.

There is voluminous litigation on the rights and duties of partners to each other—sad evidence that partnerships can go sour. Here are some representative no-no's, or things a partner cannot legally do. Notice that common sense indicates these are not ways in which honest people deal with each other:

- A partner cannot secretly obtain for herself an opportunity available to the partnership.
- Partnership assets cannot be diverted for personal use of the partners.
- Partners cannot fail to distribute partnership profits to other members of the partnership.
- Each partner must disclose any and all material facts affecting the business to the other partners.

⚠️ **Would-be partners beware.** *The courts have often ruled that those who have seriously discussed forming a partnership must adhere to the same exacting standards of good faith that bind partners, even if they never signed an actual partnership agreement. For example, if two people seriously plan to open a saw shop and find a perfect location, it's probably a breach of fiduciary duty for one person to try and cut out the other by leasing the place as a sole proprietor. Just when this partner-like responsibility arises isn't totally clear, but when real negotiating begins, that probably means there are fiduciary duties of trust involved. Since you'll have to trust your partners eventually, it makes sense to start building that trust by full disclosure and square dealing right from the start.*

History Lesson # 4

In medieval England, the legal affairs of merchants were administered separately from the common law courts (the main English courts, where law was so extremely complex as to mock the word "common"). England, which depended heavily on trade, didn't subject its merchants, and especially foreign traders, to the expensive and tedious forms of common law. Thus, English partnership law evolved from the realities of how merchants actually conducted business, with most basic partnership principles being codifications of the customs of trade. Eventually, this codification became known as "law merchant."

Partnership lawsuits were handled in informal businessmen's courts, such as the Court Staple (a staple was a trade fair), first given official sanction by the Statute of the Staple in 1353. This law proclaimed that justice was to be done to foreign traders according to the law of the staple (or law merchant), from day-to-day and hour-to-hour (that is, speedily).

7. Partnerships and Paperwork

As you'll see further on, the technicalities of establishing and maintaining a small business partnership are not unduly burdensome. Once you agree on and create your partnership agreement, that's pretty much it as far as legal paperwork is concerned. You don't have to file any formal partnership paper with any governmental bureau, department or agency, except that the partnership must file appropriate papers with:

- the IRS, to obtain a taxpayer I.D. number (IRS Form SS-4)
- the appropriate local agency, if the partnership operates under a fictitious name (a name other than those of the partners). For example, if Wang, Olivier and Simmons call themselves Ace Electric, they'll have to meet state requirements for all businesses operating under a fictitious name. (See Chapter 3, Section A and Chapter 8, Section A for more on choosing a business name and fictitious name statements.)

Of course, partnerships have to comply with the same small business and tax paperwork common to any other business. This includes getting a state tax resale permit if they will sell goods, filing payroll and unemployment tax returns if they will hire employees, and generally dealing with all the rest of the bureaucratic procedures that go with starting and operating a business. (See Chapter 8.) And, of course, there's internal recordkeeping, including sales, accounts receivable, general ledger and other accounting—which are required of any business.

8. Relationships That Aren't Partnerships

Just as it's important to know what qualifies as a partnership, it can be crucial to recognize a "mock" or "phony" partnership.

a. Tax Scam Partnerships

Legitimate partnerships, like any other business form, can limit or reduce taxes in some circumstances. However, partnerships are particularly vulnerable to being ruled invalid by the IRS if they are phony relationships designed primarily to lower tax liability.

For example, Daniel and Marie live together. Daniel is a poor artist who makes very little from his paintings; Marie runs a profitable dress store and pays substantial taxes. Can Daniel and Marie legally declare they're now in a partnership to run the dress store and, for tax purposes, each report half the store's profits as their separate incomes, thus lowering the total amount of taxes paid? As you might expect, if the purpose of a partnership is only to evade or reduce taxes, the IRS won't recognize it. There must be some genuine sharing, either of management and control of a business, or investment in it, for there to be a tax-valid partnership; the partnership can't exist solely in bookkeeping terms. (*IRS v. Tower*, 327 U.S. 290 (1946).)

Family Partnerships

The IRS traditionally takes a close look at any partnership involving family members or relations. (Defined under Internal Revenue Code Section 704(e).) Some tax planners tout family partnerships as a way to lower income taxes, or to shift assets to younger family members free of estate or gift tax. The truth is family partnerships won't achieve these goals unless there is a real, legal partnership business. The basic rule is that in order for there to be a valid family partnership, each participating family member, as a partner, must actually contribute something—either money or service or both—to the partnership. Of course, there are many family businesses run as partnerships that are perfectly legitimate, with several family members active in the business. These partnerships incur no wrath from the IRS.

b. Nonprofit Enterprises

Enterprises not primarily designed to make a profit also fail to qualify as partnerships. Such an endeavor is either a "nonprofit corporation," if it's incorporated or an "unincorporated association," if it isn't. This latter group includes religious, charitable, educational, scientific, civic, social, athletic and patriotic groups or clubs, and trade unions and associations.

For more information about nonprofit corporations, see How to Form a Nonprofit Corporation, *by Anthony Mancuso (Nolo).*

9. Terminating a Partnership

In addition to establishing sensible rules for you to live by during the life of your partnership, your partnership agreement will govern the basics of what will happen if the partnership ends. By termination of a partnership, we mean that the business no longer functions as a partnership. The partnership books are closed, and the partners go their separate ways. One of the other partners may continue the former partnership business in some other form, or, as is probably more common in cases of partnership termination, the business may end as well. ■

An Overview of Your Partnership Agreement

I n this chapter, we'll look at the basic elements covered in small business partnership agreements. In Chapters 3 through 6, we discuss these subjects in more detail and present specific sample clauses you can use in drafting your partnership agreement. You'll make your decisions about what you want in your agreement as you go through those chapters. Then you'll draft your own agreement, step-by-step, in Chapter 11. (The intervening chapters cover other subjects concerning partnerships and small businesses.)

A. The Spirit of Your Agreement

Let us emphasize: Partnership agreements are simply written agreements that express your understanding and your decisions about how you want your business, and the partners' relationship, to work.

Good, candid communication is essential to making a partnership work, and that starts at the beginning. Indeed, one of the primary reasons to prepare a written partnership agreement is to see if or where the partners might disagree and to fully air those concerns. There's no magic legal formula you can plug in to create a partnership agreement. If you see a lawyer—and she's competent—she can help you focus on issues and will probably suggest a variety of possible solutions. But no lawyer can make basic choices for you. If she tries to do this, you almost surely will get a very expensive, lawyer-drafted agreement that is legally impeccable but fails miserably to address your real needs.

Partnerships are (very) human enterprises. As you read through this book, try to relate what you're learning and discussing to your own personal dynamics. We're not masters of the human psyche, but our experiences have taught us a few questions prospective partners should consider.

- Do you all understand and agree that you're going to run a business with the aim of making a decent profit? Any enterprise in which you share making money qualifies as a business. If any would-be partners are nonbusiness types who simply aren't comfortable with that, you (and they) don't want to be part of the same partnership.

- How long have you all known each other? We've seen some new friendships crumble fast under partnership decision-making stresses. Don't enter any partnership casually.

- Are all prospective partners roughly on the same economic plane? If not, how do you feel about the possibility that some partners' decisions may be made not on the basis of the business's economic realities, but on their outside financial resources?

- Finally, what's the chemistry of the people involved? (We can't resist adding what one lawyer friend told us he'd learned about partnerships: "Never prepare one for a group of psychiatrists. Six years later they're still arguing over the wording.") There are no rules at all here. Sometimes people with different natures work out very well as partners. And sometimes people who are longtime friends with very similar personalities can't develop a harmonious business relationship. Probably, the best you can do is to ask yourself if you can imagine being in a close business relationship with your prospective partners ten or 20 years from now. If you can't, think twice about going forward.

B. Preparing Your Agreement

Use this book as a workbook. Make notes or other comments as you go along. As you go through the next chapters, use a pencil to fill in any clause you think you want to use. Place a check mark in the box next to that clause. When you prepare your final agreement, this checked box will enable you to quickly locate the clauses you want.

We've done our best to both cover the basics and make our clauses direct and clear. Your partnership agreement doesn't need to be (indeed shouldn't be) a gobbledygook-filled monstrosity stuffed with abstruse lawyer language. It should be clearly written, in plain English, to express decisions you've made which meet your needs.

Your situation may require you to alter and revise one or more of our clauses. Or you may want to cover one or more matters we don't discuss, which means you'll have to draft partnership clauses on your own. Fine, but we do urge caution. You do not want any change or new clause to create ambiguity—not a good thing in a partnership agreement, whatever its value in modern poetry. If you do make significant changes or add new clauses, be sure they clearly and concisely express everything all partners have agreed to—no long-winded, lawyerly language is necessary.

If we wanted to give the most cautious advice possible, we'd urge you never to prepare a new clause without discussing the matter with a lawyer. (See Chapter 10, Section A.) But such extreme caution isn't usually necessary. We trust that readers will be able to use their intelligence to draft a new clause that fits their needs and to sensibly judge if a lawyer's review of that clause might really help.

We suggest that you be cautious and selective regarding the amount of detail you include in your partnership agreement. (Remember, the U.S. Constitution is much shorter than many lawyer-drafted partnership agreements.) You do need to cover the basics—and you do get to decide what those basics are. As tempting as it might be to try, it's never possible to cover every conceivable contingency in your partnership agreement—not that some lawyers don't attempt to, presenting their client with an 80-page document and a bill for thousands of dollars.

Legally, your partnership starts when you agree that it does. As we noted in Chapter 1, in some circumstances partnerships can be based on an oral agreement or can even be implied from the operational realities of a business. But for obvious reasons, implied or oral agreements are such a lousy idea that from here on we'll assume that you'll adopt our commonsense approach of putting your partnership agreement in writing. Moreover, the laws of many states effectively compel partnership agreements to be in writing. For example, under New York law, any partnership agreement must be in writing if:

- the agreement is to last for more than one year
- real estate is involved
- an arbitration clause is included, or
- there are guaranteed payments to partners.

A written partnership agreement becomes effective when it's signed, unless the agreement itself specifies a different date. (As we've noted, prospective partners owe a full fiduciary duty of trust to each other even before the partnership legally exists.)

C. Basic Topics Covered in a Partnership Agreement

What's normally covered in a partnership agreement? The list below itemizes the major areas. In Sections D through J of this chapter, we look more deeply at decisions involved in actually working out a partnership agreement. Usually, you'll draft or hammer out your agreement between the heady day you first realize that you're going to take your business dream seriously and the even headier day when you open for business.

In this chapter, you won't be picking clauses for your agreement or making final decisions about it. Instead, use this chapter to begin to become familiar with the types of decisions you will have to make, including:

- the authority of a partner
- the name and purpose of the partnership
- contributions to the partnership (cash, property or services)
- payments from the partnership to the partners (profits, losses and draws)
- management duties of the partners

- expansion (admission of new partners)
- withdrawal/death of a partner: buy-out agreements, and
- resolution of disputes (mediation and arbitration).

1. The Uniform Partnership Act

As we've said, there's a body of law, primarily the Uniform Partnership Act or the Revised Uniform Partnership Act, which establishes some basic legal rules applicable to partnerships, such as the liability of partners.

The Uniform Partnership Act or Revised UPA

One of these acts has been adopted in all states except Louisiana. In most states, however, there are some variations, usually slight, between most states' partnership acts and the original uniform act. Uniform Acts, as the name indicates, are standardized laws created by a legal commission. However, when it adopts a uniform law, a state legislature can make changes in the uniform version.

The legal citation for each state's UPA or RUPA law is set forth in a chart in Appendix 1. With basic legal research skills you can use this citation to find your state's laws in a local law library. We discuss how to do your own legal research in Chapter 10, Section C.

All but a few of your state's UPA or Revised UPA rules can be varied, if you decide to do so, by an express statement in the partnership agreement. Even if you know your state's UPA rules and decide they are what you want, it is not wise to rely on the UPA to define key clauses in your partnership agreement. You should create those clauses yourself and express your decision explicitly in your agreement.

2. Joint Ventures

To remind you, a joint venture is a partnership for a specific limited purpose, such as building one house or giving one series of dance performances. People involved in joint ventures should also have an agreement covering the basics of partnerships and some additional matters, including:

- extent of the venture
- staffing and control of hiring
- conflicts of interest
- management control, and
- tax issues.

D. Partners: Their Authority and Relationship

The first and most important decision you'll make in organizing your business will be choosing your partners. Once you've done that, you need to set down in your partnership agreement exactly how you'll work together and how each partner will work for the partnership.

1. Authority of a Partner

The rights and powers of partners can be defined in your partnership agreement with any degree of specificity you desire. Indeed, some partnership agreements contain pages and pages defining the authority, duties and restrictions on partners. However, this type of endless detail is usually not helpful. In fact, one or more partners' insistence on this approach can signal serious mistrust between the partners. Remember, trust is the central ingredient in any partnership, and no number of legal clauses can compensate for its absence. If you have so little trust in your prospective partners as to think pages of detailed clauses defining the partner's authority are necessary, you should seriously question whether creating a partnership with these people is advisable at all.

As we said, in the absence of a specific limitation, any partner can bind the partnership by decisions made in the ordinary course of partnership business.

> **EXAMPLE:** Herb, Frank and Connie own a music store. Herb, an offbeat country music freak, gets carried away and orders twelve times as many Emmy Lou Harris CDs as the store can normally sell. Herb didn't consult Frank and Connie; if he had, they wouldn't have allowed him to order so many CDs. Nevertheless, the partnership (and each partner) is liable for the bill for all the CDs.

As discussed in Chapter 1, while the rights and duties of the partners between themselves are primarily controlled by the partnership agreement, that's not necessarily true for other people dealing with a partner. After all, outsiders usually don't have any idea what's in the partnership agreement. So, in the above example, even if Herb, Frank and Connie's partnership agreement specifically limited the number or type of CDs a partner could commit the partnership to buy, a third party wouldn't be bound by this unless they had actual notice of the provision. To translate this into lawyer lingo would be to say that an outsider can legally rely on the "ostensible" or "apparent" authority of a partner. This is authority that's been demonstrated by the partner in the course of the business or authority that's normally granted partners in similar business partnerships.

Silent Partners

The term "silent partner" can mean a partner whose involvement isn't revealed to the public, or it can mean a partner who contributes only cash to the business and won't work in it, or both. In either case, we advise you to be exceedingly wary when considering having a silent partner as part of your partnership. Indeed, we think it is rarely a good idea, and we urge you to see a knowledgeable lawyer and review your situation carefully before agreeing to a general partnership with a partner who isn't going to take a publicly acknowledged role in the business, or who won't work in it.

What's troublesome about a silent partner? If a partner's involvement won't be revealed to the public, the question at once arises: Why this secrecy? There's rarely a valid reason for it. Regardless of what is revealed to the public, if the silent partner will contribute only cash to the business, not work, this creates inherent conflicts. The other partners are working, usually very hard, to keep the business alive, while the silent partner isn't. Yet, as a full-fledged owner, the silent partner is entitled to a share of profit of the business and has an equity share of the business. If the business prospers because of the work of the other partners, they're likely to become increasingly resentful of benefiting the silent partner. Also, from the silent partner's point of view, she has potentially unlimited liability for partnership debts but may not find out about a problem because she isn't around the business.

But what about having a silent investor in capital-intensive partnerships, such as those that purchase real estate and don't need too much management? This goal can be achieved without making the investor a partner. Structure the investor's contribution as an interest in a limited partnership, specifically defining the investing partner's role and return, which can include a share of the profits. (See Chapter 9 for an outline of how limited partnerships work.) Or treat the investment as a loan. But don't give away an ownership share of your business to someone who won't work in it.

2. Partnership Decision-Making

What is the authority of the partners between themselves to make decisions about normal partnership business? The short answer is that partners may make decisions any way they agree upon. Often, decision-making is done democratically: one partner, one vote. The UPA provides that each partner has an equal vote, but this can be altered in the partnership agreement. (Note that the UPA calls for this approach even if the partners haven't contributed equal amounts of assets to the partnership.) We usually recommend this one-partner, one-vote approach, since it's more likely to promote harmony and goodwill among the partners. However, some situations—or some people—call for a different approach. How you decide to structure voting power in your partnership isn't a mechanical matter. Rather, it is a reflection of how the partners feel about each other and what each is actually contributing.

Many partnerships have only two partners. Others have an even number of partners. Obviously, in these partnerships, there's a possibility of deadlock under a one-partner, one-vote rule, so you'll need to take special care regarding dispute resolution methods. (See Chapter 6.) In theory, having an unequal number of partners eliminates the possibility of deadlock. In the real world, however, you haven't avoided a serious conflict just because there's an odd number of partners. If the three majority members of a partnership consistently outvote the two minority members, the partnership is likely to be in deep trouble. And it's no help that it got into the mess democratically.

EXAMPLE: Stephanie, Alison and Lori decide to set up a modeling agency. Stephanie contributes $20,000 to start the business and will work full-time. Alison contributes $10,000 and will work only occasionally at the business. Lori will contribute only $500 and will work halftime. Obviously, Stephanie is contributing the most to the business. Should she nevertheless have just one vote, only one-third control in the partnership? That's up to the three partners.

If Stephanie insists she doesn't want to risk being outvoted by the two other partners, and they agree, here are two possible approaches to solve her problem:

- The partnership agreement can provide that each partner's vote is in proportion to her contribution of the partnership capital. This approach leaves Lori without any significant say in the management of the business, since she contributed such a small amount of capital. It might well be fairer to proportion voting rights according to each partner's share of profits, since they (presumably) will reflect contributions of services as well as initial capital to the partnership.

- Another approach is for the partners to agree on what proportion of voting power each partner should receive. For example, the partners could agree that Stephanie will have 60% of the voting power, with Alison and Lori each receiving 20% (and decisions to be made by majority).

Note that both methods leave Stephanie in complete control. Although her problem has been solved, if she ever adopts policies that

Alison and Lori don't care for, there's little they can do but resign and try to liquidate the partnership. This often isn't easy to do, even if, as we urge, specific clauses have been included in the partnership agreement covering what happens if any partner leaves. (See Chapter 5.) Another approach, which can work well for small partnerships, is to require that all major decisions be unanimous—that is, every partner has veto power.

As you can see, deciding on a clause involving the control and management of a partnership can be tricky. Sometimes partners try to handle this by going into great detail about how, when and who makes decisions—down to specifying just when meetings will occur and what types of issues must be decided by all partners. We believe a more common sense approach is to require that major decisions be made and voted on by all partners, with less formal requirements for minor decisions.

Of course, how you define major and minor will depend on the personalities of the partners and the type of business. Some partners do it by adopting money as a yardstick to define the authority of each individual partner (for example, "all decisions involving the expenditure or potential expenditure of more than $5,000 shall be discussed and voted on by all partners"). Others handle it in some other way (for example, "a decision as to what jobs to bid on, the design specifications and the amount of the bid shall be unanimously agreed to by all partners").

3. A Partner's Authority to Borrow Money

It is not uncommon for a partnership to borrow money, either to get started or to expand. Normally, the lender will insist on the signature of all the partners to make sure that each partner is aware of the partnership's obligation. Banks are particularly careful about this.

Some lenders, however, won't be so fussy; so, the question can arise—does one partner have the power to borrow money and obligate the partnership to pay it back without the express approval of the other partners? This is something that should be covered in your partnership agreement. We recommend that you adopt a partnership agreement that requires all partners to approve all loans, unless there are special circumstances in your business that compel a different approach. It's simpler and less risky that way.

Partnership No-No's

A partner has considerable authority to bind the partnership in the ordinary or normal course of the partnership's business. Does this mean that one partner can bind the others no matter what she does, unless there's a specific clause prohibiting the particular activity in the partnership agreement, and it's brought to the attention of someone dealing with the partner? No. There are a number of things the Uniform Partnership Act says that a partner can't do. Members of the outside world are presumed to know a partner can't do these things "in the ordinary course of business." Here is a list of the actions that a partner cannot take without partnership approval unless the agreement specifically provides otherwise:

- convey one's interest in any partnership property ("Convey" is legalese for any type of transfer, whether by sale, gift or exchange.)
- mortgage or otherwise subject partnership property to a lien to cover one's personal debts or borrowing
- attempt to dispose of specific partnership property (rather than one's own interest in the partnership) through one's will after death
- assign partnership property in trust for creditors or on the assignee's promise to pay the debts of the partnership
- dispose of the "goodwill" of the business
- commit any act that would make it impossible to carry on the ordinary business of the partnership
- agree to a judgment for the other side in a lawsuit against the partnership.

We do not think that any of these acts should be permitted in a partnership agreement. However, if you disagree and want a single partner to be able to mortgage property or take any of the other steps listed above, you'll have to state this expressly in your partnership agreement when defining partners' powers. (See Chapter 3, Section D.)

There's another risk here that you should be aware of. No matter what the partnership agreement states, partners in what have traditionally been called "trading partnerships" have the apparent authority to borrow money or execute loans on behalf of the partnership. Apparent authority means that outsiders can lend money to the partnership on the say-so of one partner, unless they actually know that other partners must approve the loan.

Trading partnerships are, as the name states, those directly involved in trade, like merchants selling a product. Examples of nontrading partnerships include service businesses like law firms, theaters, banks, real estate enterprises or farms. Partners in nontrading partnerships traditionally don't have the apparent authority to borrow money on behalf of the partnership. This distinction between trading and nontrading partnerships sounds clear, but deciding which label fits a particular business is often quite difficult. Indeed, one commentator has stated that the distinction between trading and nontrading partnerships has haunted partnership law for generations. The UPA doesn't make this distinction; however, it doesn't outlaw it, so the courts in many states still adhere to it.

⚠ Be especially careful if you run a retail business. *What all this means is simply that, in many partnerships running a retail business, there is an additional danger if you have an unreliable partner. Without actual authorization by you, this partner can borrow money and leave you and the other partners stuck for the loan.*

4. Liability of the Partnership to the Public

Conventional legal rules of responsibility are applicable to partnerships. For example, partners must perform any services provided to the public competently, or the partnership can be liable for negligence. Competence means a partner must use the level of professional skill, care and diligence generally applicable in the profession or trade. This standard usually applies to all partnership enterprises whether they're set up to fix teeth, trains or toilets, or to sell soap, soup or sawdust. So, if one partner (or an employee of the partnership) in a pest control business inspects a house sloppily and doesn't spot termites in the basement, the partnership is liable for any loss that results from that negligence.

The partnership is also liable for "any wrongful act or omission of any partner acting in the ordinary course of business of the partnership where loss or injury is caused to any person...." (UPA Section 13.) This means that if a partner negligently injures a pedestrian while driving a car on partnership business, the entire partnership is liable for the pedestrian's

damages. Similarly, the partnership is generally liable for intentionally wrongful acts—deceit, assault, trespass—committed by a partner during the course of partnership business.

The conventional way to protect against most business risks is to buy liability insurance. As we indicate in Chapter 8, Section E, obtaining insurance often means you pay a relatively high cost for protection against occurrences that are rather unlikely. However, insurance protection against traditional sorts of negligence lawsuits—someone slips and falls in your store and sues you—is obviously sensible, especially in situations where insurance is relatively affordable. Whether you want insurance against other risks, such as professional incompetence or intentional injuries, is often a more difficult choice and depends to a large degree on who you are and what you're doing. For example, legal and medical malpractice insurance has become so costly that some lawyers and doctors no longer purchase it, but choose to accept the risk that if they're sued for malpractice, they'll have to pay legal defense costs themselves—and, if they lose the case, they'll have to pay the judgment from their own assets. While this approach may make sense for dermatologists and copyright specialists (who are rarely sued), it might be too risky for brain surgeons and trial lawyers (whose work involves serious risks). As noted in Chapter 1, if you are in a fairly high-risk occupation and can't get or afford insurance, you may wish to incorporate to take advantage of limited personal liability.

Do your homework before you buy business insurance. *Deciding whether or not you need insurance by asking an insurance agent for a recommendation is a little like leaving it up to a car dealer to add on all the optional equipment he sees fit. A better approach is to talk to people in businesses like yours to see how they've solved the liability insurance dilemma. Once you decide on the insurance you want, shop around—rates will vary considerably.*

Apparent Members of a Partnership

Here's another, and more remote, area of possible partnership danger—the possibility that you might be held liable as a member of a partnership to which you don't legally belong. This liability arises if it reasonably appears to a member of the public that you're a member of the partnership, and that person takes action relying on her belief that the partnership exists.

For instance, suppose you and two acquaintances investigate forming a partnership, and even have partnership stationery printed, with all three names on it. Then you decide, for whatever reasons, to back out. Later someone who isn't paid for work by the partnership sues you for his bill, claiming, on the basis of the letterhead and statements made by the continuing partners, he believed that you were involved and relied on this in dealing with the partnership. Is this enough for him to prevail against you? Maybe—maybe not; it can ultimately depend on what a jury decides, based on all the facts of the situation. Certainly, your name on a letterhead can be enough to cause someone to sue you. Who needs that worry? The point is simple—if you discuss a partnership that you don't actually join, be sure that there's no chance that you'll subsequently be held out as a member of the partnership. If stationery or cards have been printed, destroy them. If third parties have been informed about the partnership, write to each to inform them of the true state of affairs.

5. Legal Rights of a Partner Against a Partnership

You should realize it's at least theoretically possible that—despite your good intentions—you and your partners will end up having a spat. If you can't resolve your problems, you should know that partners do have some formal legal rights vis-a-vis their partnership. These include:

- the right to an accounting of the partnership assets; that is, an examination of the books by an outside accountant. Periodic accountings are often provided for in partnership agreements. They are generally paid for by the partnership itself. But if an accounting is made as part of a lawsuit, a court has the right to apportion the cost of an accounting in a way it decides is fair.
- a right to a legal action for dissolution of the partnership under certain circumstances
- a legal action for an injunction to restrain illegal partnership acts and the appointment of a receiver to handle partnership assets, and
- ordinary breach of contract actions.

E. Name and Purpose of the Partnership

A partnership business must have a name—an identity by which it presents itself to the public and the IRS. Some partnerships, such as law or accounting firms, simply choose the last names of some partners. Many partnerships choose two names—their own last names for their partnership, and a separate business name (called a fictitious business name) that, hopefully, will enhance their business. You can choose any name you want for your partnership or your business—except you can't pick one that's already in use or is very similar to one in use. If you create a fictitious business name you must comply with the applicable state laws governing such names. These aren't generally onerous. (See Chapter 3, Section A and Chapter 8, Section A.)

The partnership agreement also normally contains a short statement of the purpose of the business, such as:

- "The purpose of the Milliflower partnership is to engage in retail flower sales and any related commercial activity."
- "The purpose of the A-G partnership is to purchase, renovate and sell residential real estate."

Generally, it's best for partners to broadly state the purpose of the partnership. There's no sensible reason to unduly narrow your scope.

You can also state the date the partnership is to start and, if appropriate, when it will end. Most partnership agreements, of course, don't specify a termination date. The duration of a partnership is generally open-ended and will last as long as the partners desire it to.

When you and your prospective partners sit down and prepare your statement of the purpose of the business, you should also take this occasion to discuss—or review—each partner's personal goals for the business. What are each partner's dreams, hopes and fears? Surely, you'll have already voiced these concerns, but a focused summation is a good idea. Generally, we don't think you need to write your thoughts or conclusions down (no transcript is required), though there's certainly no prohibition against doing so. If you do, one good approach is to have a section in your agreement that covers each partner's sense of the goals of the business and his or her hopes for it, while making it clear this isn't intended as a binding legal provision but is offered in the spirit of making a written record of shared intentions.

F. Financial Considerations

Whatever your feelings about money, we've learned that a healthy, sensible respect for it is essential for a partnership business to work. Money is funny stuff; conflicts revolving around it can destroy a partnership with astounding speed, so it's essential that all prospective partners reach an honest understanding of how you'll handle money matters, and then pin down that understanding in your partnership agreement.

1. Initial Contributions to the Partnership

Your partnership will need some assets to commence business. The initial contributions, obviously, are made by yourself and your partners. In the simplest situation, each partner will contribute cash only. Often partners contribute equal amounts, but it is equally common that they don't. In any case, if your partners are all contributing cash, you create a specific clause in your agreement that states how much money each partner has contributed, or will contribute.

It's also common for partners to contribute property as well as (or instead of) cash to a partnership. Property contributions can range from the simple to the highly complex. In simple situations, the major matters to be covered in the partnership agreement are the value the partnership puts on the property contributed and the conditions, if any, placed on its transfer to the partnership. As with all elements of a partnership agreement, a two-step process is involved here: First the partners discuss and agree how to value property a partner contributes (and decide on any other issues pertinent to acquiring that property); second, that agreement is written in a specific clause in the partnership agreement.

Partners may also contribute their personal services. This is often a specific skill (not simply working on partnership business). For example, three partners decide that a fourth partner will receive an owner's (partner's) interest (not just wages) in a business because of a promise to donate needed bookkeeping and paperwork skills. However, contributing services can have adverse tax consequences for the contributing partner if it's not handled properly. We'll discuss this in more detail in Chapter 7, Section E.

A partner can sell, loan, lease or rent property to the partnership, as well as contribute property to it. Lending property to a partnership can be particularly appropriate in a situation in which one partner possesses an item that the partnership wants to use (for example, a valuable set of antique restaurant furniture), but the partner doesn't wish to give it to the partnership, and it's too expensive for the partnership to buy.

2. Profits, Losses, Draws and Salaries

If your partnership agreement doesn't state how profits and losses are to be divided, the UPA provides that all partners share both equally, even if they contributed unequal amounts of cash, property or labor to the partnership. If the partnership agreement defines how profits are to be distributed, but doesn't mention losses, the UPA provides that each partner must contribute toward the losses according to his or her share of profits. (UPA Section 18(a).) However, even if profits and losses are to be shared equally, you should state this expressly in your partnership agreement, rather than rely on the UPA. This will prevent the possibility of later disagreement over what your understanding was.

Many partnerships choose to divide profits and losses unequally. This can be done for all sorts of reasons, such as when one partner contributes more work or more money to the partnership. There's no one formula for distributing profits or losses, no simple rule to tell you when it's sensible to give one or more partner a larger or smaller share. Once again, it's your business and you can divide the profits and losses any way you all agree is fair. What's crucial is that you all discuss what you want and then come to an agreement.

Sometimes partners decide that one or more partners will receive what's called a draw. The term "draw" means a periodic payment against future partnership profits. Rather than wait, say, until the end of the taxable year to divide up profits, each partner takes a draw each month, or whatever period you've agreed on. If one partner, in particular, doesn't have a financial reserve and needs money to live on each month, the partnership may decide that only that partner will receive a draw. This policy creates the risk that those who don't receive draws will resent payments to a partner who gets them.

⚠️ **Be sure to address partner salaries in your partnership agreement.** *Working partners can also receive salaries from the partnership. These salaries are not draws, but normal partnership business expenses. The salary must be reasonable, in light of industry standards. The IRS has rules on what is permissible for partners' salaries and what must be paid out as profits. If this subject concerns you, review it with an accountant.*

In some states, oral agreements for partners' salaries are valid. It's wise to state explicitly in your agreement whatever you've decided about partners' salaries. You generally can't spell out the dollar amount of salaries partners will be paid for the next five years, but you can state whether salaries will be allowed or not.

3. Owning Property

Property owned by a partnership is held in the partnership name. (UPA Section 25.) Partners, however, are free to decide whether property used by the business will be partnership property or will be owned by an individual partner and merely used by the partnership (that is, rented, leased or loaned and used free). Unless the partners expressly agree to the contrary, property acquired with partnership funds is partnership property.

> **EXAMPLE:** Eduardo and Louise are partners in a local parcel delivery business. Eduardo has two cars of his own, which they occasionally use in the business. Eduardo enters into a

simple written agreement with the partnership, which states that the partnership will compensate Eduardo so much money per mile for use of the cars. In this situation, there's no implication that the cars belong to the partnership. But if Eduardo's cars wear out and the partnership buys a car with partnership assets, and Eduardo uses the car once in a while on the weekends, this new car is clearly a partnership asset.

Property held in the partnership name can logically and legally only be sold and transferred by the partnership itself. There are advantages to this. Aside from protection against unethical partners, partnership property isn't subject to attachment or execution to satisfy a creditor's individual claim against one partner.

If the partnership agreement or the partners haven't defined what's partnership property, here are the four questions courts usually ask in determining the nature of possible partnership property.

- What was the source of funds used to buy it?
- Was it purchased in the partnership name?
- Was it used in the partnership business?
- Was it reflected on the books as a partnership asset?

4. Taxes

We discuss partnership taxation, especially as it concerns a beginning partnership, in Chapter 7. There are, however, a few tax matters we want to make sure you're aware of from the start of your consideration of partnerships.

- The partnership doesn't pay taxes itself, but it must file an "informational" partnership tax return (IRS Form 1065).
- Partners pay taxes on all net profits, whether actually distributed to the partners or not.
- Partnerships must use the accrual method of accounting "whenever inventories of goods are maintained." (The accrual method of accounting means debits and credits are

counted when accrued, not when money is actually received or paid. For example, if a business sells flowers and bills for its services, the sale is counted when it is invoiced, not when the customer actually pays.)

- Partnerships or partners are only allowed to deduct money spent organizing or promoting a partnership over a period of years (rather than in the partnership's first tax year).

- Contributions of property or services to a partnership can raise complex tax problems. See below and read Chapter 7 carefully before making any decisions.

The tax implications of contributions to a partnership, especially property contributions, can become quite complicated. For example, if one partner wants to contribute property he bought long ago at a low price—property that is now worth far more—does that partner have to pay taxes on this gain when the partnership gets ownership of the property? Is this transfer a taxable event? The answer is generally no. However, if the transferred property is subject to a mortgage, the tax situation becomes murkier, and the contributing partner may be assessed a taxable gain.

Note for existing businesses. *Problems with contributions can also arise if a merchant decides to take in a partner and the merchant's inventory will be legally transferred to the partnership. This type of bulk transfer must comply with provisions of your state's Bulk Sales Act unless—as is often the case—the new partnership assumes all the debts previously owed by the merchant. (Uniform Commercial Code Section 9-103 et seq.)*

History Lesson # 5

Partnership law was slowly merged into the conventional English legal system but has always retained the flexibility of its practical roots. In England, equity courts first took on partnership cases. Equity courts evolved from the tradition that the King, acting through his chancellor, could do justice on an ad hoc, individual basis, without the limits of the common-law rules. Then, under Lord Coke (in the 1600s) and Lord Masefield (1700s), the common law courts themselves consciously began to change and develop streamlined procedures for dealing with commercial disputes.

The roots of most law in the United States are English (except in Louisiana, where law is based on the Napoleonic Code). After the American Revolution, the states passed laws which provided that they "received" (adopted) the English common law as American law, except when the state specifically varied English rules. That received law includes English partnership law, which is the basis of our current law.

G. Expanding Your Business

We urge you to discuss how you and your partners will handle it if your business takes off and prospers greatly. There are many ways to define success, from making gobs of money to doing enjoyable work to being free as a bird. Ask yourself now whether the additional burdens that are bound to accompany running a bigger business would be worth it.

We have friends whose small consulting business grew rapidly, far beyond their original expectations. They just went with the flow—and soon were mired in high overhead and many unanticipated problems. With demanding customers, tight deadlines and employees knocking on their office doors asking about vacation policies, sick-leave plans and pension options, they found themselves growing more and more dissatisfied. Eventually they scaled their business down to near its original size. They were a lot happier, even though they earned less. While these are personal, not legal, matters, we believe that discussing your dreams and plans for the future of the business must be an integral part of creating any partnership. It's one excellent way for you to determine whether you and your partners are sufficiently compatible to press ahead.

So discuss and review what you and your partners want to happen if your business does very well. How much income is sufficient before each of you will feel satisfied? Will any of you want to kick back and develop other interests, or will you all redouble your efforts to become more prosperous? Think about how each of you will feel: hiring employees; hiring more employees; moving to a new store or office; adding a second store, warehouse or factory; expanding into a related business; buying additional machinery; financing a larger staff or inventory; taking over an ongoing operation; etc. If individual partners feel very differently about many of these issues, it's an indication that perhaps they should rethink the idea of going into business together.

While you should talk about these matters, we don't feel it's normally advisable to put specific provisions in your original partnership agreement that provide an expansion game plan, with one important exception: adding partners. The reason that there's not much point in incorporating details of how you'll handle future growth in your original agreement is that generally it's quite futile to try to predict the specifics of your business future. Whatever the future holds, it's almost surely going to be different from what you think it will be now. As Napoleon put it, "First you commit yourself, and then…you see."

As a practical matter, any specifics regarding expansion that you put in your agreement now aren't likely to be of any use in legally binding a partner. If a couple of years down the road your partner doesn't like the way the business is expanding, all the legal clauses in the world aren't likely to make him more cooperative. Courts won't issue orders compelling a partner to live up to a clause agreeing to work productively for an expanded business; how could the court enforce it? Remember, the essence of partnership is voluntary cooperation. If you and your partners begin to fundamentally disagree about the direction your partnership business should take, it's time to go your separate ways. A well-drafted partnership agreement can help you by containing provisions governing a split-up of the partnership, but it can't make you continue to work together productively, no matter how detailed it is.

H. Operational and Management Responsibilities

It's desirable, and usually essential, that each partner be actively involved in managing and operating the partnership business. Aside from the practical, common sense reasons for this, it's generally desirable for income tax purposes. (See Chapter 7, Section I.)

When preparing your agreement, you should be sure everyone feels comfortable with how work and responsibilities have been divided up. As for the specific clauses in your agreement, there's no iron-clad rule about how you should describe each partner's work responsibilities. If there are only two or three partners, and they will all be involved in all phases of the business, a simple statement to that effect will usually suffice. On the other hand, if your business will involve more separation of management roles, or if, whatever the work duties involved, you feel more comfortable with precision on this subject, feel free to define the details of management responsibilities in your agreement.

If you decide to be specific about management responsibilities, here are some key issues you will probably want to cover:

- skills to be contributed by each partner
- hours worked
- work duties of each partner (the specific tasks and functions of the business for which each partner has primary responsibility), and
- management roles (aspects of the business that each partner has primary responsibility to control and direct, either by his own efforts or by supervising employees).

If you think it's advisable, you can be even more specific, covering matters like:

- expense account rules, and
- check-signing procedures.

I. Withdrawal of a Partner, Buy-Outs and Ending a Partnership

It's absolutely essential that you set out in your original agreement rules for what happens if a partner leaves—whether by withdrawal, death or illness or expulsion. How much notice of withdrawal must a departing partner give? Can that partner sell his or her interest? To whom? Do the remaining partners have the right to buy out the departing partner? How is the buy-out price determined? What is the payment schedule? What happens if there are only two partners and one leaves? Or suppose there are an equal number of partners divided into two opposing groups, both of which want to continue the business?

1. Rules for a Partner's Departure

At the beginning of a partnership, when everyone is excited, it's often psychologically hard for partners to pay adequate attention to rules that deal with what happens if a partner withdraws from the partnership. What a downer to worry about buy-outs or valuation of the business at a time when you really just want to talk about who's going to put up money or whether to take on a particular lease or how great everything's going to be. Unfortunately, ignoring the problems a departing partner can cause is foolish. Sooner or later you are very likely to have to handle these problems. Our experience in talking to many partners and former partners convinces us that it's likely to be sooner than you might think. In a footloose age, very few shared ownership businesses retain the same owners for more than a few years. And even if your partnership business does endure unchanged for a long time, eventually one of you will retire or die, and you or your loved ones will have to deal with what to do next.

EXAMPLE: Sumi, Yollanne and Avril are partners in a bakery. For years their business prospers, and all three enjoy their work, at least much of the time (those 3 a.m. baking shifts can get anyone down). But Sumi is 20 years older than the other two, and in her 50s she decides she wants to do something else. Now what? How can she cash in for her share of the bakery? If there's nothing covering this in their partnership agreement, Sumi could try to sell her share of the partnership to anyone she wants to. Also, she has the legal right to seek a formal dissolution of the partnership and distribution of partnership assets. If she does this, Yollanne and Avril are powerless to protect the existing business. If they'd created a buy-out provision in the partnership agreement, they would already have a mechanism in place to deal with this.

When you're preparing your agreement, you must focus on problems raised by the departure of a partner. Now is the time to let yourself be a little paranoid. Indeed, we've heard lawyers refer to partnership buy-out agreements as divorce agreements signed while the parties are still in love. Imagine partner departures, even disasters. How would you cope with them? For example, if a partner leaves, it's quite possible there will be a conflict over the value of her interest if you haven't already established a method to determine that worth. Not surprisingly, the departing partner could conclude that her interest is worth a lot more than the partners who remain would. Or, if a partner dies, his heirs might likewise often feel his interest is worth more than the surviving partners say it is. So you need to specify in your partnership agreement how the value of a departing partner's interest is determined. Also, do the remaining partners have the right (or option) to buy a departing partner's interest? Usually, it's a good idea to provide for this. We'll get into this in depth in Chapter 5, Sections A and B. Here you don't have to resolve these issues, just realize they're important.

Once you decide on how to value a partnership share, there's the question of payment. Naturally, a departing partner usually prefers to receive payment for her entire share in cash, immediately. However, the remaining partners may face the destruction of the business unless time payments are allowed. A prior agreement on how payments are to be made eliminates these conflicts.

While Chapter 5 discusses buy-out basics, see Buy-Sell Agreement Handbook: Plan Ahead for Changes in the Ownership of Your Business, *by Anthony Mancuso and Bethany K. Laurence (Nolo) for even more in-depth information on this topic.*

2. Ending a Partnership

The legal term for the ending of a partnership is "dissolution." When a partnership ends, the partnership business ends too. The partners can't undertake new partnership business. They must pay all the bills and distribute any remaining assets to the soon-to-be ex-partners. (This is discussed in Chapter 5, Section F.)

By definition, a partnership ends if there were only two partners, and one leaves. By contrast, with any larger partnership, the departure of one partner usually doesn't result in a termination of the business; the other partners carry it on.

The ending of a partnership doesn't necessarily mean you've failed. In several partnerships we know of, substantial success led to the eventual breakup of the partnership. For example, two friends of ours started a restaurant in Northern California. Their first place was tiny, with delicious vegetarian food and friendly service. The restaurant prospered sufficiently so that the owners could move to a much bigger place, which they later bought. As they continued to prosper, the owners realized that their dreams had begun to diverge. One wanted to continue to run the existing restaurant, while the other dreamt of a stylish seafood restaurant in San Francisco. Both dreams held—so their partnership was terminated on a friendly but businesslike basis. Eventually, the San Francisco restaurant proved very successful, while the other one continued on its small scale.

J. Disputes

The last major area to cover in your agreement is what happens if the partners have a dispute that they can't resolve. Certainly, when you're starting your business, you don't envision serious disputes, but it would be absurd to assert that it won't occur. It's common sense to work out your method for handling disputes that the partners can't resolve between themselves far in advance of their occurring. Reliance on a dispute-resolution clause is definitely a last resort. It is no substitute for the day-to-day give-and-take we all use to prevent small annoyances from turning into big problems. But having a formal dispute-resolution clause in your agreement can be essential if compromise proves to be impossible. We want to reassure you that we know of very few partnerships that haven't been able to work out their problems themselves and had to resort to mediation or arbitration.

Now and throughout the existence of your business, do all you can to avoid having to resolve disputes in a formal way. Some partners discuss these issues over a civilized lunch and good wine and find that this works wonders. Other partners go on annual retreats or schedule a "play day" to remove the partners from the tensions and dulling effects of day-to-day pressures, and open them up, relax them and help them remember why they all went into business with each other in the first place. Some busy people are inclined to resist scheduling the time these activities take. In our view, this is short-sighted. Business isn't just about hard work; it's also about working well with people. Good communication may sound like a cliché, but it's essential for a business to prosper. Setting aside a few hours to relax and talk is a wise use of time.

However, despite your best efforts, it's conceivable that a dispute will arise that the partners can't resolve between themselves. For this reason, we urge you to include a mediation/arbitration clause in your partnership agreement. (See Chapter 6.) Mediation and/or arbitration are your best options for resolving conflicts that can't be solved informally. Basically, both procedures involve using a private (non-court) structure to handle disputes. The advantage is that the cumbersome, expensive process of our court system is replaced by a procedure that is cheaper, more humane and perhaps—most importantly—vastly faster.

Of course, you all hope that you'll never need to have recourse to your mediation/arbitration clause. And you probably won't. Most partnerships don't wind up in such serious fights. But if for some reason yours does, you'll be glad you have the clause.

No clause can prevent a partner from leaving a partnership. If the partners have become so enmeshed in conflict that mediation/arbitration procedures are called for, it's likely that at least one partner will want out permanently. Not even a court would order a person to remain active in a partnership if she doesn't want to. But with mediation/arbitration, at least the issues between the partners will be settled reasonably, and promptly, without a court fight.

1. Mediation

Mediation is a process in which an outside party—the mediator—attempts to assist two or more people in resolving their dispute by reaching a mutually satisfactory compromise or resolution. A mediator has no power to impose a decision, which means there's no guarantee you'll resolve the matter unless you and your partners can find some common ground. However, if mediation is successful, the partners will generally have reached an agreement into which everyone's had input, and which hasn't been imposed on them by a court or an arbitrator. This can help all the partners feel good about the legitimacy and fairness of the compromise.

For more information on mediation, see How to Mediate Your Dispute, *by Peter Lovenheim (Nolo).*

2. Arbitration

Arbitration means that your dispute is submitted to an arbitrator, who the has power to make a binding decision. The arbitration process is usually fairly informal, depending on the arbitrator's personality and any arbitration rules you have agreed on. An arbitrator's decision is exceedingly difficult to challenge successfully in court. The contesting party usually must demonstrate that the arbitrator's behavior has been extreme—such as provable bias or a decision clearly outside the scope of her authority.

Your partnership agreement can provide for binding arbitration by various methods, from naming a trusted friend to selecting a group of three colleagues. It can be wise to name a specific arbitrator, who all the partners respect, in the initial agreement.

3. Combining Arbitration With Mediation

We suggest that you include both mediation and arbitration clauses in your agreement. Any dispute is first referred to a mediator. But if the partners fail to agree, you'll next present the dispute to an arbitrator rather than go to court. For example, you could state that if mediation proved unsuccessful after a certain period of time, arbitration would follow.

History Lesson # 6

By the start of the 21st century, America's regular civil courts had become overly complicated, overly expensive and overburdened with huge numbers of lawsuits. As a result, practical business people increasingly abandoned them as sensible places to resolve disputes. As in the Middle Ages, business has come to rely increasingly on what amounts to a private court system. Thus arbitration and, more recently, mediation clauses have become increasingly popular in business circles. Having an arbitrator render a decision is comparatively inexpensive and fast. It remains to be seen whether the civil court system will respond to this challenge by modernizing its old-fashioned rules, procedures and language. There are some signs that this is happening, as some larger states are beginning to make arbitration a part of their system. Also, several states have passed "plain English" statutes, requiring standard legal documents—such as leases, insurance contracts, etc.—to be phrased in clear, everyday English, not legalese. And in some states, retired judges can be hired by private parties to hear and decide their case. This procedure is often called "rent-a-judge."

K. Short-Form Partnership Agreements

For some people, there is a significant time gap between starting a partnership, perhaps with a handshake, and the final signing of their comprehensive partnership agreement. Human nature being what it is, it's simply too easy to put off preparing your agreement and end up with nothing at all in writing for a significant period of time. If you're like most of the new business partners we know, you feel like you're entering, or have just entered, one of the most exciting times of your life. Starting up, you'll find yourself going in many directions at once—bills! orders! jobs!—and may put off preparing your agreement. So, with some trepidation, we include here two sample short-form partnership agreements that say little more than the fact that a partnership has been established and that there is more to come. We also include one blank short-form agreement you can complete. This short-form agreement is reproduced in Appendix 3, so you can remove it from the book, fill in the blanks and complete it.

Why do we do this with trepidation? Well, we'd prefer it if no one ever used a short-form agreement at all. It's much better to get your complete agreement quickly and finally done—drafted, typed and signed. We're a little afraid that some people will try to substitute the short agreement for a longer one and use it as an excuse not to design something that will work over the long term. So, let us emphasize that a short-form agreement is a stopgap device and should never be used for longer than one to three months.

SHORT-FORM PARTNERSHIP AGREEMENT

Arnold Presnor and Imogene Grange agree as follows:

1. That as of April 1, 2004 they are partners in a business to be known as Acme Illusions. Acme Illusions will operate an interior design business in the greater Dallas, Texas metropolitan area;

2. That Arnold Presnor and Imogene Grange will each contribute $20,000 to get the business going and will be 50-50 partners;

3. That all initial decisions regarding business location, advertising, price, etc., will be made jointly;

4. That neither partner will obligate the business for any debt in an amount more than $1,000 without the other's consent;

5. That within two months from the date of this agreement, a formal partnership agreement shall be prepared, which will cover what happens if a partner dies or quits, as well as partnership decision-making, a dispute resolution mechanism, etc.

Signature: _____ Dated: _____

      Arnold Presnor

Signature: _____ Dated: _____

      Imogene Grange

SAMPLE SHORT-FORM PARTNERSHIP AGREEMENT

Olga March, Randy Graham and Bill Obie make the following temporary partnership agreement with the express intention of replacing it with a detailed agreement prior to January 1, 2005. The partners agree:

1. That they are equal partners in the Happy Clam, a seafood restaurant to be located on the waterfront in Baltimore, Maryland;

2. That Olga and Randy will each contribute $53,000 to refurbish an existing restaurant which has been known as Toni's Terrific Tostadas;

3. That Bill obligates himself to serve as chef of the new restaurant for two years in exchange for his one-third share;

4. That all major business decisions involving getting the new restaurant operational will be made by Olga and Randy, and all decisions having to do with the kitchen, including the menu, food ordering, hiring kitchen assistants, etc., will be made by Bill;

5. That the formal partnership agreement, which will be drafted prior to January 1, 2005, will include clauses covering the following matters:

   - the purpose of the partnership business

   - the terms of the partnership

   - the contributions made by each partner

   - distribution of profits and losses

   - management powers and responsibilities

   - admission of new partners

   - provisions for continuing the business if a partner departs, dies, etc., including valuation and buy-out terms, and

   - arbitration

Signature: _____ Dated: _____
            Olga March

Signature: _____ Dated: _____
            Randy Graham

Signature: _____ Dated: _____
            Bill Obie

BLANK SHORT-FORM PARTNERSHIP AGREEMENT

_____, _____,

_____, _____,

and _____ agree as follows:

1. That as of _____, 20____, they are partners in a business known as _____ _[business name]_ _____.

2. That the general purpose of the business is _____ _[describe]_ _____

   _____

   _____

   _____.

3 That the partners now agree that _____ _[include all specific agreements made]_ _____

   _____

   _____

   _____.

4. That the partners further agree that they will prepare, by _____, 20____ (or, "as quickly as they can"), a final and complete partnership agreement governing the partnership, and that the agreement will cover at least:

   - contributions of each partner to the partnership
   - distribution of profits and losses
   - management powers and responsibilities
   - admission of new partners
   - the departure of a partner for any reason, and
   - arbitration

To formalize this short-form partnership agreement, each partner has signed his or her name on the date below:

Signature: _____ Dated: _____

Signature: _____ Dated: _____

Signature: _____ Dated: _____

Signature: _____ Dated: _____

Signature: _____ Dated: _____

L. Will You Need a Lawyer or an Accountant?

After you've worked out the substance of your agreement with your partners, you may decide you want to see a lawyer. (See Chapter 10, Section A.) Obviously, we're proponents of doing the work yourself if you can; since this book was first published in 1981, we know that many thousands of readers have prepared their own partnership agreements without needing attorneys' help. However, we certainly won't tell you that it could never be useful, or even necessary, to see a lawyer. Whether it is depends on several factors: How complicated is your business? How much time and effort have you expended on your agreement? How complicated is that agreement? How much money are partners investing? How complex are your tax issues, particularly regarding contributions of property or services? Are there any issues you want to cover in your agreement that still trouble you? How confident do you feel that you understand partnerships and that your agreement is sound and complete?

Oh yes, one more thing: If all partners are fairly savvy people, with at least a modicum of business experience, dispensing with professional help may make sense. However, if one or more partners, especially one who plans to make a major investment, is much less sophisticated than the others when it comes to business matters, all partners have a real interest in seeing that that person gets professional advice. The reason is simple: If problems develop down the road, no one wants a situation in which the inexperienced person claims (rightly or wrongly) that he was taken advantage of.

Even if you do use a lawyer, it's best not to dump the whole problem of creating your partnership on her desk. Remember, it's your business. We suggest you use this book and other available resources to figure out how to structure your partnership, and seek professional help only for the few areas you can't resolve unaided or want to have double-checked. Why pay lawyers' fees merely to get an authority figure's stamp of approval?

Almost all small businesses will need the help of an accountant, at least at tax time. But particularly as you start up, don't get hooked into paying for a more complicated accounting system than you need. A beginning partnership needs two things above all: income and a good relationship between partners. For practical purposes, you can get all the accounting you need from a business checking account. If there is consistently sufficient cash in the bank, you're doing okay. ■

Partnership Name, Contributions, Profits and Management

In this chapter, we discuss and present clauses for basic issues concerning the creation of a partnership. Have your pencils and note pads ready and be prepared to talk to each other, because you'll be starting to pin down what will actually be in your final agreement.

Completing Sample Clauses

In this chapter and Chapters 4, 5 and 6, you'll find sample clauses you can use for your agreement. As you proceed through these chapters, hash out what you want to do about each basic subject covered. Then select the clause, or clauses, you want and fill in the blank lines with the appropriate information (using pencil, of course). When you select a clause and complete it, place a check in the box to the left. Doing this will aid you when it comes time to assemble all the clauses you've chosen into one coherent document (which you'll do in Chapter 11).

A. Name, Term and Purpose

Your partnership, your business and your product (if you have one) need names. You also need to state the term of the partnership—how long it will last—and its basic business purpose.

1. Naming the Partnership, the Business or a Product

You will give your partnership a name in the partnership agreement. Your business or product also will have a name, which may or may not be the same as the partnership name. As for the titles the partners take for themselves, you're legally free to let your imaginations take flight. You can call yourselves partners, managing partners, or dukes or barons for that matter. (There were three members of Denis's law firm; they all had business cards identifying themselves as "senior partners.")

The name of the partnership is often the last names of the partners. For example, "The partnership shall be called Smith, Weiss and Fong." However, this isn't mandatory. The partnership can have a more imaginative or fictional name. For example, "The partnership shall be called the Merry Mongoose." If the partnership business will use a fictitious name (a name other than the names of its partners), the partners may decide to give the partnership the same name, so the enterprise has only one name. If the partnership chooses a fictitious name for itself or its business, it must follow all the steps discussed below to make sure that name is legally available.

There is also one legal restriction on the name of a partnership you must be aware of: A partnership cannot legally hold itself out to be a corporation. This means that you can't use the words "Inc.," "Ltd.," "Corporation," "Incorporated" (or in some states, "Company" or "Co.") or "Foundation" after your name. However, terms that don't directly imply that you're incorporated, such as "Associates," "Affiliates," "Group" and "Organization," are normally okay. Check with your Secretary or Department of State's office or take a look at your state's UPA or Revised UPA to determine which terms you may (or may not) use in your partnership's name.

As discussed, the partnership is a business, and that business itself needs a name. That name can be the same as the name of the partnership. For example, like the partnership, the business can be called "Smith, Weiss and Fong." But the business can also have a different name. Smith, Weiss and Fong (the partnership) could call their business "Rive Gauche Wines." This is a fictitious business name. By the way, don't be thrown off by the word "fictitious." In this context, it has no negative implications whatsoever and simply means you've decided to call your business something different—usually, more descriptive or imaginative—than your own last names.

If you do choose to use a fictitious business (or partnership) name, however, you're entering into an area where you can face serious problems if you choose a name another business is already using. So, let's take a closer look at how you can sensibly choose a name for your business.

Use of "He or She" in Sample Clauses

In some sample clauses, individual partners are identified as "he or she." Obviously, we can't know if all members of your partnership are the same sex. Even if they are, we suggest that it's wise to leave the phrase "he or she" in your agreement rather than eliminating the reference to one sex so the clause reads simply "he" or "she." After all, it's hard to be absolutely sure you'll never take in a partner of the other sex. And leaving the clause reading "he or she" won't cause any harm if all partners are the same sex.

---

a. The Importance of Your Business or Product Name

Your business or product name may turn out to be one of your most important business assets, as it can come to represent goodwill of your business. We don't mean this just in an accounting or tax sense, but primarily that the people and institutions you do business with will identify you mostly by your business name or associate certain characteristics with the name of your product. For this reason, as well as a number of practical reasons, such as not wanting to print new stationery or checks, change promotional literature, create new logos,

etc., you will want to thoughtfully select a name you'll be happy with for a long time.

If your business has a product, the name you choose for that product can also be vitally important. (Certainly we're all familiar with "brand names.") Once your business has a product, or even a clear idea of a product, it's wise to decide whether you will market the product nationally, or at least in several states. If so, you should also check on the legal availability of the name you choose for that product. And if your business offers a service, consider whether you might ever sell that service to a broad, not local, market. Multistate or national marketing is far more common than in the past. Many marketing devices, from the Internet and World Wide Web to "national yellow pages," allow customers throughout the country to learn of your product or service. Clearly, you don't want to begin marketing your product or service nationally and then learn, perhaps via a lawsuit, that some business in another state or area already has a trademark on the name you are using.

Finding an appropriate and available name for your business and product requires patience. It's often best not to act on your first impulse—try a few names before making your final choice. Ask others for feedback. Remember, you will have to live with this name for a long time.

b. Checking on the Legal Availability of a Name

Whatever name you decide to use for your partnership, product or both (even your own names), check to be sure another business isn't already using that name, or one confusingly similar. This matter isn't, unfortunately, just legal nitpicking. Business names can be, and often are, legally protected trademarks, or service marks. This means that a business with a prior claim to a name identical or similar to yours can sue to enjoin (stop) you from using the name or can force you to change it. A court may even award money damages to the name's rightful owner for any sales or goodwill it loses due to your use of the name. If you violate a trademark or service mark registered with the U.S. Patent and Trademark Office, a court may even award the rightful owner treble damages (three times the actual money damages suffered as a result of the infringement), defendant's profits and court costs, and a judge may order the goods with the offending labels or marks confiscated and destroyed.

Checking on the legal availability of a name can take some work. Perhaps the easiest thing to do is to go to the U.S. Patent and Trademark Office's website, www.uspto.gov. From there, click on "Searchable Databases" and choose the "Trademark Electronic Search System" link. This will take you to the USPTO's registered trademark database, which you can search for free. In addition, from the main USPTO website, you can download forms and get answers to frequently asked questions. If you don't have access to a computer, you can also conduct a name search by locating a Patent and Trademark Depository Library. All states have at least one of these libraries. To locate them, you can ask help from a local research librarian.

You can obtain much more information on naming your business or product and conducting name searches from Trademark: Legal Care for Your Business & Product Name, *by Stephen Elias (Nolo). This book covers just about everything you might need to know about trademark law. In addition to educating you about trademark law, the book should aid you in choosing a strong marketing name, and, if the circumstances warrant, help you register your business or product name as a trademark with state and federal trademark agencies.*

One way to create a name that doesn't conflict with another business's trademark can be to geographically limit your name, adding a particular

limitation, such as "of Georgia" or "in Northern Wyoming" or "in downtown Los Angeles." So, if you call yourself Southern Oregon Lumber, and you are the only one, you should be okay. But even here, it pays to check. If there is an Oregon Lumber Co., and they operate in Southern Oregon, they might object that your name is confusingly similar. Also, this approach works best only if you're sure your business will not offer goods or services outside of your local geographic area.

Without discussing the intricacies of federal and state trademark, service mark and trade name law, the basic rule (if there is a conflict among the users of a name) is that the ultimate right to use a particular name will usually be decided on the basis of who was first to actually use the name in connection with a particular trade, business, activity, service or product. In addition, a court will usually take into account the similarity of the types of businesses or organizations and their geographical proximity. The more local your business (for example, a gardening service or house painting business), the less you have to worry about. But even at the village square level, you can run into problems if you aren't careful. For example, Benjamin and Jerry Fisher would very likely hear from the lawyers of another Ben & Jerry if they put their first names on an ice cream shop. However, if they open Ben & Jerry's Plumbing, their name should be legally okay (at least as far as the famous Ben & Jerry's goes), since fixing pipes can't really be confused with making or selling ice cream. But they should still check to be sure no other Ben & Jerry used that name or anything similar (B & J, for instance) in their area, or that no national plumbing franchise uses it.

c. Protecting Your Name

Once you've decided on a fictitious product or business name that you have concluded is available for you to use, you may want to register it either with your Secretary or Department of State or, more likely but costlier, with the U. S. Patent and Trademark Office as a trademark or service mark.

Federal registration costs $325 and can be accomplished on one of two grounds:

1. You have actually used the name in interstate commerce (that is, in two or more states) in connection with the marketing of goods or services; or

2. You intend to use the name in interstate commerce in connection with the marketing of goods or services.

If you specify the second reason in your trademark application, you must file an affidavit (sworn statement) within six months stating that the name has been placed in actual use. This costs an additional $100. Simply stated, it is possible to reserve ownership of a trademark before actually using it, but you have to pay at least $100 extra for the privilege.

You might wonder if there are any benefits to registering your business or product name as a trademark. First, if you register your business or product name as a trademark or service mark, it will be placed on the Principal Register of all registered trademarks maintained by the USPTO. This means that other would-be users are on notice that you own the mark, and that you have the exclusive right to use the mark nationwide. And, once it's registered, the law presumes that you are the legal owner of the trademark, which means you won't have to prove ownership if you get into a dispute with another business over its use. So while it may seem a bit expensive, if you're going to market your services or products nationally, it might be worthwhile.

In addition to picking a business and product name, you may want to choose and register a domain name for your website. This can be either your business or product name, or even one you dream up. To learn even more about picking a domain name that doesn't conflict with someone else's trademark, see Domain Names: How to Choose & Protect a Great Name for Your Website, *by Stephen Elias and Patricia Gima (Nolo).*

d. Filing a Fictitious Name Statement

If you use any or all of the partners' last names for your business, you do not have to register the business name with any government agency (but as mentioned, it may be a good idea to file trademark registrations). If you use a fictitious business name, state law or local ordinances normally require you to register that name. (See Chapter 8, Section A.) Happily, this is neither a complicated nor particularly expensive procedure. Registering a fictitious business name at the state or county level typically involves filing a single statement, often referred to as a dba or d/b/a (doing business as), and in many states, publishing a series of brief notices in a local newspaper. Contact your Secretary or Department of State, city or county clerk or tax and license officer for more information.

In unusual circumstances, a partnership using a fictitious name may not have to file a fictitious name statement. If the partnership will not conduct business or earn income, no statement is required. What type of partnership, you may ask, doesn't intend to make money? They are rare, but occasionally people create a partnership for an informal club. For instance, a group of investors who wish to share advice may want to create a partnership agreement to define how they'll work together, but the partnership itself will not buy or sell stocks. If the partnership is given a fictitious name in this type of agreement, no fictitious name statement is necessary.

Many state and local government agencies are now on the Web. *It's easier and often less time-consuming to download government forms and information from a state or local government agency's website. To find state and local government on the Web, check out www.piperinfo.com, which provides links to state, county and city websites.*

e. Who Keeps the Name if the Partnership Splits Up?

Who gets the right to continue to use the business name, product name or a website domain name if the partners split up? An obvious example of a business with a desirable name is a successful rock band, but don't ignore this concern because your business is more mundane. The name of a successful bakery, restaurant or dry cleaner can also have real value. It's best to assume your business name will have value in the marketplace, and define in your partnership agreement who will retain rights to the name if a partner leaves or the partnership ends. (See Chapter 5, Section E.)

 Think about potential ownership issues before you put your name on a partnership. *Putting your own name on a business can cause problems if you sell out or leave and the business continues. You may have sold the right to use your own name for that type of business. If you decide to use your name for the name of your partnership, make sure you and your partners agree on who will get the right to use the name when and if the partnership ends.*

f. Choosing Your Partnership and Business Names

Aside from warning you about what you can't do, there's nothing beyond the obvious we can tell you about choosing your partnership and business names. "Main Street Books" could be a problem if you lose your lease on Main Street. "The Food Conspiracy" sounded hip in 1968 and peculiar by 2002. "Nolo" (the publisher of this book) chose a name that sounded peculiar to some people 30 years ago (and now), but we're still fond of it.

Following is a clause you can complete to state your partnership and business names.

NAME

The following clause is in the file **NAME**, *in directory* **Clause01**.

☐ The name of the partnership shall be

_____ .

The following clause is in the file **NAMEBUS**, *in directory* **Clause01**.

☐ The name of the partnership business shall be

_____ .

2. Term of the Partnership

Many partnership agreements do not state how long the partnership will last, or provide a termination date. Legally, this means partnerships last indefinitely—usually until one partner departs or dies, or the partners agree to dissolve the partnership. Even so, it is best to clearly state the circumstances under which the partnership will terminate. You can also, of course, decide that the partnership will end at a certain date.

Here's a basic open-ended term clause:

The following clause is in the file **TERMDEA**, *in directory* **Clause02**.

Lasts Until Dissolved on Death of Partner

☐ The partnership shall last until it is dissolved by all the partners, or a partner leaves, for any reason, including death.

Whether you wish to state a specific date when the partnership will end or that it will last until ended by a partner's death or departure, be sure your duration clause is coordinated with your buy-out clause. (See Chapter 5, Sections A and B.)

Here's a more specific clause which requires an explicit cross-reference to the numbered section you will eventually give your buy-out clause. (See Chapter 11, Section A, Step 6, which explains how to number the clauses of your agreement.) Frankly, we don't think this type of cross-referencing to other clauses is necessary. But if you don't mind a little extra verbiage in your agreement, it doesn't hurt, either. It can make your agreement seem more lawyerlike and conventional.

The following clause is in the file **TERMWITH**, *in directory* **Clause02**.

Lasts Until Dissolved or Partner Withdraws

☐ The partnership shall last until it is dissolved by all the partners or until a partner withdraws, retires, dies or otherwise leaves the partnership, under Sections _____ and _____ of this Agreement.

Sometimes partners decide they don't want an open-ended agreement. This is particularly true in joint ventures (partnerships for a specific limited purpose or project). Here are some sample clauses to limit the term of a partnership.

The following clause is in the file **TERMSET**, *in directory* **Clause02**.

Lasts for Set Term of Years

☐ The partnership shall commence as of the date of this Agreement and shall continue for a period of _____ years, at which time it shall be dissolved and its affairs wound up.

The following clause is in the file **TERMDATE**, *in directory* **Clause02**.

Lasts Until Set Date

☐ The partnership shall continue until [*specify an event, such as "the sale of 126 Venture Street, Albany, New York"*], at which time it shall be dissolved and its affairs wound up. ·

3. Purpose of the Partnership

Your partnership agreement should contain a short statement of the basic purpose of the business. Generally, it's wise to state the purpose broadly, to allow for possible expansion of the business.

> **EXAMPLE:** Three partners plan to start a consulting business to provide specialized advice on the employment problems of county governments in Colorado. At first, they decide to call the business "Colorado County Government Consulting Service." Then they ask themselves what happens if the business does well. Perhaps the next step would be to do consulting for governmental entities generally or for a mix of governmental and private clients in fields other than employment and outside of Colorado. After considerable discussion, they decide it makes sense to define the business purpose as consulting in the public and private sectors, and leave out limiting words like "employment," "county governments" and "Colorado."

Another way to deal with the same problem would be to include both definitions as to the scope of the business. That is to say you might draft something like this:

> The original purpose of our partnership business is to provide high-quality consulting services to county governments in the State of Colorado concerning employee relations. However, it is also contemplated that in the future, general consulting services may be offered to governmental and private business units at all levels within and without Colorado.

There's not much specific help we can give you in drafting your purpose clause, since it all depends on the nature of your business and what you want. Just state what you want to do in everyday, plain English, and you'll be fine. Imagine you are describing your business to some friends, write those words down, maybe do a bit of editing, and you've got it.

Some partnerships don't want a broad purpose clause. For instance, if you're engaged in a limited enterprise, such as a joint venture, it's likely you will want to limit that business by purpose as well as by time. If a partner will also work in a closely related business, you'll need to exclude that type of work from your "purpose" to prevent possible conflict of interest problems later. (See Section D of this chapter for specific clauses related to partners' possible conflicts of interest.)

Here's a basic form for your purpose clause:

 The following clause is in the file **PURPOSE**, *in directory* **Clause03**.

Statement of the partnership's purpose

☐ The purpose of the partnership is:

_____

4. Statements of Partners' Goals

As we discussed briefly in Chapter 2, Section E, the partners can decide to include in their partnership agreement a short written statement of each partner's goals and hopes for the partnership. While these are clearly matters the partners should discuss, there's no real reason to put them into your agreement. However, there's no harm in including them either, as long as you make it expressly clear that this clause is not intended to be a binding legal provision.

One method for doing this is to include a short recital in the agreement. A recital is a statement about the partners or the partnership; often it explains how and why the partnership came into being. A recital normally has no legal effect; its purpose is simply to state, in writing, facts that the partners want to stress.

> **EXAMPLE:** The partners have each worked making women's clothing. They've decided to combine their skills and energies and open a women's clothing store selling handmade clothes. Danielle will be the partner who makes the clothes and supervises any employees who help with this task. Li-Shan will run the store and coordinate all relationships with other clothing makers who leave their goods at the store on consignment. Danielle and Li-Shan hope to make a very comfortable living. However, Li-Shan wants it on record that she does not want to sacrifice her weekends and vacations to the job. Both partners understand that this clause is an expression of intention and is not legally binding.

Here's a basic clause you can use or adopt to state partners' goals, if you decide you want that.

 *The following clause is in the file **GOALS,** in directory **Clause03**.*

Statement of Partners' Goals

☐ The specific purposes of the partnership are set out above. In addition, the goals and dreams of each partner are set out below. The partners understand that this clause is not legally binding, but include it in the Partnership Agreement as a record of their hopes and intentions: _____.

B. Contributions

One of the first things you and your partners will need to decide is how much cash, property or service each partner will contribute to the partnership, as well as what happens if the partnership eventually needs more money.

If each partner contributes an equal amount, each will (presumably) be an equal owner of the business. But what if the partners make unequal contributions? Then you need to decide how you want ownership to work. You can all still be equal owners as far as equity in the business goes, but later on, when it comes to division of profits, you can provide for unequal division. Or you can provide for this in unequal ownership.

Capital Account

You will encounter the term "capital account" often in your partnership business. Simply stated, a partner's capital account is the dollar value of her ownership interest in the business. Another way of phrasing this is that a capital account reflects a partner's total equity in the business. A partner's capital account will be adjusted over the life of the partnership to reflect profits allocated to that partner, distributions made, and each partner's share of losses and liabilities. It's important for partners to keep good records so that when the partnership is dissolved or a partner sells his or her interest, the partner pays the correct amount of income taxes on any gain in the value of his or her partnership interest.

> **EXAMPLE:** Merv and Hayden start a business booking nightclub comedians. Each contributes $40,000 cash, so each partner's capital account starts out at $40,000. Now suppose the business loses a net $10,000 the first year, or $5,000 a partner. Each partner's capital account will now be $35,000.

Determining the value of a partner's capital account can be far more complex if, for instance, the partnership owns appreciated property or inventory. Once a business is underway, it often requires an accountant experienced with partnership issues to determine the current value of a capital account.

Regarding contributions, we've already stressed that if there's a significant disparity between work and money contributed by different partners, there's a real potential for conflict. The person who contributes the most of either may come to resent the others, especially if the business gets off to a slow start. At the very least, you need to recognize that unequal contributions can cause problems in the partnership, and talk out what's mutually comfortable—or at least acceptable—so you can resolve these issues before you go into business together.

If one partner will work much more than the other, it's permissible, under tax laws, to pay that partner a salary. Compensating a working partner is a deductible business expense, as long as the salary is reasonable in light of what's generally paid for similar work in the industry. In other words, the salary cannot be a disguised distribution of profits. However, this can create complicated taxes for both the partnership and the partner who receives the salary, so if you're interested in doing this, get some help from a knowledgeable tax attorney or accountant experienced with partnership issues. In addition, keep in mind that this salary won't be tied to whether the partnership actually makes a profit. For this reason, you should carefully consider whether you want to commit the partnership to paying this money.

1. Cash Contributions

Frequently, each partner contributes cash to a new business. A key decision here is whether each partner contributes an equal amount. If this is possible, we think it's desirable; otherwise, the partners who

contribute the most cash may want more than an equal say in management decisions, which can lead to problems down the road.

But sometimes partners simply can't afford to contribute the same amount of cash. There are many ways to handle the problems inherent in this disparity. One is to have what would otherwise be the excess cash contributed by one partner converted to a loan; in other words, all partners make equal contributions, and one partner also loans money to the business.

> **EXAMPLE:** Naomi and Toni open a modern dance studio. They both contribute $20,000, and Naomi loans the business an additional $30,000 at 10% annual interest, to be repaid over three years.

Another solution is to have the partners who contribute less cash work more, often at a set rate, to equalize contributions.

> **EXAMPLE:** Jake and DJ open a massage-and-relaxation business. DJ contributes $30,000, but Jake can only contribute $26,000. They agree that Jake will work ten more hours a week than DJ, at $22 per hour, until he's worked the equivalent of $4,000 worth. Then they will work equal amounts.

 The following clause is in the file **CONTEQ**, *in directory* **Clause04**.

Equal Cash Contribution

☐ The initial capital of the partnership shall be a total of $_____. Each partner shall contribute an equal share amounting to $_____, no later than _____, 20__. Each partner shall own an equal share of the business.

 The following clause is in the file **CONTUNEQ**, *in directory* **Clause04**.

Unequal Cash Contribution

☐ The initial capital of the partnership shall consist of cash to be contributed by the partners in the following amounts:

Name	Amount
_____	$_____
_____	$_____
_____	$_____
_____	$_____

Each partner's contribution shall be paid in full by _____, 20____.

Each partner's ownership share of the business shall be:

Name	Share
_____	_____
_____	_____
_____	_____
_____	_____

 The following clause is in the file **CONTCASH**, *in directory* **Clause04**.

Equal Cash Contributions, With a Partner Loaning Additional Cash

☐ The initial capital of the partnership shall be a total of $_____. Each partner shall contribute an equal share amounting to $_____, no later than _____, 20__. In addition, _____*[name]*_____ shall loan the partnership $_____ by _____, 20__. The partnership shall pay ___ % interest on the loan.

It's prudent to see a lawyer before allowing a partner to lend money to a partner or the partnership. *Having a partner lend money to partners or the partnership is unusual with most beginning businesses. A complicated financial transaction like that is far beyond what most partners need or want. If you are seriously considering having a partner loan money to your business or to the partners individually, it's wise to see a lawyer regarding that transaction.*

 The following clause is in the file **CONTWORK***, in directory* **Clause04***.*

Unequal Cash Contributions, to Be Equalized By One Partner's Extra Work in the Business

☐ The initial capital of the partnership shall consist of cash to be contributed by the partners in the following amounts:

Name	Amount
_____	$_____
_____	$_____
_____	$_____
_____	$_____

Each partner's contribution shall be paid in full by _____, 20__. In addition, to equalize the contributions, _____[name]_____ shall contribute an extra ___ hours of work ____[per hour or week, etc.]___ valued at $_____ until the amount contributed by all partners is equal.

Contributions are one area of partnership agreements that can get very complex. Clauses for some of the more common types of complexities are set out below.

a. Deferred Contributions

If a partner cannot initially contribute the desired amount of cash, one method for handling this is for the partnership to require him to make deferred contributions—in other words, payments over time. These deferred payments can be arranged any way you decide upon, including equal monthly installment or payments from business profits. (When "he/she" appears in these paragraphs a specific partner is referred to, and you should identify that partner as "he" or "she," crossing out or deleting the reference to the inappropriate sex.)

 The following clause is in the file **DEFMON***, in directory* **Clause04***.*

Monthly Installments

☐ _____ shall be a partner, but shall not make any contribution of cash or property to the initial capital of the partnership. *[He/she]_____* shall subsequently contribute to the partnership capital, and _____*[his/her]* capital account shall be credited, in the amount of $_____ per month, beginning _____, 20__, until _____*[he/ she]*_____ has contributed the sum of $_____.

The following clause is in the file **DEFOUT***, in directory* **Clause04***.*

Contribution Out of Profit

☐ _____ shall be a partner, but shall not make any contribution of cash or property to the initial capital of the partnership. *[He/she]_____* shall subsequently contribute to the partnership capital, and _____*[his/her]* capital account shall be credited ____ % of _[his/her]_____ share of the partnership profits for each fiscal year, beginning _____, 20__, until _____[he/she]_____ has contributed the amount of $_____._

b. Paying Interest on Contributed Capital

Should partners receive interest payments from the business on contributed capital? Generally, the answer is no. Why pay money to yourselves from your own business for the money you put in? If you decide no partner can receive interest for contributions, it's best to state this explicitly in your agreement, as provided in the clause below.

 The following clause is in the file **CAPNOINT**, _in directory_ **Clause04**.

No Interest Paid

☐ No partner shall be entitled to receive any interest on any capital contribution.

In rare instances, partners decide they want to pay interest on capital contributions. Perhaps one partner has contributed more cash to the business than others and wants to receive interest on his contributions. In effect, this turns that contribution into a loan. Rather than pay interest, it's usually better to be direct and call the extra portion of the contribution a loan. After all, why should a partner both receive an ownership interest and the bonus of money interest for his contribution? If interest is paid, many payment variations are possible. For example, you might specify that partners only receive interest in years when net profits exceed a specified percent, that only a certain partner receives interest or that interest is optional and shall be decided upon yearly by the partners, etc.

If despite our suggestion you decide to pay interest on contributions, use or adapt the following clause.

 The following clause is in the file **CAPINT**, _in directory_ **Clause04**.

Interest to Be Paid

☐ _[Each partner]_ or _[Name of individual partner]_ shall be entitled to interest on his or her capital contribution accruing at the rate of ___ % per year from the date the contribution is paid. This interest shall be treated as an expense to be charged against income on the partnership books and shall be paid to the partner entitled to it _____[specify terms, for example, "quarterly" or "only upon termination of the partnership"]____._

2. Contributions of Property

As discussed in Chapter 2, it's common for one, some or even all partners to contribute property as well as, or instead of, cash to a partnership. This can be real property (real estate) or personal property (everything else). Also, a partner can sell or lease personal or real property to a partnership. Obviously, property contribution scenarios can range from the simple to the exceedingly complex. In simple situations, the major matters covered in the partnership agreement are the value the partnership puts on the property contributed and the conditions, if any, placed on its transfer to the partnership and use by it.

⚠ _Be sure to check the tax aspects of contributions of property carefully, especially if the property has appreciated in value. If a partner will contribute appreciated property, you may well need the assistance of a partnership tax expert before finalizing your agreement. We discuss these tax issues in Chapter 7._

a. Contributions of Real or Personal Property

Following is a sample clause that can be used, or adapted, when a partner contributes property to the partnership. Of course, this clause (or any other property contribution clause) can also be combined with a cash contribution clause, if you have one.

 The following clause is in the file **PROPSPEC**, *in directory* **Clause04**.

Specific Property Contributed

☐ _____ shall contribute property valued at $_____, consisting of ___*[If the property is difficult to describe, describe it in detail on a separate sheet of paper marked "Exhibit A" and add here "and more particularly described in Exhibit A, attached to this Agreement."]___* by _____, 20__.

(If more than one partner contributes property, repeat this clause for each partner.)

A partner may loan specific items of property, such as tools or antiques or vehicles, to the partnership. Often, the partnership won't pay a fee to use the property (though you can provide for that if you decide to). You also need to decide when the items are to be returned. This could be when the partnership ends, when the lending partner wants the property back or after a set period of time, such as one year.

Here's a clause for loans of property to the partnership.

 The following clause is in the file **PROPLOAN**, *in directory* **Clause04**.

Loans of Property Made to the Partnership

☐ In addition to the capital contributions defined in this Agreement, some partners have or will loan to the partnership additional items of property, as specified below:

_____ shall loan ___*[item identified]*

_____ shall loan ___*[item identified]*

(If the property is not simple to describe, you can add "more particularly described in Exhibit A, B, etc., attached to this Agreement.")

Each item of property lent to the partnership shall remain the separate property of the lending partner and shall be returned to that partner____*[insert whatever terms you've agreed on—for example, "upon dissolution of the partnership, or "upon demand," etc.]____* .

b. Contributions of Intellectual Property, Such as a Patent or Copyright—Ownership Retained by Individual Partner

These days, one distinct form of property partners may contribute to a partnership is intellectual property—legal rights to a copyright, patent, trademark or trade secret. Since these are unique forms of property, it's better to clearly define what that contribution means. For example, is the partner transferring all rights to the business? Or just the use of the intellectual property during the existence of the business? And who controls derivative rights, including the right to license the intellectual property to others?

The following clause is in the file **IPOWN***, in directory* **Clause04**.

Intellectual Property—Ownership Transferred to the Partnership

☐ ____[Name]____ , the owner of _____[describe, such as "patent #_____ for [describe patented subject]" or "the copyright to [name] dated "]_____ hereby agrees to transfer all ___[his/her]___ interest in this [patent/copyright]__ to the partnership with the understanding that all _[his/her]_ interest in the ___[patent/copyright]___ , including the sole right to license derivative works, shall vest in, and be owned by, the partnership and shall not be ___[his/her]___ separate property. In exchange for this transfer, it is agreed that [name]__ shall be credited with a contribution of $_____ to the partnership. No sale or assignment of, or grant of license under the [patent/copyright]__ shall be made without the consent of all the partners. Any monies resulting from any such sale, assignment or grant of license shall be divided_[equally among the partners] or [among the partners in accordance with the allocation of profits specified in this Agreement]_.

 The following clause is in the file **IPUSE***, in directory* **Clause04**.

Intellectual Property—Only Use Transferred to the Partnership

☐ ____[Name]____ , the owner of __[describe, such as "patent #___ for [describe patented subject]" or "the copyright to [name], dated"_____] hereby contributes to the partnership the nonexclusive use of that [patent/ copyright]__ , to the partnership, with the understanding that ___[he/she]___ shall retain sole ownership of the ___[patent/copyright]___ , along with the sole right to license its use to third parties, and it shall not become a partnership asset. _[Name]_ further agrees that until the termination of the partnership, or until ___[his/her]___ death or retirement from it, ___[he/she]___ will not, without the consent of all other partners, sell, assign or grant licenses under this ___[patent/copyright]___ . Any money accruing from a sale or assignment of, or the grant of licenses under such _[patent/copyright]__ , which are so authorized, shall be the sole property of [name]__ . For the purpose of profit-sharing only, and not for participation in the distribution upon the termination and winding up of the partnership, the partnership will credit [name]____ with a contribution in the amount of $_____.

3. Contributions of Services

As we've already noted, in some cases, one or more of the partners will receive an owner's (partner's) interest in the business, at least in part because of a promise to donate personal services to the business. For example, Elsa and Daphne form a partnership owned 50% by each to cater parties. Each will spend equal time on food preparation and service. Elsa contributes $10,000 to get the business going. Daphne agrees to contribute unpaid labor as a bookkeeper and business manager for nine months over and above the time she spends on parties, instead of contributing cash, which she doesn't have.

Here's a clause covering the contribution of services:

 The following clause is in the file **SERVCON**, *in directory* **Clause04**.

Contribution of Services

☐ ____[Name]____ shall make no cash or property contribution at the commencement of the partnership. ___[Name]___ shall donate *"[his/her] full work time" or "hours per week,"* *etc.]* , and energies to the partnership for a period of ___ and for those services ___[he/she]___ shall be entitled to ___ % ownership of the business.

Sometimes, the partners contributing cash or property want the service partner to eventually equal their cash contributions. One way to do that is to require that the service partner not receive a full share of the profits she's otherwise entitled to until her cash contribution equals a set amount. These situations are very individual, and there's no simple, set clause to cover it. You need to create a solution you all think is fair, then write it down, by using or adapting the following clause.

 The following clause is in the file **SERVPROF**, *in directory* **Clause04**.

Contribution of Profits from Service Partner

☐ Should *[service-contributing partner's]* share of the profits, as defined in this Agreement, exceed ___*[insert whatever you've agreed upon]*___ , ___*[he/she]*___ shall contribute the excess to *[his/her]* capital account in the business until the total amount of *[his/her]* capital account shall *[equal the separate capital contributions made by* _____ *and* _____] *or [insert specific dollar amount].*

 There may be adverse tax consequences for a partner who contributes services. See Chapter 7 for more information.

4. Failure to Make Initial Contribution

What happens if a partner simply fails to contribute the initial cash or property required of her by the partnership agreement? The first question here is whether you want to concern yourself with this as part of your agreement. After all, don't you trust your partners to put up what they say they will? On the other hand, if for some reason one partner proves unwilling or unable to abide by her commitment, you'll probably be in better shape if you've provided in advance for what you want to do. Does the business break up or not? Is that partner expelled from the partnership?

Here are three approaches to this issue of failure to make cash or property contributions.

 The following clause is in the file **FAILDIS**, *in directory* **Clause04**.

Partnership Dissolves

☐ If any partner fails to pay his or her initial contribution to the partnership as required by this Agreement, the partnership shall immediately dissolve and each partner who has paid all or any portion of his or her initial contribution to the partnership's capital shall be entitled to a return of the funds and properties he or she contributed.

In the following clause, you're agreeing that if one partner doesn't make the required capital contributions, that partner is expelled from the partnership. The expelled partner's interest is then allocated pro rata to the other partners.

The following clause is in the file **FAILNO**, *in directory* **Clause04**.

Partnership Continues for Partners Who Have Made Contributions, and No Additional Contribution Required

☐ If any partner fails to pay his or her contribution to the partnership's capital as required by this Agreement, the partnership shall not dissolve or terminate, but it shall continue as a partnership of only the partners who have made their initial capital contributions as required and without any partner who has failed to do so. In that case, the share in the partnership's profits and losses allocated under this Agreement to any partner who has failed to make his or her initial contribution shall be reallocated to the remaining partners in proportion to their respective shares of partnership profits and losses as specified in this Agreement.

In the next clause, you're also agreeing that a partner who fails to make a required capital contribution is expelled from the partnership. However, instead of the partnership doing without that money, you're requiring the other partners to contribute that money in proportion to their respective partnership interests.

The following clause is in the file **FAILREQ**, *in directory* **Clause04**.

Partnership Continues—Additional Contributions Are Required

☐ If any person fails to pay his or her initial contributions to the partnership's capital as required by this Agreement, the partnership shall not dissolve or terminate, but shall

continue as a partnership of the partners who have made their initial capital contributions and without any person who shall have failed to do so, but only if the remaining partners pay the initial capital contribution that was to have been made by the noncontributing partner or partners. The partnership shall promptly give written notice of this failure to all partners who have made their initial capital contributions. The notice shall specify the amount not paid. Within ____ days after the notice is given, the remaining partners shall pay the amount of the defaulted contribution in proportion to the respective amount they are required to pay to the partnership's capital under this Agreement. That share of the profits of the partnership belonging to noncontributing partners shall then be reallocated to the remaining partners in proportion to their respective shares of partnership profits and losses under this Agreement.

Finally, there's the often more troubling question of service contributions. These can be more difficult because they're made over time, not at once. What happens if a service partner quits on the first day? That's easy. He hasn't contributed anything, so he does not become a partner. But what happens if he quits after contributing 90% of what he promised? Or (as is more likely) suppose he doesn't quit, but regularly contributes only 70% or 90% of the hours he promises? These questions indicate one more type of problem you take on when you accept a service-contributing partner. Here again, there's no automatic clause to handle the issue. You have to work out what you think is fair. You may well provide for different results, depending on how nearly the service partner did as promised. When you have a meeting of the minds, write it up using or adapting the clause below.

*The following clause is in the file **FAILSERV**, in directory **Clause04**.*

Failure of Service Partner to Actually Perform Service

☐ If ___[service partner's name]___ fails to contribute the services promised, the partnership shall proceed as follows: _[insert what you've agreed on]_ .

5. Future Contributions

We don't think it makes sense to worry now about what will happen in the future if you need more money. Adopting a partnership provision to require future cash contributions makes even less sense. If a partner doesn't have the cash needed three years from now, what good is a clause you drafted long in advance? Nevertheless, despite our views, we know some people like the sense of commitment that required future contributions provide. If you really want to require future contributions, you're not prohibited from doing so.

You can provide that additional contributions can be decided upon by a less-than-unanimous vote—perhaps a simple majority, or two-thirds—of the partners, or partnership interest, can be given the authority to require that more cash be put up. But in a small partnership, this isn't really feasible. If one partner can't—or won't—put up additional cash, it's likely to be destructive to try and bludgeon her into it.

In an additional contribution clause, you can add more detail, such as how notice of the need for increased capital is to be given, how much time the partners have to make the contributions, etc.

Another way to handle the problem of the need for additional cash is to have a partner, or partners, make loans to the partnership, on whatever terms the partners agree upon.

However, having a partner make loans to a business can raise a number of complicated issues. Is the loan to the partnership itself? If so, could there be a conflict between the lending partner's right to collect defaulted loans, and her duties of loyalty to the partnership? Or is the loan a "personal" loan to the other partners? Can a loan that the lending partner knows will ultimately be used by the borrowing partners for partnership business be reasonably called "personal"? Is interest charged on the loan? Will there be security for the loan?

See a lawyer before a partner makes loans to a partnership. *As noted, having a partner loan money to partners or the partnership is unusual with most beginning businesses. A complicated financial transaction like that is usually far beyond what the partners need or want. If you are seriously considering having a partner loan money to your business or to the partners individually, see a lawyer.*

If you think that any future contributions may be needed, use or adapt this clause.

The following clause is in the file **CONFUT**, *in directory* **Clause04**.

If Future Contributions Needed

☐ If, at any future time, more money is required to carry on the partnership business, and all partners vote to increase the capital contributions required by partners, the additional capital shall be paid in by the partners *["in equal shares" or "in the proportions as they have respectively contributed originally," etc.]*

Here is another type of specific clause we think is usually not warranted. It assumes that more money will be needed and that all partners will be willing and able to contribute it (without taking a vote first). In a business that will surely need more capital to expand, putting a portion of profits back into the business can make sense, but it's usually better to determine how much at the end of each year, not at the beginning. Note that if you decide to include this clause, you will have to figure out a way to deal with partners who can't or won't make these additional contributions. Will you reduce the noncontributing partner's interest in the partnership and allocate it to the partners who do make capital contributions? Will you expel the noncontributing partner? Will you allow another partner to make the contribution and increase his or her interest in the partnership accordingly? Unfortunately, there's no set answer to this question: you and your fellow partners will have to sit down and figure out what seems most appropriate to your situation, and work from there.

The following clause is in the file **CONTANN**, *in directory* **Clause04**.

Requirement of Annual Contribution by Partners

☐ Each person shall contribute annually ____ percent of his or her share of each year's profits [or $_____] to the partnership's capital for a period of _____ years. If any partner fails to make such contribution, *[insert remedy you've decided on]*.

💡 **Consider prohibiting voluntary contributions.** *Assuming the distribution of profits and control of the business is tied to the balances in the partners' capital accounts (for example, a one-third contribution means one-third ownership), you may want to state expressly what all should understand anyway—no partner has the right to gain more power without the others' consent by making unwanted, voluntary contributions.*

The following clause is in the file **CONTCON**, *in directory* **Clause04**.

No Voluntary Contributions Without Consent

☐ No partner may make any voluntary contribution to the partnership without the written consent of all other partners.

C. Profits, Losses, Draws and Salaries

Clearly you'll want to decide how the partnership will compensate the partners. Realistically, over the long haul, you'll need to make a profit for any partners to get paid. But after all, you're going into business to make money, so figure out what will happen when you do.

The first issue here is how you'll divide profits. This can be one of the thorniest issues in creating a partnership agreement. To determine this, you have to decide what the foundation of your partnership is. Is it the classic "all for one and one for all" of the three musketeers, with all profits shared equally, no matter what? Suppose one partner consistently brings in twice as much business as each of the others; should the "rain-making" partner be paid more? Does it matter if all the partners work equally hard, even though one brings in more money? What resentments might simmer, or erupt, if one partner is, or is not, paid more?

Next, you should determine if one or more partners can receive a draw against their share of the profits—that is, be paid sooner than the other partners. This might be appropriate if one partner had less savings than the others and was counting on partnership profits to meet his or her living expenses. In theory, you could even provide that one partner gets paid a draw from contributed cash or the other partners' capital accounts, but this is quite undesirable. In effect, some partners are having their ownership share of the business eaten up to pay another.

Finally, you will want to decide if one or more partners will receive a salary for work done in the business. As noted, salaries are not draws. Salaries, including partners' salaries, are paid as normal business expenses for work done and do not come out of a partner's share of profits. Indeed, by law, salaries cannot be a disguised payment of profits. Salaries must be reasonable pay for the work done, in light of industry norms. If equal partners will all work in the business an equal number of hours, there is no particular need to pay salaries—an equal division of profits (with or without a draw) should be adequate. However, if one partner will work more hours than others, paying that partner a salary might make sense. Or you could deal with the disparity by giving the hard-working partner a larger share of the profits.

Paying partner salaries is rare. *Because most partners agree they should all be paid out of the partnership's profits, and because it can complicate the partnership's and the salaried partner's taxes, most partnerships do not pay partner salaries. In addition, remember that you are essentially guaranteeing payment to a partner, even if the partnership doesn't make money. Consider this issue carefully before you decide to pay partner salaries.*

1. Basic Profit/Loss Clauses

If your partnership agreement doesn't state how profits and losses are to be divided, the UPA provides that all partners share both equally, even if they contributed unequal amounts of cash, property or labor to the partnership. If the partnership agreement defines how profits are to be distributed but doesn't mention losses, each partner must contribute toward the losses according to his or her share of profits. (UPA Section 18(a).)

If profits and losses are to be shared equally, it's better to state this expressly in your partnership agreement, rather than rely on the UPA. This will minimize any possibility of later disagreement.

 The following clause is in the file **PROFEQ**, *in directory* **Clause05**.

Equal Shares

☐ The partners will share all profits equally, and they will be distributed *[insert whatever you agreed upon, such as monthly or yearly]* . All losses of the partnership shall also be shared equally.

Some partnerships will choose to divide profits and losses unequally. This can be done for all sorts of reasons, such as one partner contributing more work or more money to the partnership. There's no formula that defines when you want to give one or more partner a larger or smaller share—it's your business and you can divide the profits and losses any way you all agree is fair.

Here are some clauses for defining the distribution of profits and losses on an unequal basis.

 The following clause is in the file **PROFSET**, *in directory* **Clause05**.

Unequal Shares: Set Percentages

☐ The partnership profits and losses shall be shared among the partners as follows:

Name	Percentage
_____	_____%
_____	_____%
_____	_____%

This clause is straightforward enough, but what do you do if you decide to make different allocations of profits and losses? In that situation, the following clause would be appropriate.

 The following clause is in the file **PROFDIF**, *in directory* **Clause05**.

Unequal Shares: Different Percentages for Profits and Losses

☐ The partnership profits and losses shall be shared among the partners as follows:

Name	Percentage of Profits	Percentage of Losses
_____	_____	_____
_____	_____	_____
_____	_____	_____

⚠ **Be careful if you make different allocations of profits and losses.** *The IRS calls these "special allocations" and they must have a legitimate purpose, or a "substantial economic effect" for the IRS to recognize them. If the IRS decides that you*

have made these special allocations for the sole purpose of lowering income taxes (say, by allocating all of the losses to the partner in the highest tax bracket), it will disallow the allocations. If you are interested in making different allocations of profits and losses, consult a partnership tax expert.

In some partnerships—such as investment real estate agreements—capital contributions may be the most important factor in distributing profits, especially if all partners will work in the business roughly the same amount of time. Here's a clause for this type of situation.

 The following clause is in the file **PROFCAP**, *in directory* **Clause05**.

Unequal Shares: Profits and Losses Keyed to Capital Contributions

☐ The partnership's profits and losses shall be shared by the partners in the same proportions as their initial contributions of capital bear to each other.

2. Draws Paid to Partners

As mentioned, a draw is an advance of anticipated profits paid to a partner or partners. Many small business partnerships handle draws informally. If all partners decide that all can take a draw, they do. If the partners divide profits equally, each takes an equal draw. If there's an unequal division of profits, there's usually an unequal draw.

The situation is different if only some, but not all, partners receive a draw. This can be done if one, or some, partners actively work in the business and the others don't, especially if the working partner needs an ongoing income from the business. A draw can, if the business is profitable, provide this income.

It's usually not advisable to allow draws for some partners and not others. *One reason for this is that it's hard for most new small businesses to accurately track their profits and losses on a weekly or monthly basis, so determining an appropriate figure as a draw against profits is often very difficult. If a working partner needs an income from the business, consider providing the partner with a moderate salary. (See Section C4 of this chapter.)*

If only some partners will receive a draw, you need to state that in your agreement. We advise against specifying the amount that will be paid in draws. You cannot be sure now what your profits will be, so it's premature, if not rash, to contractually bind the partnership to pay, by draw, one or more partners according to a set schedule.

If despite our advice you want to authorize draws for certain partners only, here's a sample clause.

 The following clause is in the file **DRAWAUT**, *in directory* **Clause05**.

Draws Authorized

☐ Partners _____ and

_____ are entitled to draws from

expected partnership profits. The amount of

each draw will be determined by a vote of the

partners. The draws shall be paid _[insert_

whatever time schedule you've agreed upon,

such as monthly, etc.] .

You can also prohibit draws. We think this is too extreme. If all partners want to take an equal draw, and the profits are there to support it, why shouldn't they? Nevertheless, there are partnerships where partners agreed only to regular—say quarterly—distribution of profits and do not permit draws. In the interest of thoroughness, here's a clause prohibiting draws.

 The following clause is in the file **DRAWPRO**, *in directory* **Clause05**.

Draws Prohibited

☐ No partner shall be entitled to any draw

against partnership profits. Distributions shall

be made only as provided in this Agreement,

or upon unanimous written agreement of the

partners.

What happens if the amount a partner draws in a year turns out to exceed her actual share of partnership profits? Do you think you'd simply ignore that fact because that partner needed all that money to live? Or does it seem fair that the partner who received more in draws than her yearly share of partnership profits have this amount treated as a loan, with an obligation to repay the partnership? Speculating over this possible problem will be unnecessary for partnerships that don't allow unequal draws. However, if you do, you may want to consider the issue.

At first, converting part of what appeared when paid to be a draw against profits into a loan may seem harsh, but the alternative may be worse for the rest of the partners. If the partner with the excess draws can simply keep the money, you're, in effect, rewriting the basic profit distribution clause of your agreement.

If you allow unequal draws in the first place, here's a clause you can use or adopt to cover draws in excess of profits:

 The following clause is in the file **DRAWLOAN**, *in directory* **Clause05**.

Draws Exceeding Partners' Actual Shares of Profits to Become Loans to Partners

☐ Notwithstanding the provisions of this Agree-

ment governing drawing permitted by partners,

to the extent any partner's withdrawals for

draws under those provisions during any fiscal

year of the partnership exceeds his or her share in the partnership's profits, the excess shall be regarded as a loan from the partnership to him or her that he or she is obligated to repay within _____ days after the end of that fiscal year.

3. Retention of Profits for Business Needs

We've been asked if there's a standard percentage of profits that are retained by a partnership business—for new equipment, expansions, employees' bonuses, whatever—before any remaining profits are distributed to the partners. It's a good question. Obviously, most businesses won't last long if they don't plan for the future and keep a reserve against unexpected problems. But the answer, as you might expect by now, is no, there's no set formula. Here, too, you must decide how you want your business to run. You can include a clause in your agreement to acknowledge that you'll retain some profits for future business needs. Or you can simply do it as the need arises and all agree on it.

 The following clause is in the file **RETGEN**, *in directory* **Clause05**.

General Limitation on Distribution to Retain Cash Business Needs

☐ In determining the amount of profits available for distribution, allowance will be made for the fact that some money must remain undistributed and available as working capital as determined by _[for example, "all partners" or "a majority of partners"]_ .

Here's a more mathematical approach to the problem of retaining earnings for business needs.

 The following clause is in the file **RETLIM**, *in directory* **Clause05**.

Specific Limitation on Distribution to Retain Cash Business Needs

☐ The aggregate amounts distributed to the partners from the partnership profits shall not exceed ____ % of any net income above $_____.

4. Salaries

As we discussed, although it's rare, you can decide to pay one or more partners a salary for work actually performed in the business. (In tax lingo, a salary is sometimes called a guaranteed payment.) If you decide to do so, state that generally in your agreement.

 The following clause is in the file **SALARY**, *in directory* **Clause05**.

Salaries to Partners

☐ Partners can be paid reasonable salaries for work they perform in the partnership business.

You can also decide, as most partnerships do, especially where all partners will work in the business, that no partner will receive a salary; instead, all money will be paid to partners as profits. (Since a partnership isn't taxed itself, the tax consequences to a partner are generally the same whether the partner receives payment as income or as profits. However, the tax consequences to the partnership are different, since a salary is a deductible business expense that reduces the total partnership income. (See Chapter 7.))

In some states, oral contracts for partners' salaries are valid. So, if no salaries are to be paid, it is wise to state this explicitly.

The following clause is in the file
SALARYNO, *in directory* **Clause05**.

No Salaries to Partners

☐ No partner will be paid any salary, except those that may in the future be decided on by unanimous written consent of all partners.

D. Management Responsibilities

In this section, you'll pin down the basic ways in which you'll operate the business. This can include matters like work duties of partners (such as hours to be worked and skills contributed), supervision responsibilities and other possible business activities permitted or prohibited to partners. Clearly, these are topics all partners will need to discuss and agree upon.

You do not need to pin down designated roles in your partnership agreement or in running your business. You are not required to have a president, vice president, treasurer or any other officers—but of course you can have them if you want to.

A related concern is how specific to make your partnership agreement. Clauses involving management of a partnership can get very detailed, down to specifying just when office meetings should be held, or what type of pens you'll buy. There's no lawyer's rule for determining how much precision is the right amount. However, it's probably best to avoid excessive detail. After all, minor matters may well change; if your computer doesn't function well and you purchase another, you don't want to have to amend your partnership agreement. Obviously, deciding how much detail to include is a subjective decision. Some partners in a restaurant might feel strongly about the type and quality of coffee to serve and want to include it in their partnership agreement, while others would find putting this level of detail in a partnership agreement laughable. Certainly, in your conversations, you should explore any area in which you uncover potential for disagreement.

1. Managing the Business

You may want to specify that all, or some, of the partners will contribute specific skills, such as working as a salesman, computer programmer, bookkeeper or cook. If so, use or adopt the following clause:

The following clause is in the file **SKILLS**, *in directory* **Clause06**.

Skills Contributed

☐ Each partner named below shall participate in the business by working in the manner described:

Partner	Type of Work
_____	_____
_____	_____
_____	_____
_____	_____

To prevent, or at least curtail, arguments over who is goofing off, you might want to include a clause specifying how many hours a partner is expected to work. Again, note how continually the issue of trust reappears throughout the drafting of an agreement. If you really trust your partners, do you need to specify hours worked? Maybe not, but we know of partnerships that sank into discord when one partner suddenly wasn't around much but still wanted his full share of the profits. If this occurs, you'll be glad to have your expectations in writing.

The following clause is in the file **HOURS**, *in directory* **Clause06**.

Hours Worked

☐ Except for vacations, holidays and times of

illness, each partner shall work _____ hours

per week on partnership business.

Do you want to spell out what happens if a partner wants to take a leave of absence or sabbatical? Are they permitted at all? If so, how much time off is allowed? How far in advance must notice of a partner's desire to take a leave be given? Can a partner take leave no matter what the financial condition of the business? Does the partner receive any pay, or right to profits, while on leave? Must all partners approve of the leave?

Because there are so many questions here, there's very little we can give as a sample clause— just a heading and some blank lines for you to create your own leave clause.

 The following clause is in the file **LEAVES**, *in directory* **Clause06**.

Leaves of Absence

☐ Any partner can take a leave of absence from

the partnership under the following terms and

conditions:

_____

_____

_____

_____

In many small business partnerships, all the partners are involved in management and supervision (if there are any employees to supervise). This is simply stated in the agreement.

As we've said, it's generally desirable to have all partners' income be "earned" under IRS rules. This requires that each partner materially participate in the business, which the IRS defines as "regular, continuous and substantial involvement in partnership business operations." Tax law provides different tax treatment for income received from earned and passive activities. To oversimplify, receiving passive income (income from investments) can be less advantageous than receiving earned income (income from labor) for several reasons. Because most partners who participate in the partnership business generally receive earned income, there is no reason to belabor this distinction here.

 The following clause is in the file **ALLWORK**, *in directory* **Clause06**.

All Partners Work in Business

☐ All partners shall be actively involved and

materially participate in the management and

operation of the partnership business.

a. Decisions

This preceding clause does not specify how management decisions are made. Many small partnerships require all decisions to be unanimous; that is, every partner has veto power.

 The following clause is in the file **DECALL**, *in directory* **Clause06**.

All Decisions Unanimous

☐ Except as otherwise provided in this Agree-

ment, all partnership decisions must be made

by the unanimous agreement of all partners.

Some small business partnerships distinguish between major and minor decisions, allowing a single partner to make a minor decision but requiring unanimity for major ones. In a practical sense, you'll allow this anyway. You're not going to require a partnership meeting and vote each time a partner wants to buy a box of paper clips.

How you define major and minor will depend on the personalities of the partners and type of business. Some partners adopt money as a yardstick to define the authority for each individual partner (for example, all decisions involving the expenditure or potential expenditure of more than $1,000 shall be discussed and voted on by all partners). Others handle this in some other way (that is, a decision as to what jobs to bid on, the design specifications and the amount of the bid shall be unanimously agreed to by all partners; or decisions about the types of food to serve, particular recipes to use and the formula by which to price catering jobs shall be agreed upon unanimously by all partners).

 The following clause is in the file **DECMAJ**, *in directory* **Clause06**.

Major/Minor Decisions

☐ All major decisions of the partnership business must be made by a unanimous decision of all partners. Minor business decisions may be made by an individual partner. Major decisions are defined as: ___ *[write in how you've agreed to define a major decision].*

Here's one example of a clause defining major acts.

☐ The following acts may be done only with the consent of all partners:

a. Borrowing money in the partnership's name, other than in the ordinary course of the partnership's business or to finance any part of the purchase price of the partnership's properties;

b. Transferring, settling or releasing any partnership claim, except upon payment in full;

c. Mortgaging any partnership property, or pledging it as security for any loan;

d. Selling or leasing any partnership property other than in the ordinary course of the partnership's business; or

e. Knowingly causing anything to be done whereby partnership property may be seized or attached or taken in execution, or its ownership or possession otherwise be endangered.

b. Unequal Management Powers

In some partnerships, where the partners agree that contribution of capital is the most important factor, management decisions may be based in proportion to contribution. For example, in a partnership to purchase real estate, with little ongoing management required of the partners, a partner who put up 70% of the cash may well not want to share power equally with two partners who each put up 15%. Here are two clauses for distributing management power.

 The following clause is in the file **POWCAP**, *in directory* **Clause06**.

In Accordance With Contributed Capital

☐ Each partner shall participate in the management of the business. In exercising the powers of management, each partner's vote shall be in proportion to his or her interest in the partnership's capital.

The following clause is in the file **POWFIX**, *in directory* **Clause06**.

By Fixed Percentage as Agreed on by Partners

☐ In the management, control and direction of the business, the partners shall have the following percentages of voting power:

Name	Percentage
_____	_____%
_____	_____%
_____	_____%

Either of these methods may result in one partner having more than 50% of the authority in the business. With majority control, one partner can completely run the show, unless there's a specific clause requiring more than a simple majority to make decisions. Or put more clearly, unless there is such a clause, the minority partners may have no effective power in the business. If this is what you're considering, be careful. Are you sure it's a partnership you want? Are the minority partners really akin to investors, not owner-managers? If so, would a limited partnership or a corporation better suit their interests? (See Chapter 1, Section E, and Chapter 9.) Even the majority partner may not benefit if minority partners feel frozen out of management. A disaffected partner can always quit the partnership business, which presumably isn't what the majority partner wants—after all, why were the minority partners included in the first place?

2. Financial Matters

How your partnership business will deal with money is obviously something you need to talk through, and reach agreement on. After that, you can be as definite about financial matters in your agreement as you want to. Here, we look at some of the financial matters often covered in partnership agreements.

It's wise to provide for periodic accountings so that all of the partners can keep up with what's going on. This is especially true when some partners don't have easy access to, or ready understanding of, bookkeeping and financial records. Also, if you borrow money from a bank, the bank will likely require quarterly financial statements. Quarterly accountings should be adequate for many businesses, although others will want monthly statements. Assuming you take our advice (see Chapter 10, Section B) and work with a CPA or other small business financial expert, you will want to get her advice on this one.

 The following clause is in the file **ACCTPER**, *in directory* **Clause06**.

Periodic Accountings

☐ Accountings of *[specify what, such as "partners' capital accounts" or "profits or losses since the last accounting"]* shall be made every *[specify time period]* .

In a very small business partnership, you may well not want to obligate yourselves for the cost of monthly or quarterly accounting, but prefer, instead, to handle this on a yearly basis. Still, each partner may want the explicit right to an accounting, if she requests one. (Normally, partners have this right under the UPA, but it's prudent to spell that out in your agreement, so all partners are clear on the subject.)

 The following clause is in the file **ACCTREQ**, *in directory* **Clause06**.

Accounting on Request by a Partner

☐ Accountings of any aspect of partnership business shall be made upon written request by any partner.

At the very least, you will need to provide for a yearly accounting.

The following clause is in the file **ACCTDET**, *in directory* **Clause06**.

Accountant to Determine Profits and Losses

☐ The partnership's net profit or net loss for each fiscal year shall be determined as soon as practicable after the close of that fiscal year. This should be done by a certified public accountant, _[specify who, if you know]_ in accordance with the accounting principles employed in the preparation of the federal income tax return filed by the partnership for that year, but without a special provision for tax-exempt or partially tax-exempt income.

Be careful when borrowing money to establish or quickly expand a small business, unless the partners have lots of experience running the same type of business. Too often money borrowed to set up a business is spent on the wrong things. In our view, it's best to borrow only for absolutely essential items and, even then, to borrow as little a possible. For example, leasing used equipment will cost a fraction of purchasing it new and gives you a chance to determine what you really need and what you can do without. If you do decide to borrow money, or provide for the possibility, it's best to require the consent of all partners.

 The following clause is in the file **BORROW**, *in directory* **Clause06**.

Power to Borrow Money

☐ A partner can borrow money on behalf of the partnership in excess of $_____ only with prior consent of all partners.

 The following clause is in the file **EXAUT**, *in directory* **Clause06**.

Expense Accounts Authorized

☐ An expense account, not to exceed $_____ per month, shall be set up for each partner for his or her actual, reasonable and necessary expenses during the course of the business. Each partner shall keep an itemized record of these expenses and be paid once monthly for them on submission of the record.

 The following clause is in the file **EXNOAUT**, *in directory* **Clause06**.

Expense Accounts Not Authorized

☐ The partners individually and personally shall assume and pay:

- All expenses for the entertainment of persons having relations with firm.
- Expenses associated with usual business activities.

The following clause is in the file **SIGNCHK**, *in directory* **Clause06**.

Signature Required on Partnership Checks

☐ All partnership funds shall be deposited in the name of the partnership and shall be subject to withdrawal only on the signatures of at least _____ partners.

"Commingling" means mixing funds together when they should be kept separate and distinct. If a partnership business receives a check, it must go into the partnership account, not any partner's personal account. Even though this is a fundamental aspect of partnership law, it's wise to provide it explicitly.

The following clause is in the file **NOCOMMG**, *in directory* **Clause06**.

Prohibition Against Commingling

☐ All partnership funds shall be deposited only in bank accounts bearing the partnership name.

A "trust account" means money one person or business controls that is legally, and morally, the property of someone else—for example, when a lawyer receives a settlement check, a portion of which belongs to a client. Money belonging to third parties should always be put in a trust, not a partnership account. Of course, many businesses will never have occasion to receive money belonging to others, so they needn't worry about this provision.

 The following clause is in the file **TRUSTACC**, *in directory* **Clause06**.

For Businesses Receiving Funds to Be Held in a Trust Account

☐ All trust and other similar funds shall be deposited in a trust account established in the partnership's name at _____ bank, and shall be kept separate and not mingled with any other funds of the partnership.

How often do you need to meet? In most small business partnerships, you'll be meeting each other daily, maybe hourly, so do you really need a formal meeting clause? We doubt it. But if you want to specify that you'll have regular, formal meetings at time intervals that seem sensible to you (every month, every three months, etc.), there's surely no harm in doing so.

 The following clause is in the file **MEETINGS**, *in directory* **Clause06**.

Meetings

☐ For the purpose of discussing matters of general interest to the partnership, together with the conduct of its business, partners shall meet _[describe time and days, etc.]_ or at such other times agreed upon by the majority of the partners.

 The following clause is in the file **MAINTREQ**, *in directory* **Clause06**.

Maintenance of Records

☐ Proper and complete books of account of the partnership business shall be kept at the partnership's principal place of business and shall be open to inspection by any of the partners or their accredited representative at any reasonable time during business hours.

 The following clause is in the file **VACATION**, *in directory* **Clause06**.

Vacation

☐ Each partner shall be entitled to _____ weeks paid [or unpaid] vacation per year.

Do you want to make an express provision governing what will happen if a partner becomes seriously ill? This is a subject you should discuss, of course. But how can you know now how you'd want to handle it if it occurs? There are so many variables, including the needs of the ill partner, the income of the business and the duration of the illness. However, if you decide you do want a provision, at least a general one, stating you do or do not allow sick leave, you can include it here.

*The following clause is in the file **SICKLEAV**, in directory **Clause06**.*

Sick Leave

☐ The partnership's sick leave policy for partners is:

_____

3. Outside Business Activities

A key partnership question is whether any partner can engage in outside business. Often, of course, they usually must, at least at first, because the partnership business income is unlikely to be sufficient to support the partners. If a partner can engage in outside business, what types are permitted? Allowing a partner to directly compete with the partnership obviously risks serious conflicts of interest. But if you prohibit directly competitive businesses, how do you determine what is direct competition? If the partners are running a restaurant, can a partner be an owner of a delicatessen? Work in a delicatessen?

Remember, the first priority is that each partner must be able to survive financially while the partnership business has time to become profitable. Put another way, this is an important area to cover, because people can feel vital interests are at stake, including the integrity of the partnership and the ability to make enough money to live, or live comfortably. So take the time to talk this out and be sure you all agree on what clauses like "materially interfere with the partnership business" mean. Surprises and misunderstandings here can lead to much unpleasantness among the partners.

Here are four clauses for different approaches to this issue.

 *The following clause is in the file **OUTNOCOM**, in directory **Clause06**.*

Permitted, Except for Direct Competition

☐ Any partner may be engaged in one or more other businesses as well as the business of the partnership, but only to the extent that this activity does not directly and materially interfere with the business of the partnership and does not conflict with the time commitments and other obligations of that partner to the partnership under this Agreement. Neither the partnership nor any other partner shall have any right to any income or profit derived by a partner from any business activity permitted under this section.

 *The following clause is in the file **OUTPERM**, in directory **Clause06**.*

Permitted

☐ It is understood and agreed that each partner may engage in other businesses, including enterprises in competition with the partnership. The partners need not offer any business opportunities to the partnership, but may take advantage of those opportunities for their own accounts or for the accounts of other partnerships or enterprises with which they are associated. Neither the partnership nor any other partner shall have any right to any income or profit derived by a partner from any enterprise or opportunity permitted by this section.

The following clause is in the file **OUTSPEC**, *in directory* **Clause06**.

Specific Activities Permitted

☐ The list below specifies business activities that each partner plans or may do outside of the partnership business. Each partner is expressly authorized to engage in these activities if he or she so desires: _____

_____

_____.

The following clause is in the file **OUTREST**, *in directory* **Clause06**.

Restricted

☐ As long as any person is a member of the partnership, he or she shall devote his or her full work time and energies to the conduct of partnership business, and shall not be actively engaged in the conduct of any other business for compensation or a share in profits as an employee, officer, agent, proprietor, partner or stockholder. This prohibition shall not prevent him or her from being a passive investor in any enterprise, however, if he or she is not actively engaged in its business and does not exercise control over it. Neither the partnership nor any other partner shall have any right to any income or profit derived from any such passive investment.

4. Ownership of Business Assets

If a partner leaves or the partnership dissolves, it's vital to know who owns the partnership's assets. The question here is: Was the asset owned by the partnership, or separately by an individual partner? Obviously, property that is held in the partnership name—real estate, a car, etc.—is partnership property. But what of more sophisticated types of property, such as trade secrets, patents, copyrights or the partnership name itself (which, as we've noted, can be very important to many businesses, from restaurants to fashion designers). Here are clauses that state that certain assets are partnership property. You can, as we hope you know, adapt or modify any of these clauses to suit your needs.

The following clause is in the file **OWNTS**, *in directory* **Clause06**.

Trade Secrets

☐ All trade secrets used or developed by the partnership, including customer lists and sources of supplies, will be owned and controlled by the partnership.

The following clause is in the file **OWNPAT**, *in directory* **Clause06**.

Patents

☐ Any ideas developed by one or another of partners pertaining to partnership business that are the subject of an application for a patent shall be partnership property.

The following clause is in the file **OWNCOPY**, *in directory* **Clause06**.

Copyrights

☐ All copyrighted materials in the partnership name are, and shall remain, partnership property.

The following clause is in the file
OWNNAME, *in directory* **Clause06**.

Business Name

☐ The partnership business name of ___[specify]___ shall be partnership property. In the event of the departure of a partner and/or dissolution of the partnership, control and ownership of the partnership business name shall be determined pursuant to this Agreement.

5. Provision for a Managing Partner

Managing partners are common in large partnerships, such as big restaurants or service businesses. Especially where some or most of the partners don't want to be involved in day-to-day management, you'll need a managing partner. Having a managing partner can be appropriate if all or most of the partners will work in the business in other capacities (for example, ten architects choose one as the managing partner). However, if most partners won't work in the business, they may want to consider a limited partnership (see Chapter 9) instead of a general partnership with a managing partner. One big advantage is that the financial liability of a limited partner is limited to the amount of his contribution, while a general partner in a partnership with a managing partner has unlimited financial liability. We realize that most of our readers aren't in this situation, but for those few who are, we offer several possible clauses. First, here is a clause where the managing partner has wide powers.

The following clause is in the file **MANPART**, *in directory* **Clause06**.

Authority of Managing Partner

☐ The managing partner shall be ___[name]___. The managing partner shall have control over the business of the partnership and assume direction of its business operations. The managing partner shall consult and confer as far as practicable with the non-managing partners, but the power of decision shall be vested in the managing partner. The managing partner's power and duties shall include control over the partnership's books and records and hiring any independent certified public accountant the managing partner deems necessary for this purpose. On the managing partner's death, resignation or other disability, a new managing partner shall be selected by a majority of the partners.

Next is a clause granting more limited power to the managing partner. To make this work, you'll need to define what a "major" or "basic" partnership business decision is.

The following clause is in the file **MANLIMIT**, *in directory* **Clause06**.

Limited Authority for Managing Partner

☐ The managing partner shall be ___[name]___. The managing partner shall have control over routine business transactions and day-to-day operating decisions. The managing partner shall not make any major or basic decisions without consent of a majority of the partners. A major or basic decision is defined as ___[state the definition you've agreed on]___ .

The following clause is in the file **MANSAL**, *in directory* **Clause06**.

Salary of Managing Partner

☐ The managing partner shall be paid a monthly salary of $_____ or such other amount that may be determined by the unanimous written agreement of the partners. This salary shall be treated as a partnership expense in determining its profits or losses.

The following clause is in the file **MANALL**, *in directory* **Clause06**.

Managing Partner Handles All Money of the Partnership

☐ All partnership funds shall be deposited in the partnership's name and shall be subject to withdrawal only on the signature of the managing partner.

The following clause is in the file **MANOPER**, *in directory* **Clause06**.

Managing Partner Handles Operating Fund Only

☐ All partnership funds shall be deposited in the partnership's name and shall be subject to withdrawal only on the signatures of at least partners, except that a separate account may be maintained with a balance never to exceed $_____. The amounts in that separate account shall be subject to withdrawal on the signature of the managing partner. ■

Changes and Growth of Your Partnership

In this chapter, we focus on anticipating and planning for business growth. You and your partners want to explore how compatible your plans for the business are. How much do you each want your business to grow? If it's a retail business, how does, say, owning two, five or ten stores sound—like progress or a nightmare (albeit, hopefully, a profitable nightmare)? How much income does each partner hope for? Do you want employees? Roughly how many? How many might be too many? How much vacation time does each partner dream of?

We don't think it's sensible to try to pin down in your partnership agreement details of business growth. To point out the obvious, the future is always uncertain. For this reason, five-year plans haven't proven very useful. But whatever you decide about the growth of your business, you'll surely have to deal with change. Your partnership agreement should address at least two concerns involving change and growth. First, you'll want a clause stating how your agreement can be amended. Second, you should focus now on the question of admitting a new partner and figure out what's required to take someone into your partnership.

A. Amending the Partnership Agreement

Some types of business growth will necessitate a change in your partnership agreement. For example, as discussed in the next section, the addition of a new partner necessarily entails revisions of (at least) the clauses listing the partners' names and those covering contributions and distribution of profits. Also, the admission of a partner may necessitate changes in your agreement in other ways. For example, in a business we know, a former employee became a partner by purchasing a partnership capital interest. Since he had no actual cash, he paid for this purchase by having part of his weekly salary deducted. All this was put into the revised agreement the partners prepared when he was admitted into the partnership.

Even if you don't admit any new partners, growth of your business may require changes in your partnership agreement. You and your partners may decide that the expanded business should be run differently than the original business. Or perhaps the business will need additional cash contributions, and you'll decide that they should be made in proportions different from those originally agreed to. Any significant change in the structure or operation of your business should be reflected by a change in the partnership agreement. There is no need to become fussy over day-to-day developments and inevitable small changes—significant changes should be relatively unusual occurrences. Just what amounts to a significant change is up to you to decide. Some changes, such as an alteration in the distribution of profits a partner receives or assets he contributes, are obviously significant. Others, such as the decision to have more formal partnership meetings or change the accounting protocol, may or may not seem significant enough to you to warrant changing your partnership agreement.

The important thing is that you have set rules from the beginning as to how your agreement can be amended. The great majority of small business partnerships require written consent by all partners to amend the agreement. This is simply one application of a basic partnership philosophy requiring unanimity. Here's a sample clause permitting amendment only if all partners agree.

 The following clause is in the file **AMENDALL**, *in directory* **Clause11**.

By Unanimous Agreement

☐ This Agreement may be amended only by written consent of all partners.

In theory, you can create any amendment clause you desire. You could specify that the agreement could be amended by a vote of 51% of the partners, or by 51% of the capital accounts. We believe it's unwise for small business partnerships to allow their agreements to be amended by less than a unanimous vote of the partners. Other methods could leave one or more partner powerless—the dominant partners could simply amend the original agreement out of existence. This could leave the powerless partners with no recourse except to quit the partnership. If this kind of breakup is going to occur, it's far better to have the partners face the issue directly, through clauses that specifically address what happens when a partner leaves, than by the indirect route of amending the agreement. (See Chapter 5.)

 You may want to modify the rule of unanimity for amending the agreement if you're setting up a partnership with a lot of members. *We know of some collective businesses, for example, where there are 15, 20 and even 30 partners. In this situation it may make sense to allow a change in the agreement if, say, 75% of the partners approve. However, many collectives or large partnerships, such as good-sized accounting or architecture firms, still retain the requirement of unanimous consent to change the agreement.*

If you want to allow amendments by less than unanimity, use the following clause:

 The following clause is in the file **AMENDSPE**, *in directory* **Clause11**.

As Specified

☐ This Agreement may be amended by _[whatever method you've decided upon]_ .

B. Admission of a New Partner

Now let's focus on one specific aspect of growth that you should definitely handle in your original partnership agreement—the admission of a new partner or partners. Growth of a partnership business may lead to the opportunity, or even the necessity, of taking in a new partner or partners for any of a number of reasons. To name a few of the more common ones:

- desire (or need) for the new partner's contribution of cash
- need for skills contributed by the new partner
- need for additional management
- need to retain a key employee by allowing her to become a partner, or
- desire to expand your business to new locations or customers offered by the new partner.

The admission of a new partner is such a vital issue that it's better not to rely on your general amendment clause to cover it. Instead, state expressly in your partnership agreement how a new partner can be admitted. The major question to face is whether all existing partners have to agree to do this. We believe that it's wise to require unanimous consent, particularly in small partnerships.

 The following clause is in the file **ADDALL**, *in directory* **Clause11**.

Addition by Unanimous Written Agreement of All Partners

☐ A new partner or partners may be added to the partnership only by unanimous written consent of all existing partners.

1. Admitting a New Partner to Large Partnerships

If a large partnership requires unanimity to admit a new partner, there can, in theory, be serious problems if one or more partners refuse to accept the majority decision. Most larger partnerships we know (mostly big cooperatives) have nevertheless handled this issue by specifying in their agreement that unanimity is required for admission of a new partner. They try to avoid conflicts over this by other means. First, in reality, such conflicts rarely occur. Second, there are ways to test out a potential partner to see if she'll fit in. For example, one food sales collective we know of invites prospective partners to work for the enterprise for several weeks. After that time, the partners vote on whether the newcomer will be accepted into the business. If it's

unanimous, the hours he or she has worked are credited toward his or her buy-in amount. However, if the partners reject the prospective partner after they get to know him or her, the partners pay him or her for this work at the going rate (agreed upon before they start).

Further, if one or a few partners of a large partnership attempt to regularly thwart the will of the majority regarding the admission of new partners, peer pressure can often curtail this obstructionism. If peer pressure fails, large partnerships almost invariably have expulsion provisions in their agreement, so a partner who consistently or arbitrarily stands alone, preventing new partners from being admitted, may find himself rejected.

If, despite our advice, a large partnership decides that less than unanimity will be required to admit a new partner, here's a clause you can use or adapt to accomplish that goal.

The following clause is in the file **ADDLESS**, *in directory* **Clause11**.

Addition by Less Than All Partners

☐ A new partner may be admitted to the partnership with the written approval of___*[state method agreed upon—for example, partners holding 75% of the capital interest of the partnership; or, 80% of the votes of the partners, etc., or whatever you decide]* .

2. Adding a New Partner When You've Failed to Plan Ahead

Okay, so much for all our good advice about planning ahead to cover the question of admitting a new partner. Suppose you didn't? How do you proceed if you have nothing but an oral partnership agreement, or a written one that simply doesn't provide for the admission of a new partner and you now want to? Assuming that you and your partners have talked your situation over and are in agreement on future actions, now is the time to draft a comprehensive partnership agreement. If you can't agree on future plans, things won't be so simple; the fact that you have no written agreement including a procedure to handle disagreements will almost surely aggravate your problem. Bluntly put, if you can't at least agree on a mechanism to arrive at an agreement, there's little you can do except dissolve your partnership.

If, however, you do agree to expand and want to admit a new partner, this can be an excellent time to review your partnership agreement. If possible, you will want to replace whatever existing understanding you have with a written agreement that is both current and comprehensive. In a sense, you are in the same position as people adopting an agreement for the first time. One nice thing about a partnership—as opposed to a corporation—is that it can be changed easily at any time all partners

agree. To clarify the situation, you could begin the new partnership agreement with a general introductory clause, such as the following:

 The following clause is in the file **ADDFAIL**, *in directory* **Clause11**.

Admitting a New Partner When You've Failed to Plan Ahead

☐ ____*[Names of old partners]*____ have been engaged in business at ____*[location]*____ as a partnership under the firm name of _____. They now intend to admit *[name of new partner]*____ to their partnership, and all the members of the expanded partnership desire to amend and clarify the terms and conditions of their Partnership Agreement and to reduce their agreement to writing.

3. Dissolution of the Partnership When a New Partner Joins

Admitting a new partner causes a technical "dissolution" of the original partnership. A dissolution of a partnership need not imply the sort of negative consequences that we associate with the term dissolution of marriage (that is, termination of the relationship). In the context of adding a new partner, a partnership "dissolution" is simply the legal term used for a change in the membership of the partnership. Even if the business otherwise continues as usual, there has been a technical dissolution of the old partnership and the simultaneous continuation of that business by the newly created partnership. In other situations, however, the dissolution of a partnership may signal a much more fundamental change—up to and including the partnership's ceasing to do business.

Legally, from the moment of dissolution of a partnership business, no new partnership business can be undertaken by the old partnership. The original partners only have legal authority to wind up the business as rapidly as is feasible. (UPA Sections 30, 33, 35 and 37.) But since in the case of the addition of a new partner, the "dissolution" of the old partnership is basically a technical matter, the major problem is to close out an old set of books and start another. The business itself can go happily on. To make this clear, use the following clause in the section of your agreement on admitting a new partner:

 *The following clause is in the file **ADDNEW**, in directory **Clause11**.*

No Dissolution of the Partnership When a New Partner Joins

☐ Admission of a new partner shall not cause dissolution of the underlying partnership business, which will be continued by the new partnership entity.

4. The Incoming Partner's Liability for Existing Partnership Debts

Most of the issues the partners must deal with when a new partner is welcomed to your business family are the same as those that you resolved in your original partnership agreement—who gets what, who contributes what, who does what. However, one important additional matter must be resolved. Will the incoming partner be personally responsible for the existing debts of the partnership? Under the Uniform Partnership Act, a new partner is personally liable for partnership debts incurred before he became a partner, up to his share of (that is, contribution to) partnership property. (UPA Section 17.) Of course, once someone becomes a partner, he or she has unlimited personal liability for partnership debts incurred after his or her admission to the partnership.

EXAMPLE: Raul contributes $50,000 when he joins Elaine and Beverly in a partnership to produce pet food. When Raul joins the partnership, the two women owe $100,000. Raul's maximum liability for the preexisting debts would be the $50,000 he contributes.

The partners can vary this rule in the partnership agreement. This means that Beverly and Elaine could agree to release Raul from any liability for partnership debts that existed before he became a partner. Even so, the $50,000 he put up would be part of the business, and creditors could go after it if the business had no other assets. Or, at the other extreme, Raul could assume full personal liability for all existing debts. But to do this, Raul must clearly assume such liability.

Whatever the legal rules, it is risky to join a partnership that has substantial debts. Creditors tend to sue anyone who's an owner of an insolvent business, no matter when the owner came on board. Whether you're a new incoming partner or a member of the original partnership, you certainly hope that existing debts will be an academic problem and that your business is sufficiently profitable to pay debts from operating revenues. But, of course, this isn't always true. Indeed, one reason to bring in a new partner is precisely because the old partners need more cash. This is one example of how it's impractical to put detailed future plans in your partnership agreement before you start the business. It's impossible to know what sort of debt situation you will face two years from now. Sure, you could put a clause in your original agreement saying that all new partners must be ready to assume personal liability for all partnership debts no matter when incurred, but what good does that do? What happens if the only suitable person you can find balks? A custom-tailored clause regarding a new partner's liability for existing debts is likely to be necessary, so there's no point in trying to anticipate the problem before you face it (which you may well never need to do).

Here are three clauses for handling the issue of partnership debts and the incoming partner, as far as the partners are concerned. The first limits the incoming partner's liability; the second states the UPA rule that the incoming partner is liable for existing debts up to her investment in the business; and the third imposes maximum liability by providing the incoming partner is responsible for all partnership debts, no matter when the partnership incurred them.

 The following clause is in the file **DEBTNO**, *in directory* **Clause11**.

Not Responsible for Partnership Debts Before Becoming Partner

☐ ____[Incoming partner]____ shall not be personally responsible for, or assume any liability for, any debts of __[name of partnership business]__ incurred on or before _____, 20__.

or

 The following clause is in the file **DEBTDATE**, *in directory* **Clause11**.

Responsible for Partnership Debts From Set Date

☐ ____[Incoming partner]____ hereby expressly assumes personal liability for debts of [name of partnership business] incurred on or before _____, 20___, equal to the amount of his or her contribution to the partnership, totaling $_____.

or

 The following clause is in the file **DEBTALL**, *in directory* **Clause11**.

Responsible for All Partnership Debts

☐ ____[Incoming partner]____ hereby expressly assumes full personal liability equal to the personal liability of all other partners in the partnership of ____[name of partnership business]____ for all partnership debts and obligations whenever incurred.

5. Tax Liability of Incoming Partners

If a new partner receives a capital (that is, equity) interest in a partnership in exchange for services rendered or to be rendered to the partnership, she will be taxed immediately for the fair market value of the interest received. (The interest the partner receives must be without substantial risk of forfeiture for this tax rule to apply. Cases where there is a substantial risk of forfeiture are somewhat rare—they include instances where the partnership property has already been liened by a creditor.) This can be a real problem for newly admitted partners to professional partnerships, because the new partner will probably receive an interest in the (taxable) assets of the partnership, including accounts receivable and earned (but unbilled) fees.

EXAMPLE: Phillip and Betty operate a successful accounting firm. They decide to invite Janice, who has worked for them for years, to join their partnership because she's a good worker and a good friend, but also because they fear that if they don't give her a better deal, she'll open her own competing business. Janice receives 25% interest in the partnership and is not required to pay anything for it. The partners calculate the fair market value of this interest to be worth $50,000. Although Janice doesn't receive $50,000 cash—just her ownership interest in the business assets (that is, fixed assets, accounts receivable, unbilled fees and goodwill)—the IRS takes the position that she's received ordinary income amounting to $50,000, which is subject to income tax. In sum, come tax payment time, Janice will be out-of-pocket a substantial amount because she received her partnership ownership interest.

Because of this harsh tax rule (and often because it makes practical sense as well), it can be wiser for a service partner to sign a contract with the partnership that she'll receive her ownership (equity) interest in the business over time, after her services are performed. Or perhaps the partnership will agree to pay the taxes. But as we discuss in Chapter 7, it's not easy to solve this problem so that all partners are fully satisfied, and you'll likely need to consult an accountant or other tax advisor experienced with partnership tax issues.

6. Outgoing Partners

We discuss the problems caused by departure of a partner in Chapter 5. Here we just want to remind you that it's not unusual for the admission of a new partner to a business to coincide with the departure of another. The two occurrences can overlap.

Problems caused by the departure of a partner are usually much more complicated than admission of a new partner. Normally, unless the new partner directly purchases the departing partner's interest, that interest must be valued. Arrangements are often made by the remaining partners to buy that interest. Clauses specifying how this is to be handled should be in the original partnership agreement, so be sure to check the next chapter carefully. Also, remember that outgoing partners remain personally liable to the business's creditors for all debts of the partnership incurred up to the time they leave. As we've said, an incoming partner may or may not assume personal responsibility for those debts. But even if an incoming partner does assume full responsibility for old partnership debts, this doesn't release the departing partner from potential liability to existing creditors. Likewise, even a written release and assumption of liability by the new partner for the old partner doesn't automatically leave the old partner in the clear. If all the partners (including the new one) are broke, creditors of the old partnership can still go after the departed partner.

EXAMPLE: Al and James are partners in A-J Auto Body Repair. Al leaves, selling his partnership interest to Peter, who assumes personal liability for all existing debts of A-J. On the date Al leaves, A-J owes $36,000 to Nifty Paints, a major paint supplier. A-J never pays the bill, and six months later, the business goes broke. Neither James nor Peter has any personal assets. Al can be held liable by Nifty for the full $36,000 owed. Of course, Al has a claim for this amount against Peter (who assumed that debt); but if Peter is broke, it doesn't seem likely he will collect on it. ■

Changes: Departure of a Partner, Buy-Outs and Business Continuation

This is very likely the most important chapter in this book, yet it's one that many people will be tempted to skim. When you're excited and full of energy about establishing a new business, it probably seems trivial, or even destructive, to worry about a partner leaving. What a drag. But hopefully, you know enough now about life with a capital "L," to agree with our emphatic urging that you relax and remind yourselves that changes will happen. You owe it to yourselves to consider what you'll do if one of you—a partner—voluntarily leaves, becomes disabled or dies, or is even expelled from the partnership.

Sooner or later—and our experience tells us it's more likely to be sooner—the makeup of your partnership will change. A partner may want to leave for all sorts of reasons—to start another business, to move to Paris, to teach yoga. Or, if you all stay together for many years, a partner will inevitably retire or die. However a partner leaves, the same fundamental issues come up. To whom can the departing partner sell his interest? Do the remaining partners, or partner, have the right to buy it before anyone else can? How is the purchase price determined? Can the departing partner force the remaining partners to buy her interest, if she cannot find an outside buyer? What happens to the partnership business when a partner leaves? What are the departing partner's rights and duties to the remaining partners and partnership business? Finally, what happens if the partnership ends because all partners agree to do so?

It's essential you set up in your initial partnership agreement a structure to handle what will happen if a partner leaves or your partnership ends. It's simply not good business sense to leave these questions open and unresolved. If you haven't provided a structure to deal with them, and they arise in reality, there's a serious risk of conflict—a departing partner's interest is often directly opposed to that of those who remain. Simply put, the departing partner often wants a much higher price for his interest than the remaining partners think it is worth. And if, as has been known to happen, either side or both

sides harbor grievances against the other, matters can become dangerously hostile and conflicted.

You need to reach agreement about three basic issues:

- Does the partnership or the remaining partners have the right, or even the obligation, to buy a departing partner's interest? This is called a "buy-sell" agreement.
- If there is no outside buyer, how is the value of a departing partner's interest determined?
- How are payments to a departing partner to be made?

Some people worry that focusing on problems of a partner's leaving casts a pall over their discussions. Well, it should cast a shadow of possible reality, but it doesn't need to be a pall. Squarely facing the fact that problems can arise is a good indication that you and your partners will deal with these issues sensibly if or when they do. In hashing out your views with those of your other partners and writing down your decisions about a departing partner, you'll be making rules for your shared endeavor—rules that are legally enforceable. This is a valuable security to have, even if you all remain partners for decades.

Now let's look at some examples of problems that can arise if a partner leaves a partnership.

- Joe, your partner in your Florida consulting business for five years, decides to move to Austin because his wife, who's working on her Ph.D., gets a job at the University of Texas. He wants to take his money out of the business. How much money is he entitled to? Does he have the legal right and expectation of getting it all now? What if you go broke in the process of paying him off?
- Four partners run a successful Cincinnati café (cappuccino hits it big in Southern Ohio). Three want to expand; one decides she wants to cash in and finally become a full-time artist. Can she sell her share of the business to anyone at all? If she must sell to the remaining partners, how is a fair buy-out price determined? And what is a fair payment schedule?

- Your partner in your plumbing business, Janine, is killed in an auto accident, and her will leaves everything to her abrasive sister, Laticia. There's got to be a way to prevent Laticia from trying to fix pipes with you for the rest of your life, or from forcing a sale of the business. What are your rights to buy Janine's interest?

Here are a number of other partner-departure problems that can arise, some horrendous. Read them with a sense of humor as well as attention. All these things can't happen to one person.

- What happens if a partner quits?
- Does the remaining partner have the right to buy the departing partner's interest? If so, how is the purchase price determined?
- Does the reason why he quits matter? Would you be willing to pay him the same amount of money as his buy-out price whether he becomes ill with rheumatoid arthritis or runs off to Hawaii?
- What happens if the departing partner wants to sell her interest to someone you don't know, or even worse, do know and can't stand?
- Can a partner take a leave of absence? If she does, and stays away a year and a half, can you tell her she's out?
- What happens if a partner becomes disabled and can no longer work in the business? Who determines that a partner has become disabled within the meaning of your partnership agreement?
- What happens if your partner becomes mentally ill, gets Alzheimer's or is killed?
- What happens if one of your partners becomes alcohol or drug dependent, and you want to kick him out?
- Suppose your partner gets divorced and his wife ends up with a share of the business as part of a property settlement. If they're not speaking, what do you do?

- What if the partners all want to end the partnership, but each wants to continue the business on their own?
- What happens if a partner dies and her share is inherited by her spouse, who wants to cash in as fast as possible?

Do we have your attention? Good. Now, to work. To prepare sensible partnership clauses governing partners' departures, go though this chapter carefully: talk, discuss, argue, speculate—do everything you can to pin down what seems fair if a partner leaves. Today, no one knows if he or she will be the person who wants to leave or a person who wants to stay, so all partners should look at the question from both positions.

We'll cover a lot of ground here. While we urge you to seriously consider what will happen if a partner leaves, that doesn't mean you need to spend weeks right now conjuring up every conceivable possibility, no matter how remote. Your business is just starting. You can draft basic partner-departure clauses that fit your needs now. If your business prospers and grows, you can amend your partnership agreement later to reflect your new realities.

A. Buy-Sell Clauses

In this section, we'll cover issues concerning the sale of a departing partner's interest in the business, including:

- the right of the remaining partners to buy that interest
- what happens if the remaining partners decline to buy that interest
- requiring advance notice of withdrawal, and
- conflicts regarding which partner can buy out which others.

Sometimes buy-sell agreements, especially when they're very complex, are prepared as separate documents. We see no reason for this additional paperwork in most cases. You should be able to keep your buy-sell agreement succinct enough so it can be included in your partnership agreement.

To avoid the scary possibility that an unwanted person might buy, or otherwise acquire, a departing partner's share of a business, most buy-sell agreements contain what's called a "Right of First Refusal." This clause requires a departing partner to offer her share to the remaining partners before selling or transferring it to anyone else. (If you've ever dealt in real estate, it's kind of like buying an option on a building.)

 In a couple of states, right-to-buy agreements are risky when applied after a partner's death. *In Alabama and Mississippi, buy-out agreements were held void in cases where one partner died, on the grounds that the agreement was "testamentary in character" and did not conform to the state law on wills. Gomez v. Higgins, 130 Ala. 493, 30 So. 417 (1901); Thomas v. Byrd, 112 Miss. 692, 73 So. 725 (1916). If you are in these states, see a lawyer.*

1. The Right of First Refusal

Do you want to allow a partner to be able to freely sell or transfer her partnership interest to an outsider no matter what the other partners want? Your answer should probably be no. You need a very persuasive reason (we can't think of one) to exclude a right of first refusal clause from your agreement. If one partner leaves, the remaining partners normally want at least an option to buy her share and continue the business. Otherwise, if one partner withdraws, there can be unfortunate consequences, such as:

- The business may have to be liquidated. Selling off your used computers and machinery, and the sofa in the waiting room, isn't going to make much money for anybody. Most businesses are worth far more as operating entities than they are as carcasses up for sale to the highest bidder.

- The withdrawing partner may attempt to sell or transfer his interest without all partners' consent. Obviously this raises the possibility of all sorts of unhappy scenarios.

To avoid all these unhappy possibilities, a well-drafted partnership agreement normally contains a right of first refusal clause. Under this clause a departing partner who receives a bona fide offer from an outside buyer will be able to get that price, either from the partners or the outside person. (Bona fide is Latin for "good faith.") Using this term in your agreement prohibits a partner from getting an unreasonably high dummy bid to jack up the sale price to the remaining partners.

Some partners decide that they do not want to have a right of first refusal clause in their agreement. Instead, they provide that a departing partner's interest shall be valued only as determined under a method set forth in their agreement. (The different methods for doing this are set forth in Section B.) They believe that if a partner leaves, it makes more sense to keep the remaining partners happy and functioning, even if the departing partner could have received a higher price by selling to an outsider. This means the remaining partners can never be forced into business with someone they don't like. Of course, if the time comes, the remaining partners could still permit the departing partner to sell to an outsider if they did like this new person. There is, after all, a real incentive for this—the remaining partners won't have to pay any money

(from the business or from their own personal assets) to the departing partner.

But most partnerships decide that it is too unfair to a departing partner to deny him a higher price that could be paid by a bona fide buyer. So they include a right of first refusal clause in their partnership agreement. If you want one in your agreement, use or adapt the one below. To complete the clause, you need to agree upon and then insert the number of days the partnership has, after it's been notified of the outside offer, to buy the departing partner's interest.

 The following clause is in the file **TRANOUT**, *in directory* **Clause07**.

The Right of First Refusal Upon Offer From Outsider

☐ If any partner receives a bona fide, legitimate offer, whether or not solicited by him or her, from any person to purchase all of his or her interest in the partnership, and if the partner receiving the offer is willing to accept it, he or she shall give written notice of the amount and terms of the offer, the identity of the proposed buyer, and his or her willingness to accept the offer to each of the other partners. The other partner or partners shall have the option, within _____ days after the notice is given, to purchase that partner's interest on the same terms as those contained in the offer.

More detailed provisions for buy-sell clauses are contained in Buy-Sell Agreement Handbook: Plan Ahead for Changes in Ownership of Your Business, *by Anthony Mancuso and Bethany K. Laurence (Nolo). For example, if you want a specific clause on buy-outs if a partner becomes disabled, covering such matters as how disability is defined and how long a disability must exist before a buy-out can or must occur, see that book.*

Right of first refusal clauses can get complicated very quickly. *You could include provisions requiring extensive details about any outside offer and would-be buyer, plus precise requirements for what makes an offer "bona fide," as well as what happens if a departing partner wants to sell only to one remaining partner (not to the partnership itself) and whether a partner can make gifts of his interest. Here we provide a clause that covers the basics, which should cover the needs of a beginning partnership. If you want to create a clause that that goes into considerable detail and covers many contingencies, you'll likely need to see a lawyer.*

2. The Right of the Partnership to Buy a Partner's Interest

The right of first refusal clause only applies if a departing partner receives a bona fide outside offer. But suppose a departing partner doesn't get any outside offer? Or suppose a partner leaves because of disability, or death, or goes bankrupt or is expelled? Or suppose a partner's interest, or a portion of it, is transferred by gift, or agreement between the partner and an outsider, or by court order, as in a divorce case? Then what? In all these cases, the remaining partners will normally want the right to buy, at their option, the interest of a departing partner.

Below, we provide a right-to-buy clause. Under this clause, the partnership has the right to buy the interest of a departing partner, no matter what the reason for the departure. An outsider who receives a share of a business has no right to force himself into the partnership. He must sell, assuming the partnership enforces the clause, which is not mandatory for the partnership. The remaining partners could decide, if they wish, to take the outsider in as a new partner. This is an example, and a reminder, that rules in a partnership agreement don't have to be binding if none of the partners want them to be. Agreement rules should protect partners and define their rights, not freeze them in a legal straightjacket.

What happens if someone receives a share of the business and would prefer not to be bought out by the remaining partners? First, realize that this is unlikely. How often does a person insist on becoming a member of a business when the other owners don't want him? (Especially when the alternative is to receive money for the ownership interest.) On balance, we feel it's best to protect the existing partners and partnership from being compelled to accept a co-owner they don't want.

The following clause allows the partners to buy in any case, except for the case where a right of first refusal applies.

 The following clause is in the file **TRANSALE**, *in directory* **Clause07**.

Sale to Partnership at Its Option

☐ If any partner leaves the partnership, for whatever reason, whether he or she quits, withdraws, is expelled, retires, becomes mentally or physically incapacitated or unable to fully function as a partner, or dies, or if the partner attempts to or is ordered to transfer his or her interest, whether voluntarily or involuntarily he or she, or his or her estate shall be obligated to sell his or her interest in the partnership to the remaining partner or partners, who have the option, but not the obligation, to buy that interest. However, if the departing partner receives a bona fide offer from a prospective outside buyer, the Right of First Refusal Clause of this Agreement shall apply.

> ### Drafting Two-Person Partnership Clauses
>
> The preceding clause refers to a partnership, or partners, that remains after one partner leaves. But if there were only two partners originally, and one departs, there's only one partner left—so there can't be "remaining partners" left. Therefore, when drafting an agreement for a two-person partnership, you must vary the sample clauses to refer to the "remaining owner," or "remaining partner" as shown below. Similarly, two-person partnerships should vary the sample clauses throughout this book to refer to the remaining owner rather than the partnership, when only one person will remain if a partner leaves.

The preceding clause for a two-person partnership should read as follows:

Sale to Partner at His or Her Option

☐ If any partner leaves the partnership, for whatever reason, whether he or she quits, withdraws, retires, becomes mentally or physically incapacitated or unable to fully function as a partner, or dies, or if the partner attempts to or is ordered to transfer his or her interest, whether voluntarily or involuntarily he or she, or his or her estate shall be obligated to sell his or her interest in the partnership to the remaining owner, who may buy that interest, under the terms and conditions set forth in this Agreement.

3. Forced Buy-Outs

What happens if a partner leaves and cannot find an outside buyer? What happens if a partner leaves for any reason, and the remaining partners don't want to buy out that departing partner's interest? If there's no clause governing the refusal of the remaining partner or partners to buy, the departing partner may be stuck.

A friend of ours who was a partner in a successful bakery faced this problem. After a number of years of long hours, struggle, growth and modest prosperity (most of their profits went into expanding the business), our friend decided she wanted to try other things. But the other partner wasn't interested in making payments for the departing partner's interest. Their agreement contained no clause governing what happened if the remaining partner didn't want to buy out the departing one. So the departing partner could only try to sell her share on the open market, not an easy job. Most people are understandably hesitant to buy into a partnership with another owner they don't know well, or at all. After trying unsuccessfully to sell her share by herself, our friend hired an agent—and many months later sold her interest for far less than she believed it was worth.

A sensible approach toward the refusal-to-buy problem is to start by understanding that an entire business is often much more saleable than a share of that business. So if the remaining partners refuse to buy the interest of a departing partner, the best solution, at least from the departing partner's point of view, is to sell the whole business and divide the proceeds. This gives the remaining partners a choice—buy the departing partner's share of the business or lose their own. An important decision here is how long the remaining partners have to make up their minds after the departing one is gone. A common period is six months. That gives them a reasonable time to see how the business works without the departing partner. But you are definitely free to choose any time period you all agree on.

Here is a clause covering refusal-to-buy:

 The following clause is in the file **TRANREF**, *in directory* **Clause07**.

Refusal of Remaining Partners to Buy

☐ If the remaining partner or partners do not purchase the departing partner's share of the business, under the terms provided in this

Agreement, within *[time period after the departing partner leaves]*, the entire business of the partnership shall be put up for sale, and listed with the appropriate sales agencies, agents or brokers.

Notice that this clause does not cover outside buyers, because it doesn't have to. If the partnership agreement contains a right of first refusal clause and there's an outside buyer, then the departing partner can sell to that buyer, unless the remaining partners exercise their option. So it's only where no outside buyer for one partner's share can be found that this clause comes into play. And if the partnership agreement prohibits the departing partner from reselling to an outside buyer, then it doesn't matter if one appears.

There's another approach to the refusal-to-buy problem, which is to have a clause compelling the remaining partners to buy, called a "forced buy-out." In theory this protects a departing owner from being stuck with a partnership interest she no longer desires. But this drastic solution may not be workable. If the remaining partners don't have the cash and are unwilling or unable to borrow it, how can they be made to pay for the departing partner's interest? Even if they could pay for it, if they choose not to, what will happen if a departing partner attempts to force a buy-out? At best, dragged-out negotiations, conflict, and slow payments. At worst, a lawsuit attempting to enforce a forced buy-out clause, then more legal work to enforce any court judgment. And looming over all these hassles are two clichés that remain distressingly true: possession is nine-tenths of the law, and you can't get blood from a stone.

We think a far more desirable way to handle the reluctance or refusal of the remaining partners to buy is a clause requiring the forced sale of the entire business. This forces the remaining partners to face up to a financial reality: either they let the business go, or they buy out the departing partner's interest. But they cannot simply ignore her.

4. Advance Notice of Withdrawal

Many partnerships decide they want advance notice, if possible, before a partner leaves. Obviously, this isn't normally possible if a partner suddenly becomes seriously injured, mentally incompetent or dies, but the vast majority of partner departures are not caused by illness, disability or death but by a desire or need to move on. In that case, a sensible advance notice clause seems fair. Of course, you get to decide how long a lead time is required.

What's the sanction if a partner doesn't comply with a notice clause? You can create any sanction you want. A common one is to provide, when you get to valuation of the business (see Section B), that the value of a departing partner's share who violates the notice provision will be reduced by a set percentage, such as 10% or 20%. Or, when inadequate notice is given, you can provide for a longer time for payment of the buy-out price (see Section C). So usually you can't define your sanction until you've been through the subsequent sections of this chapter. For now, simply provide that the sanction is "as provided elsewhere in this Agreement." But then be very sure you actually write in that sanction elsewhere, and don't simply forget about it later on.

What happens if you have an advance notice clause and a partner has an emergency and feels he has to leave suddenly? For example, he suddenly got an offer from a big New York publisher and wants to bail out of your small Maine book partnership. Well, first remember that you don't have to enforce any partnership clause, including this one. If all partners agree that it's fair to waive it, you can. But if one or more partners want to enforce the notice clause, it's important that all understand that, whatever the departing partner's emergency, the remaining partners have been surprised and must carry on the business without being properly warned of the changes they'll have to cope with. So they can fairly insist that they should be compensated for this burden by paying the departing partner a lower buy-out price than he'd normally receive. After all, here the departing partner is moving on to greener, or at least richer, pastures, so he can absorb some financial cost.

 The following clause is in the file **TRANNOT**, *in directory* **Clause07**.

Requiring Advance Notice of Withdrawal

☐ Unless physically prevented from giving notice, a partner shall give _[time period]_ written advance notice of his or her intention to leave the partnership. If he or she fails to do so [describe the sanction imposed] .

5. Conflicts Regarding Right to Buy

Now let's examine some possible conflicts regarding right-to-buy provisions and look at clauses designed to cope with them. What happens if two equal partners (or an equal number of partners on both sides) can't get along, and each wants to buy the other out? How do the partners decide who has the right to buy? The obvious answer is that it can't be decided, unless you've previously created some clause to resolve this question or, when the problem develops, you work out some sort of compromise acceptable to both. If you have no prearranged agreement, and neither side will compromise, under the terms of the UPA the business will have to be liquidated and the net proceeds distributed to the ex-partners. If there's a buy-out conflict in a multi-member partnership, it's possible that the majority could expel the minority (if allowed in the agreement) and then buy out their interest under the agreement. This is obviously a drastic solution, and the bitterness created will surely damage the business.

In a two-person or even-member partnership, there's a real possibility of a deadlock. To prevent a forced sale, you can adopt any reasonable method to see who leaves and who stays. Commonly used methods include the coin flip and auction bidding.

The coin flip method may seem simplistic, but nevertheless lots of partnerships use it because it has the great virtue of simplicity: "Heads I get to buy, tails you do." (Do be sure you all trust whoever flips the coin.)

 The following clause is in the file **COINFLIP**, *in directory* **Clause07**.

The Coin Flip

☐ If the partners cannot agree on who has the right to purchase the other partners' interest in the business, that right shall be determined by the flip of a coin [to be flipped by _[name]_].

With auction bidding, each side offers a price for the business, and can then bid their price up, until the higher bid wins.

> **EXAMPLE:** Bob and Skip each tire of the other and decide to end their boat/marina partnership. Bob wants very much to continue the business. He and Skip both believe the market value for their business is roughly $320,000 to $340,000. Bob offers to buy Skip's share of the business at $166,000, figuring Skip will decide to sell because Bob's price is toward the high side. But Skip counters with $169,000 for Bob's share. Now Bob has to decide whether to bid near maximum for the business or cash out. Bob's a gambler, so he bids $170,000. Skip decides that's good enough—he almost sold for $166,000. He sells his share to Bob and moves to Florida.

 The following clause is in the file **AUCTION**, *in directory* **Clause07**.

Auction Bidding

☐ If the partners cannot agree who has the right to purchase the other partners' interest in the business, that right shall be determined by an auction, where each group of partners shall bid on the business. The group eventually offering the highest bid shall have the right to buy the lower bidders' shares of the business. The buying group shall pay for the purchased share of the business under the terms provided in this Agreement.

Paying the buy-out price when there's a conflict. *Providing a clause that determines who has the right to buy when partners are in conflict doesn't cover how the prevailing partner will pay the losing partner the buy-out price. To accomplish that, you need a specific payment clause. (See Section C.) And if the prevailing partner is determined by coin flip, you also need a clause to determine the buy-out price. (See Section B.)*

B. Determining the Value of the Business

You need clauses in your partnership agreement to define the terms on which remaining partners can buy out the interest of a departing partner, unless a right of first refusal clause governs. (To remind you, in that case, the price and conditions of the outside would-be buyer's offer controls.) Here we focus on what's usually the most important, and thorniest, subject—valuing the business. Even for a very successful small business, finding an outside buyer who wants to buy a portion of it and will pay a fair price can be difficult, or even impossible. So how do you create a fair method for determining the worth of your business, when there's no price determined by an open market?

Even with a file of current financial data, coming up with a fair price for partnership business is not easy. Indeed, for most small businesses, there is no just-right solution. The best you can do is work up a valuation method that seems tolerable, or, at least, better than other possible methods. It's akin to Win-

ston Churchill's description of democracy as "the worst system of government ever invented, except for any other that's been tried." While no method will be perfect, working out one now, when you're setting up your partnership, allows you to discuss and agree on a method when none of you are considering selling out, and when you can all, hopefully, see both sides of the equation.

Below we'll discuss and present sample clauses for valuation approaches that we believe are as good as can be achieved. No one method is inherently superior to others. It all depends on the nature of your business, and the partners' relationship and expectations. So don't just settle on one of the methods we present if none seems to fit your situation. You can modify one, or blend two or come up with your own method altogether. Remember, the goal is to achieve as fair a method as possible of determining a buy-out price, and your own ingenuity can be used to the fullest.

We do not provide sophisticated valuation methods individually tailored to your business. Occasionally, a more industry-specific approach might seem to lead to a more accurate estimation of the worth of your business. For the vast majority of small businesses, though, especially beginning ones, such detailed methods merely bog you down in complexities, without leading to fairer results.

If you decide you now want to go beyond the basic methods we provide here, you can explore several routes:

- Consult with an expert, such as an experienced business appraiser or a trusted accountant who has experience with the valuation methods commonly used for your type of business.

- If you know other people in your business, you might also wish to discuss with them how they go about valuing their businesses. There are rough valuation norms based on profits, sales and cash flow for some types of businesses.

There are several good books that concentrate on business-valuation techniques for small businesses, including Handbook of Business Valuation, *by Thomas L. West and Jeffrey D. Jones (John Wiley & Sons).*

Revising Your Valuation Method

Now your business is just beginning. It is probably worth no more than the resale value of its tangible assets. This means that by adopting a valuation clause now, you're really making your best guess as to how you'll value your (hopefully) profitable business in the future. In that future, you may decide to reevaluate and rewrite this clause, assuming your business has become large and successful enough so that a more sophisticated evaluation method seems sensible.

Here's another important consideration. It's wise to structure your agreement so that the business is given a good chance to survive. If the buy-out price is too high, the remaining partners may simply decide to liquidate the business. If they do, and the business can't be sold to outsiders, everyone will likely receive much less than if the existing partners bought out the departing partner and the business continued. For example, if a dog-grooming business dissolves, the money received from the sale of secondhand dog-grooming equipment and other business assets should be much less than what the owners could have earned if they'd continued the business.

Also, when considering valuation methods, take into account how buy-out payments will be made (covered in Section C, below). Often a somewhat higher buy-out price may be acceptable to the remaining partners in exchange for reasonable monthly payments (instead of a lump sum). And it's

helpful—although often difficult with new businesses—to make some earnings projections and see how a buy-out method looks in the context of the amount of cash that's likely to be available. For example, if you're being bought out—or buying—in a couple of years, does what you would receive seem like a fair price if the partnership profits are $50,000 a year? $500,000 a year? What about if the business isn't profitable but it appears it soon will be?

Finally, if you are entering a partnership where the major assets are each partner's customers, and any departing partner will take her customers if she leaves, what remains for the other partners to pay for? This is a common problem in some types of service businesses, like architects or hairstylists. Normally, all that needs to be valued here are fixed assets like desks, computers and chairs.

EXAMPLE: Three hairstylists, all with their own business, decide to form a partnership. They agree that each will keep their own customers. Regarding a buy-out method, one says, "What's the big deal? If I leave, I take my customers with me. We figure out the worth of our furniture, divide it up, and that's that."

"I wish it were that simple," another answers, "but we're thinking of hiring other hairstylists, remember. And maybe leasing space and taking a cut—okay, okay, call it a commission—for each haircut given by someone we lease to. Who gets that business?"

"There's more," the third partner adds. "We want our name to catch on, get known. Who gets that? How much will it be worth? And what about our lease? Suppose it's really a good deal in two years, like we hope it is. Isn't that worth something?"

"All right," sighs the first. "No easy solutions. Back to work."

Okay, now let's look at some specific business-valuation methods.

1. The Asset-Valuation Method

The asset-valuation method of valuing a business is based on the current net worth of the business. Basically, under this method, the worth of the business is its assets minus its liabilities. The UPA requires you to use this method if your partnership agreement does not contain any specified valuation method. Here's how it works: As of the date the departing partner leaves, the net dollar value of all partnership assets is calculated and all outstanding business debts are deducted to determine net worth. The departing partner receives his or her ownership percentage of this amount (under whatever payout terms you've agreed on). The net worth of business assets normally includes:

- the current market value of all tangible assets of the business. This includes the net value of current inventory, plus the present value of other items, from manufacturing machinery to the stained glass lamps in the waiting room. You do get to decide how picky to be here. We advise against trying to value every last wastebasket or paper clip. Worrying about this level of minutiae reminds us of the divorce we heard about where the departing husband inventoried the food in the refrigerator before he left, and claimed one-half its worth as part of his community property. No wonder his wife wanted out.
- all accounts receivable that are reasonably collectable
- all earned but unbilled fees, and all money presently earned for work in progress. (This is particularly important in professional partnerships—an architectural firm, for instance— but it can also apply where construction work is being done, or anywhere else where money is earned although a bill had not yet been sent out. This, technically, is not an account receivable.)
- all cash. (If there isn't sufficient cash to cover debts, they are subtracted from accounts receivable or earned but unbilled fees.)

EXAMPLE: Lou, Wilbur and George have been equal partners in a part-time computer repair business for four years. Lou quits. Under their partnership agreement, Lou is entitled to one-third of the value of the repair shop, as determined by the asset-valuation method. The value of the assets includes all cash in the bank, fixed assets (such as tools, building, etc.), accounts receivable (money people still owe them for fixing their computers) and earned but unbilled fees, and money presently earned for work in progress. These assets are all added up and then any money the business owes (liabilities) is deducted to determine the value of the business.

The asset-valuation method can be sensible for new businesses. Aside from your hopes, what does your business really have except its fixed assets? There's no reasonable way to estimate future profits when the business has yet to establish a valuable name or reputation. This method can also make sense for a business whose worth is basically determined by the value of tangible possessions, such as an antique store. However, for many businesses that have been established and profitable for awhile, this method fails to include intangible, but still real, aspects of a business's worth. Some ongoing businesses are often worth much more than the value of assets minus liabilities. We must add that Bernard Kamoroff, author of the well respected *Small Time Operator* (Bell Springs), says that extra worth for most small businesses in Main Street America is a fantasy. Basically, he claims, they sell for the value of inventory and fixtures, period.

EXAMPLE: Suppose the computer repair business we mentioned above has a net worth, under the asset-valuation method, of $150,000, including: $46,000 worth of equipment, tools and office furniture; $82,000 in billed fees owed; $28,000 in earned but unbilled fees; $4,000 cash; minus $10,000 owed on the business's line of credit. But thanks to several very profitable service contracts, profits have averaged $180,000 a year for the past four years, and the partners have only worked a day or two a week. Under the asset-valuation method, Lou's interest is worth $50,000—one-third of the total value of $150,000. But the profits he's been earning are $60,000 a year.

When Lou leaves, the remaining two partners won't be able to simply divide up his yearly profits. They'll either have to work harder or hire someone to do Lou's work. Still, Lou's interest in the business seems worth substantially more than $50,000. Wouldn't you be glad to pay $50,000 and work a day or so a week, for $60,000 a year?

Some profitable ongoing businesses are un-doubtedly worth significantly more than the value of their tangible assets because they've earned a good business reputation. That reputation brings in continued business. This intangible asset is tradi-tionally labeled "goodwill," and is generally defined as "the well-founded expectation of continued pub-lic patronage." The concept is especially applicable for successful retail businesses (for example, a res-taurant with an excellent location and good reputa-tion) but is often less of a factor with businesses that depend primarily on individual service. A car-penter or podiatrist may have acquired personal goodwill, but it's usually hard to transfer that good-will to another person.

Beginning businesses don't have goodwill, so it can be sensible to adopt a market-value buy-out method for the first year (or some other set time), with the express provision that another more inclu-sive method will be adopted at the end of that pe-riod.

If you feel sure that you will want to include goodwill in your business valuation, you can simply add it to the list of assets to be valued. However, if you do, be aware that this just puts off the problem of valuing something that is, by definition, hard to value. If you decide goodwill is, or will soon be, a valuable asset of your business, we advise you to set up a method for calculating that value now, and

not to postpone the problem. We discuss goodwill in more depth in Section B5 of this chapter. If you think that goodwill may apply to you now, be sure you've read that section carefully before making your final decision on your business-valuation clause.

Following are clauses you can use, or adapt, if you decide an asset-valuation clause is appropriate for your business.

 The following clause is in the file **BUYASSET**, *in directory* **Clause08**.

Asset-Valuation Method

☐ Except as otherwise provided in this Agree-ment, the value of the partnership shall be made by determining the net worth of the partnership as of the date a partner leaves, for any reason. Net worth is defined as the market value, as of that date, of the following assets:

1. All tangible property, real or personal, owned by the business;

2. All the liquid assets owned by the business, including cash on hand, bank deposits and CDs or other monies;

3. All accounts receivable;

4. All earned but unbilled fees;

5. All money presently earned for work in progress;

6. Less the total amount of all debts owed by the business.

Note that this clause (and all the business-valua-tion clauses in Section B) commences with "Except as otherwise provided in this Agreement." The rea-son for this provision is that most agreements will contain a right of first refusal clause, as set forth in Section A1. Under this type of clause, you'll recall, if an outsider makes a bona fide offer to buy a partner's interest, its value is determined by this offer, not by the business-valuation clause in the agreement.

When using the asset-valuation method, you can provide now that you'll revisit your business-valuation clause after a set period, to check out if this method continues to be the best one for you. Of course, you can always amend your valuation clause, no matter what method you use, because the asset-valuation method is so rudimentary it seems particularly appropriate to specify in your agreement that you'll later check out if you still want to use it.

Following are clauses you can use or adapt to state you'll amend your agreement later to include goodwill. Of course, if you decide later there isn't any goodwill, you're not compelled to revise the agreement.

 The following clause is in the file **REVISVAL**, *in directory* **Clause08**.

Revision of Valuation Method

☐ The partners agree that _____ years after the commencement of the business, they will revise this valuation clause so that the method used will best reflect the worth of the business.

 The following clause is in the file **BUYREV**, *in directory* **Clause08**.

Revision of Valuation Method to Include Goodwill

☐ The partners understand and agree that the preceding business-valuation clause may not fully and adequately reflect the worth of the business after it has been successfully established, if the business has acquired goodwill or other valuable intangible assets. Therefore, the partners agree that ___*[time period]*___ after the commencement of the business they will meet to consider amending this business-valuation clause to include a method that will fairly reflect any goodwill earned by the business.

2. The Book-Value Method

A variation of the asset-valuation method is called the "book-value" method. This means calculating the value of all partnership assets and liabilities as they're set forth in the partnership accounting books. Basically, assets are valued at their acquisition cost. This method has simplicity to recommend it, but little else. Often, the book value of an asset has little relation to reality. And the book-value method does not, of course, cover goodwill. Worse, the acquisition cost of property is unlikely to be its current worth. Some property, particularly real estate, can be worth much more than its acquisition cost. Other property, from inventory to office furniture, is probably worth less than its acquisition cost. These assets may have been depreciated on the books, but even with depreciation, usually taken for tax purposes, the book figure may not be close to what the assets can be sold for. Finally, significant assets, such as earned but unbilled fees and money earned for work in progress, aren't included at all.

Because we believe this method is undesirable for almost all businesses, we do not provide a clause for it. We mention it only because we know it has a catchy name ("Hey, doesn't 'book value' make sense?"). There's something about the terms "the books" or the "financial books" that can sound more reliable than they are in this context. So we wanted to clear up that book value isn't a sensible way to go.

Using Capital Accounts as the Basis for Valuation

The term "capital account" means, at its most basic, the amount a partner has invested in the partnership business, less any capital distributions. You may wonder if you could use the dollar figure in each partner's capital account to determine the dollar value of that partner's interest for buy-out purposes. The answer is that this is not a wise method to use. The value of a partner's interest depends on how the business is doing, not on how much she invested. After all, investing means you are taking a risk. If the business is doing poorly, it could, at the time a partner leaves, be worth far less than the sum of all the partners' capital accounts. So you don't want to guarantee that any departing partner will automatically get back all that she's invested. By contrast, if the business has become very successful, it could be worth far more than the sum of the capital accounts.

3. The Set-Dollar Method

Under the set-dollar method, the partners agree in advance that if one partner departs from the partnership, the others will buy out his share on the basis of a pre-established price. Assigning a value to the business has the advantage of being definite, but otherwise can have serious drawbacks. Why? First, because the price selected may, from the start, be arbitrary and not related to the real current value. Second, because the worth of any partnership business will fluctuate, any predetermined buy-out figure may soon become out of date. One way to handle this second problem is to require that the partners establish a value for the partnership every year by a specified date.

A set-dollar figure can be advisable when the primary worth of the business is the energies of the partners, where there is no considerable inventory of goods and the intangible assets of the business itself (name, goodwill, etc.) have little independent value. This describes many partnership service businesses, particularly in their first few years. From computer repairs to gardening work, many new service businesses don't have costly fixed assets. What they have is the energies and hopes of their owners. Rather than bother with trying to determine the worth of each item of business property as valued by the asset-valuation method (the present value of secondhand computer repair tools or pruning tools, etc.), the partners simply determine what they think the business is worth and revise this figure periodically. After all, who knows their business better than they do?

Another occasion to use a set-dollar buy-out clause is when the partners' concern is the preservation of the business and their relationship with each other. For example, we know of a two-man partnership that runs a trucking firm. Neither partner has immediate family to inherit his interest in the firm and both want to ensure the business survives the death of a partner. So they selected what they thought was a low set-dollar estimate for the worth of the business, to be used in the event either partner died. By setting a value in advance, the deceased partner's estate does not get involved in valuing the partnership interest. And by making this amount reasonably low, the survivor should not be unduly burdened to come up with the money.

Another example where a yearly set-dollar method can make sense is when the partnership is involved in property investment—the partners hope the property will increase in value—although the amount, of course, can't be predicted. (If it could, we'd all get rich.) A prime example of this is investing in real estate. Rather than bother with annual appraisals by professionals, which can be costly and time-consuming—as well as result in surprising discrepancies between one expert's appraisal price and another's—the partners simply meet yearly and decide what they believe the partnership property is worth. Since real estate is bought and sold on an open market, the partners simply make a sensible estimation of the property's worth based on recent sales of comparable property.

If partners want to be very thorough, they can also agree on the amount or percentage rate they estimate the value of the partnership will increase or decrease over the next year. Thus, if a partner leaves six months after the last yearly valuation, they have a formula for business valuation, which includes recent price fluctuation.

The attraction of the set-dollar method for many partnerships is that it combines fairness and simplicity. The buy-out price is fair because everyone has agreed to it. Once you and your partners have determined the price, you don't need to bother with appraisals, accountants or multiples (see Sections B4 and B5) if a partner leaves. In effect, the set-dollar method says, yes, valuation of a small business partnership that can't readily be sold on a market is inherently subjective. So we—the partners—will

face that subjectivity ourselves, directly, rather than look to some other valuation method to cope with it. Since with a set-dollar method the partners must sit down regularly and work out the business's worth, this can help keep all partners up-to-date on valuation issues and quite possibly defuse potential disputes.

 The following clause is in the file **BUYSET**, *in directory* **Clause08**.

Set-Dollar Method

☐ Except as otherwise provided in this Agreement, the value of a partner's interest in the partnership shall be determined as follows:

1. Within ___[specify, for example, 90] days after the end of each fiscal year of the partnership, the partners shall determine the partnership's value by unanimous written

agreement, and that value shall remain in effect from the date of that written determination until the next such written determination.

2. Should the partners be unable to agree on a value or otherwise fail to make any such determination, the partnership's value shall be the greater of (a) the value last established under this section, or (b) __[whatever else you decide upon, such as "the net worth of the partnership"]__ .

3. __[Add any further provision you've agreed on, such as that you'll also make annual estimates of the rate of increase or decrease of the value of the business.]__

4. Post-Departure Appraisal (Valuing the Business After a Partner Leaves)

Using this method, you simply agree to have an independent appraiser (sometimes named in the agreement) determine the value of the partnership at the date of a partner's departure. At first glance, this sounds great. "Hey, why struggle with valuation now? Let an expert determine the precise value later if we ever need to." Sadly, appraisals rarely work so easily. As we've said, many small businesses aren't amenable to precise valuation, no matter how expert the appraiser. For most small businesses, all you're doing is passing the buck and hoping that somehow the word "expert" means that a tough problem will be competently solved by someone else. Or as one astute businessperson remarked, describing the difficulty of valuing most small businesses, "Use three appraisers and I guarantee you'll get three quite different numbers."

Even in an area where there is an open market that should allow prices to be determined "objectively," the reality of appraisals can be disturbing. For instance, a friend of ours was a partner in a three-man real estate partnership. Their agreement provided that a departing partner and the remaining partners would each hire an appraiser. If the appraisals differed, they'd split the difference. Sounded fine and fair, until a partner died. The partnership owned a small apartment house. The partnership's appraiser valued the building at $280,000. The deceased's estate's appraiser (legally qualified) valued the property at $410,000. Our friend remains convinced his appraiser was right, but he and his partner had to pay far more ($65,000 more!) than they thought was fair for the deceased partner's interest.

There are several other reasons to be cautious about using appraisers to determine the value of your business. It can take some time to get the appraiser's report, unless you have the good fortune of finding an appraiser who is both experienced in your business and prompt. Also, the appraisal method (unlike the other methods we discuss) makes it difficult to determine in advance what a partnership interest might be worth. This could mean partners don't have essential information when they need it, as would be the case for someone contemplating leaving a partnership. Also, appraisals don't come cheaply, and can be an added cost just when you're worrying about money most.

Having presented the possible drawbacks to the appraisal method, let us now give the other side. Since, as we've stressed, no valuation method is precise or scientific, appraisal can, in some situations, be the best of your difficult choices. Some businesses do seem more suitable to valuation by appraisal than others. Any business where there is a closely followed market that can be used to determine the price of inventory can sensibly use the appraisal method. For example, this method can be feasible for businesses that sell antiques or collectibles, such as old baseball cards, stamps or jewelry.

Beyond this, the key to making the appraisal method work is to agree ahead of time on an appraiser all partners have confidence in. For example, if you and your partners are starting a small software business, you would want to appoint someone of unquestioned integrity and judgment who knows the software industry—and probably your segment of it—intimately.

Below is a clause for the appraisal-valuation method. While it's possible to set out criteria the appraiser must use or consider in making an appraisal of your business, we don't think this is wise. If the appraiser doesn't know her business, your criteria won't teach it to her. And if she does know her business, your criteria are likely to be restrictive and not helpful.

 *The following clause is in the file **BUYAPPR**, in directory **Clause08**.*

Post-Departure Appraisal

☐ Except as otherwise provided in this Agreement, the value of the partnership shall be determined by an independent appraisal conducted, if possible, by __*[name of agreed-on person]*__ . If all partners cannot agree on an appraiser, the departing partner and the remaining partners shall each select an independent appraiser. If the two selected appraisers are unable to agree on the fair market value of the partnership business, then the two appraisers shall mutually select a third appraiser to determine the fair market value.

The appraisal shall be commenced within _____ days of the partner's departure from the partnership. The partnership and the departing partner shall share the cost of the appraisal equally.

5. The Capitalization-of-Earnings Method

"Capitalization of earnings" is a fancy term for a method that determines the value of a business based on what it makes. Often, the best estimate of what a business is really worth (without, of course, an open market to set the price) depends in large measure on its earning capacity. If the business is successful and likely to remain so even if a partner leaves, the capitalization of earnings method attempts to take into account the fact that there's a real value in the ongoing nature of the successful business. For example, take two restaurants that are each worth $150,000 according to the asset-valuation method, but one has yearly profits of $250,000 and the other has yearly profits of $30,000. Clearly, the more successful restaurant is really worth much more than the other. As we've discussed, this reality is commonly referred to as a business having "goodwill." Other intangible assets can range from a desirable lease to valuable intellectual property, including patents, copyrights and trade names. The capitalization-of-earnings method is an attempt to reflect the worth of these intangible assets when determining the worth of a business.

The theory of the capitalization-of-earnings method is simple:

1. You determine what the business earns (usually on a yearly basis) over a set period of years.
2. You multiply this earnings figure by a "multiple," a preset number to give the worth of the business.

EXAMPLE: The four partners of Ace Furniture planned their business well. They obtained a low-rent 30-year lease on their store. Now, after five years in business, that store is, as they foresaw, in the center of a rapidly gentrifying city neighborhood. The partners are astute selectors of furniture their customers want. Sales are good and profits are well over $200,000 per year the past two years. One partner decides to leave. The partners have decided the value of the business is two times the average net profits for the past two years, or $213,000. The buy-out price is $426,000.

If you're just starting your partnership, or the partnership hasn't been in existence very long when a partner leaves, it's premature to value your business by the capitalization-of-earnings method. With this method, you usually select a base period of two to five years, not just one year, because you might end up choosing a particularly good, or bad, year. Therefore, you may want to adopt another valuation provision for your first years and then switch over to the capitalization-of-earnings method later. But it's not premature for you to explore the capitalization-of-earnings method now, when your business is just beginning. If you plan or hope to switch to this method in a few years, all partners should understand now how the method they want to use in the future will work.

Suppose your business has been profitable for several years. Does the capitalization-of-earnings method necessarily make sense? Not automatically. Let's use another real world example to stress that you must first be sure the business has goodwill.

EXAMPLE: For 10 years Marianne had been a successful therapist. Energetic and affluent, she'd been getting her Ph.D. in her spare time, at the same time she worked, cared for her family and carried on an active social life. The day she received her Ph.D. she decided to open a shoe store, because she was tired of other people's problems and she loved shoes. She took in a partner, Dana, who contributed work and a small amount of money. Marianne and her financially comfortable husband put up most of the money, and when the store opened, selling very high-fashion and expen-

sive shoes, it was primarily Marianne's extended network of friends and clients who came to buy them. Nine months later, Marianne realized that she had made a mistake. She hated being in a store all day and she realized the amount of money to be made per hour of work was exceedingly modest compared to therapy. She quit the partnership to return to work as a therapist. Thinking she could make a go of the business alone, Dana borrowed money from her grandmother to buy Marianne's share, based on a price that reflected the fact that the store was profitable. But with Marianne gone, Marianne's affluent friends no longer came to buy shoes. The neighborhood in which the store was located catered to middle-class customers and couldn't support a high-priced boutique. The store failed and Dana lost her grandmother's money. The sad part of the story, of course, is that the business never really had any goodwill (Marianne did), and so Dana overpaid to buy out her partner.

Once you've determined that your business really has acquired goodwill or has other valuable intangible assets, you then can sensibly use the capitalization-of-earnings method to determine its value. There's no one set of criteria that exclusively determines how the capitalization-of-earnings method works. Rather, there are four basic areas involved. You must decide what to do in each.

1. What earnings are measured—gross income or net profits?
2. What period of time are earnings measured (averaged) over?
3. What multiplier is used to multiply average earnings to determine the capitalized earnings?
4. Are any other items, such as the value of fixed assets, also included in the valuation?

Let's look at each item individually.

a. The Measure of Earnings

The simplest way to state the issue here is: net or gross? At first blush, it seems that net earnings make the most sense, because they show what matters for buy-out purposes. After all, a business with a substantial gross income but no net earnings isn't worth much, is it? Well, maybe it is. Accounting figures don't always reflect financial reality. You need to know whether the business earns what is politely called undisclosed income. It's called "the Fiddle" in Ireland, "skimming" or "fraud" by the IRS, but by any name, it's certainly not unheard of. Especially in cash businesses, it's not unusual for an occasional sum—sometimes $20, and other times much more—to disappear into the owners' pockets, never making it to the books. Also, many businesses that honestly report all their income still find legal, if sometimes inventive, ways to consume that income as business expenses, leaving little or no net earnings. In addition, most small businesses can fairly easily inflate or deflate earnings by decisions to hire, expand, buy equipment and the like.

For these reasons, some experienced partnership lawyers often use gross income as the base figure for the capitalization-of-earnings method. Our preference is still to use net earnings—but if you do, be sure they are fairly calculated.

b. The Time Period

As we've said, using this method, you'll want to use the base of the earnings, or profits, of your business over a number of years, not simply one. You need a longer time perspective, less apt to be skewed by erratic short-term economic fluctuations. There's no set magic figure for the number of years. Sometimes partners agree to the last three years, or five, or seven—whatever gives them security that the long haul has been taken into account.

c. The Multiplier

The multiplier is the number by which the earnings, however you've defined them, are multiplied to determine the value of the business. Where does the multiplier come from? Hopefully, not out of thin air. It's not easy, though, to agree on a multiplier that will produce a fair result. No outsider can definitively say what a fair multiplier is for you. The best advice we can give you is to pick various numbers and make projections. Do any of them seem to give a fair buy-out price?

An experienced, cautious partnership advisor we know says he believes the multiplier should never be higher than three; anything more is likely to cripple a small business.

In some industries, there are somewhat established norms that help provide the multiplier. Construction companies, retail stores and restaurants are examples of businesses where there are conventional multiple norms. You can obtain standard multipliers for these and various other industries from business evaluators or brokers who specialize in that industry.

You shouldn't accept these norms without plenty of caution, however. The general economy or a particular local economy that affects your business can change so quickly that last year's multiples can become irrelevant this year. In addition, remember that no two businesses are the same. Two auto repair shops that earn $200,000 each may be headed in opposite directions.

If you use a multiplier based on gross earnings rather than profits, you will want to think in terms of a fraction (for example, in a fairly profitable business, one-third of gross earnings).

d. Other Factors Included in the Buy-Out Price

Partners can decide that they want the buy-out price to be a combination of capitalization of earnings and other factors, such as the current net value of fixed assets or the amount in each partner's capital account. Again, there are no ironclad rules. We do advise again that you be careful not to create a method that makes the buy-out price so high that no one can pay it, or the business will die if a partner leaves.

Okay, if you now or in the future want to use a capitalization-of-earnings method to determine buy-out price, here's a clause you can use, or adapt:

 *The following clause is in the file **BUYCAP**, in directory **Clause08**.*

Capitalization of Earnings

☐ Except as otherwise provided in this Agreement, the value of the partnership shall be determined as follows:

1. The average yearly earnings of the business shall be calculated for the preceding _[define this period]_ ;

2. "Earnings," as used in this clause, is defined as: ___[define, such as "net earnings: annual gross revenue minus annual expenses and all taxes" or "gross income"]__ ;

3. The average yearly earnings shall then be

multiplied by a multiple of _____ to give the value of the business, except as provided for in Section 4, below;

4. *[If you want to include additional factors in the buy-out price, do so here; such as "the value of fixed assets minus liabilities."]*

_____

_____.

6. Varying the Buy-Out Price Depending on When, Or the Reason Why, a Partner Departs

Here's one additional factor that you may want to consider regarding determining a buy-out price. Does it make a difference why or when a partner departs? Many partnerships have decided it does. How long you've been in business when a partner leaves may also be a factor. For example, if a partner leaves during the initial stage of a business (whatever time period you pick; partners often choose one or two years), she is entitled only to the book value of her interest. After this initial period, a departing partner's interest is calculated by a method that more accurately reflects the current operation and success of the business.

Also, some partnerships adopt different prices (or different methods for calculating the price) for a departing partner's interest, depending on the reason the partner leaves. For example, in a professional partnership we know, the buy-out provision varies considerably, depending on whether the departing architect:

- becomes disabled, retires over age 65, or dies (this is the highest buy-out provision, partially because insurance can cover much of the cost);
- quits to pursue some other non-architectural dream (for example, moves to Tahiti or becomes a full-time flute player); or

- quits, but remains an architect. (This results in the lowest buy-out provision, because it assumes that some of the architect's clients would likely stick with him; and if the departing partner remains active as an architect in the same county as his former partnership, the buy-out provision is even lower.)

Another reason to vary the buy-out price is in case a partner fails to give the required advance notice, as was discussed in Section A4. Some partnerships decide to impose a severe sanction here, making the price, say, one-half what it otherwise would be; others are far more lenient. And many ignore this problem altogether.

There are no set rules we can give you regarding varying your buy-out clause. You really need to create your own solutions here. Discuss this question carefully. Then write down your own decisions.

 The following clause is in the file **BUYVARY**, *in directory* **Clause08**.

Variation of the Buy-Out Price

☐ The preceding method for calculating the value of the business shall be varied as stated below, for the reasons stated below:

_____

_____.

7. Using Insurance to Value a Partner's Interest

A business or another partner can buy life or disability insurance on each partner. You can then state in your agreement that the money the policy pays to the estate of a deceased partner, or to a disabled partner, shall be the full worth of her interest in the partnership. This makes valuation very easy for disabled or deceased partners' interests—you do it when you decide what policy to buy or keep. (See Section E3 for more on life insurance.)

 The following clause is in the file **INSUREP**, *in directory* **Clause08**.

Insurance Proceeds: Disability or Death of a Partner

☐ If a partner becomes disabled, or dies, the value of his or her interest in the partnership, including for estate purposes, shall be the proceeds paid by the disability or death insurance policy maintained by the partnership, or the other partners, for that partner.

8. Other Valuation Issues

As we've said, there are many possible valuation methods. If you come up with one that is different from those we suggest, fine. Write it up and put it in your agreement. Don't worry about putting it in legalese; clear English will suffice. Some partners base the valuation on some simple formula that they find to be practical and is agreed upon by all the partners.

a. Divorce

A spouse may have a legal interest in a partnership entered into by the other spouse. This is generally true in community property states (Alaska (by spousal agreement), Arizona, California, Idaho, Nevada, New Mexico, Texas, Washington and Wisconsin), where each spouse owns one-half of all community property. It may also be true in common law states, especially at divorce, where equitable distribution laws require that marital property be divided fairly. If both spouses have legal interests in a partnership and there's a divorce, the partnership may well have to be appraised or evaluated for divorce settlement purposes. Many partnerships understandably don't want the valuation clause they've carefully prepared to be ignored in a divorce proceeding.

The best way to try to prevent this is to have all spouses sign the partnership agreement, too. Often at the end of the agreement, by the partners' signature clause, there's an additional clause for spouses.

⚠️ **Be sure your spouse understands what he or she is signing.** *If you want spouses to approve the partnership agreement and sign it, be sure that each spouse genuinely understands what's in the agreement, and what he or she is consenting to. Don't just hand them a document and say something like, "Here, dear, sign this." The goal is not, obviously, to sneak something past your spouse. Aside from the weird karma involved in trying that, you could wind up with a spousal consent that would be struck down by a court in any subsequent divorce proceeding.*

Here's a clause you can use or adapt so spouses agree to the terms of your partnership agreement.

 The following clause is in the file **SPOUSECO***, in directory* **Clause08***.*

Consent of Spouse

☐ I, _____[name]_____ , the *[husband/wife]* of *[partner's name]* , have read and understand this partnership agreement and hereby consent to all clauses and terms in it. I specifically agree that the business valuation method contained in the Agreement shall be used in any legal proceeding to determine the value of any interest I may have in the business.

[signature of spouse]

[dated]

⚠️ **Be sure to obtain a consent of spouse if one of the partners gets married after you've signed your partnership agreement.** *Once you've created your agreement, it's easy to stick it in a drawer and forget about it. But when one partner goes through a major life event, such as getting married, it's worth taking it out and looking at it to make sure your agreement still meets every partner's needs.*

b. Death Taxes

One additional possible benefit of buy-out clauses involves death taxes. You've probably heard that Congress has "repealed" the federal estate tax, or death tax. Actually, it passed a law that's much more confusing than a simple repeal. The current estate tax law:

- provides a personal exemption of $1.5 million per estate during 2004 and 2005. This exemption will rise to $3.5 million by 2009.
- repeals the estate tax entirely for one, and only one, year—2010, and
- revives the estate tax, with an exemption of $1 million, for 2011 and thereafter.

In addition to the federal government, some states impose death taxes.

If a deceased partner's estate must pay estate/death tax, the value of his partnership interest must be independently evaluated, unless there's a reasonable valuation clause in the partnership agreement. Often, an independent death tax evaluation produces a higher figure for the worth of a business than the worth determined under a valuation clause. If there is a valuation clause, the IRS will normally accept what you say your deceased partner's share is worth, as long as the clause contains the following provisions:

- The people who inherit part of the business are obligated to sell it.

- The remaining partners are obligated to purchase the business interest of their dead partner, or at least have an option to purchase it.
- The partnership agreement forbids partners from disposing of their interest during their lifetimes without first offering it to the other partners.
- The agreement is the result of an arm's length transaction; that is, it cannot be a (disguised) gift.

c. Tax Consequences of a Majority Partner Selling Out

Under federal law (Internal Revenue Code Section 708(a)), a partnership is terminated for U.S. income tax purposes if:

1. No part of the business is carried on by any partner; or
2. Fifty percent or more of the business (both partnership capital and profits) is sold or transferred within 12 months.

If the partnership is terminated, there can be serious adverse tax consequences for all concerned. All partnership property is considered distributed to the partners and is subject to tax, even if, in fact, the remaining partners want to continue the business. There are special rules for 50-50 partnerships that prevent the application of the standard tax rules here. (See Chapter 7, Section H.) If any partner will own 50% or more of the partnership business, you should consult an accountant or tax lawyer with partnership tax expertise to minimize the possibility of a formal termination of the partnership in the event the 50% plus partner sells or transfers her interest.

Some Words of Encouragement

By now, all these different considerations and options regarding buy-outs and business valuations may seem overwhelming. You may well be at the stage where you're ready to ask yourself—do we really want to bother with all of this? Or should we just hire a lawyer to do it for us? The answers are—yes and no. When the time comes to buy out a departing partner's interest, you'll be glad you took the time to resolve how to calculate the worth of that interest in advance. As any partnership lawyer can assure you, time and time again disputes over the value of a departing partner's interest lead to lawsuits and bitterness. Turning the whole problem over to a lawyer won't solve the problem either. Sure, your lawyer could say, "Okay, here's the method you should use." But a good lawyer won't be so authoritarian. Instead, she will tell you to puzzle over the same issues and possible solutions we discuss here and arrive at the substance of what you think is fair. It's your business, and no one else should decide how you determine what it's worth. This doesn't mean that you shouldn't consult a lawyer, only that you should, at the very least, understand what's involved before you do.

C. Payments to Departing Partners

How does a departing partner get paid? In a lump sum, or over time? If the payments are over time, for how long a time? These issues are closely related to which method you choose for determining the buy-out price. Think of it this way: If the remaining partners can pay the price over a number of years, they are usually willing to pay a higher buy-out price than if they must pay all cash promptly after a partner leaves.

1. Determining the Payment Schedule

It's essential that you decide on a payment schedule in the event of a buy-out of a departing partner. A lump sum payment is rarely advisable. However, if you fail to adopt a payment schedule, the UPA provides, in essence, that the departing partner has the right to collect for the full value of her interest promptly. This can become a serious problem, especially in the event of a partner's death, since the deceased partner's estate and inheritors will likely insist on exercising this right.

> **EXAMPLE:** Eric and Jack went into partnership to build a house they intended to rent. In the building stage, they became intimate friends, and the house ended up their single family home. Some years later, Eric dies suddenly, and

leaves his share of the house to his daughter. Eric's daughter demands full payment of Eric's share immediately. Since there is no payment schedule in Jack's and Eric's agreement, and Jack can't raise half the value of the house immediately, he has no choice but to sell the house he'd built and now lives in.

Paying off a departing or deceased partner's share all at once often requires the partnership to sell important partnership assets and may: (1) destroy the business; and (2) bring in much less than the full value of the sold assets because you had to resort to a hurried distress sale.

It makes good business sense to adopt a payment method that puts a premium on the survival of the business. If the payment terms are so severe the business can't afford them, everyone will lose. And even if the terms wouldn't necessarily end the business, if they're too severe, the remaining owners may still decide "the hell with it," liquidate the partnership business and go on to other things. In ending a partnership—as in starting and running one—the best approach is to have the partners share the benefits fairly. On the other hand—and, of course, there's always another side—the partner leaving (or his inheritors, if there's a death) has a real interest in getting money reasonably fast. No one wants to be hostage to someone else's business judgment for years to come. If the surviving partners make bad choices, it could wipe out money that really should go to the departing partner. This can be a particularly intense concern if the departing partner is pulling out precisely because he doesn't trust the others. So you have to balance these competing and conflicting concerns to arrive at what you think are fair payment terms.

You can adopt any installment payment schedule that fits your needs. You could agree to pay a fixed sum, or a set percentage of the total price, and then make payments each month or quarter or year. It's also possible to provide for payments to increase or decrease, over a set number of years, or payments with interest added or not. Another payment method is to obtain a bank loan to pay off the departing partner. The remaining partners pay the bank in installments. This method, obviously, requires that the business be able to obtain a substantial loan, and that the remaining partners accept the added obligation of loan interest.

So, yet once again, there's no simple, set formula. You have to create a method for payment that suits your business and your temperaments. In many situations, payments are not extended over more than two to five years. (This may seem to be a short period of time to raise all the money you'll need, but remember that if the business is prospering, you'll be able to borrow from a bank or, if necessary, you can find a new partner with capital to contribute.) A common provision is to delay the first payment for some set time, such as 90 days, in order to give the remaining partners time to start gathering the funds.

We want to remind you that as with your buy-sell clause, you're not required to stick with your payment clause when a partner leaves if none of you wants to. Again, you're creating a floor, not a ceiling—this is simply the method you'll use if you don't all agree on another one later. For instance, suppose your partnership agreement calls for a five-year payment plan, with interest at 10% per year on the unpaid balance. Now suppose seven years later, when your business is prosperous, a departing partner says, "You know, I'd like to get as much cash as I can now. If you all agree, you can give me, right now, 60% of what I would have received over five years." Obviously, if this seems fair to the remaining partners, they can substitute it for the five-year payment plan.

! If you vary the terms of the partnership agreement, put it in writing. *Just as it makes sense to draft a written amendment if you permanently change part of your partnership agreement, you should document any major, one-time*

deviations from its terms. That way, there's less of a chance that the partners will be confused or (heaven forbid) try to claim that they didn't agree to the change.

Here's a clause providing for equal monthly installment payments:

 The following clause is in the file **PAYMONTH**, *in directory* **Clause08**.

Equal Monthly Payments

☐ Whenever the partnership is obligated or chooses to purchase a partner's interest in the partnership, it shall pay for that interest by promissory note of the partnership. Any promissory note shall be dated as of the effective date of the purchase, shall mature in not more than ____ years, shall be payable in equal installments that come due monthly *[and shall bear interest at the rate of ____ percent per annum] [and may, at the partnership's option, be subordinated to existing and future debts to banks and other institutional lenders for money borrowed].* The first payment shall be made ____ days after the date of the promissory note.

As mentioned, some partnerships agree that a departing partner will be entitled to receive a set sum as part of the buy-out price upon leaving or shortly after leaving the partnership. Then she'll get payments of the balance due over time. This set sum can be a fixed dollar amount or, more commonly, a percentage of the overall buy-out figure.

If you decide on this approach, here's a clause you can use.

The following clause is in the file **PAYLUMP**, *in directory* **Clause08**.

Lump Sum, Then Equal Monthly Payments

☐ Whenever the partnership is obligated to, or chooses to, purchase a partner's interest in the partnership, it shall pay for that interest as follows:

First: It shall pay the departing partner *[define lump sum payment]* within *[time allowed]* . Second: After that initial payment, it shall pay the balance owed by promissory note of the partnership. Any promissory note shall be dated as of the effective date of the purchase, shall mature in not more than _____ years, shall be payable in equal installments that come due monthly [shall bear interest at the rate of _____ percent per annum] [and may, at the partnership's option, be subordinated to existing and future debts to banks and other institutional lenders for money borrowed]. The first payment shall be made _____ days after the date of the promissory note.

Although we do not recommend using it, we provide here a clause for full cash payment, within a relatively short time after a partner leaves the business.

 The following clause is in the file **PAYCASH**, *in directory* **Clause08**.

Cash Payment

☐ Whenever the partnership is obligated or chooses to purchase a partner's interest in the partnership, it shall pay for that interest in cash, within *[whatever time period you choose]* .

2. The Departing Partner's Responsibility for Partnership Debts

A departing partner is legally responsible for all outstanding debts and obligations of the partnership incurred up to the date she leaves. No agreement between the partnership and the departing partner can alter her potential liability to outside creditors. However, as part of a buy-out clause, the partnership can expressly assume the obligation to pay all debts of the firm, including any share owed by the departing partner. This type of clause won't protect a departing partner if the business goes broke, especially if the other partners are broke, too. But if the partnership, or any of the remaining partners, have assets to pay off old debts, the departing partner is protected.

 The following clause is in the file **ASSUMELI**, *in directory* **Clause08**.

Assumption of Departing Partner's Liabilities

☐ The continuing partnership shall pay, as they come due, all partnership debts and obligations that exist on the date a partner leaves the partnership, and shall hold the departing partner harmless from any claim arising from these debts and obligations.

It's not unusual for the departure of one partner to coincide with the admission of a new one. An incoming partner can also assume full responsibility for the old partner's share of partnership debts. The new partner, however, is under no obligation to do so. And even if the new partner does assume responsibility for the debts and gives a written release to the old partner, this doesn't automatically leave that old partner completely in the clear. (See Chapter 4, Section B.)

D. Expelling a Partner

Expelling a partner is a drastic decision, one you surely hope you never have to consider, let alone implement. It's often a subject that new partners find very difficult to consider, since they feel optimistic about their new enterprise and each other. However, part of our job is to make sure you have considered the worst as well as the best possibilities. Also, if your business expands, you may take in new partners you don't know as well, and it can be prudent to have an expulsion clause just in case they don't work out.

It's quite unusual for a small business partnership to expel a partner. We know of many partnerships that have dissolved completely, and some in which, say, two partners remain and one leaves, but personally we can't ever recall hearing of a formal expulsion of a partner. Perhaps this is because many partners in small businesses decide not to cover possible expulsion in a separate clause. They reason that since everything they decide and do must be unanimous, if they ever reach the stage where they're considering an expulsion, it's time to disband the partnership. This can make sense for very small partnerships. It doesn't for larger partnerships, where it's usually not practical to end the business because one partner is impossible to deal with. Even though they may be used infrequently, large partnerships should include an expulsion clause in their partnership agreement.

Courts hesitate to enforce expulsion clauses if there is room for ambiguity or doubt. For example, courts are reluctant to expel a partner, or enter a decree of dissolution of a partnership, based on the mental or bodily health of that partner. If it's important to you that all partners be healthy, or nonsmok-

ers, and you want them out if they're not, say so clearly and set up some sort of criteria by which the partners can make a determination. This same sort of definiteness should be the hallmark of any expulsion clause. Can a simple majority expel a partner? Do there have to be grounds justifying the expulsion? Or do you want a clause that simply says a partner may be expelled for reasons that appear to be sufficient to the other partners?

Below is a sample expulsion clause you can use or adapt. It provides that an expelled partner receives the same payment for her interest as a partner who leaves for any other reason. By doing this, you treat the partner who is expelled the same way you treat a partner who leaves for a neutral reason and probably lower the level of bitterness that is likely to surround an expulsion.

 The following clause is in the file **EXPART***, in directory* **Clause09***.*

Expulsion of a Partner

☐ A partner may be expelled from the partnership by a vote of ___*[specify vote, such as "three-fourths of the voting partners" or "the other partners holding at least 60% of the capital in the partnership," or whatever you choose]*___ .

[Here, you can also add any specific grounds for expulsion that you've agreed on.

_____

_____

_____.*]*

Expulsion shall become effective when written notice of expulsion is served on the expelled partner. When the expulsion becomes effective, the expelled partner's right to participate in the partnership's profits and his or her other rights, powers and authority as a partner of the partnership shall terminate. An expelled partner shall be entitled to receive the value of his or her interest in the partnership, as that value is defined in this Agreement.

1. Bankruptcy and Expulsion

Under the UPA, a partner's personal bankruptcy, now technically called "becoming subject to an order of relief" from the bankruptcy court, causes dissolution of a partnership, even if the business itself is still viable. In any partnership, and especially a large one, it can be appropriate to have a provision planning for immediate expulsion of a bankrupt partner. The following clause contains the technical language defining acts constituting bankruptcy and authorizes expulsion for a partner's bankruptcy. (Bankruptcy has its own rules, concepts and language. Few of you are likely to need to know about all this. If you do, rather than try and explain here what all this technical language means, we recommend the book *How to File for Chapter 7 Bankruptcy*, by Stephen Elias, Albin Renauer and Robin Leonard (Nolo).

⚠️ **Be alert for a change in the bankruptcy law.** *As of this printing of* The Partnership Book, *it's likely that Congress will pass a law that drastically curtails Chapter 7, the basic bankruptcy law. Lobbyists for credit card companies and banks have been remorselessly pressuring Congress to cut back on debtors' bankruptcy rights, and it appears that the lobbyists will soon prevail. What a surprise.*

 The following clause is in the file **EXPLBANK***, in directory* **Clause09***.*

A Partner's Bankruptcy and Expulsion

☐ Notwithstanding any other provisions of this Agreement, a partner shall cease to be a partner and shall have no interest in common with the remaining partners or in partnership property when the partner does any of the following:

1. Obtains or becomes subject to an order of relief under the Bankruptcy Code.

2. Obtains or becomes subject to an order or decree of insolvency under state law.

3. Makes an assignment for the benefit of creditors.

4. Consents to or accepts the appointment of a receiver or trustee to any substantial part of his or her assets that is not vacated within _____ days.

5. Consents to or accepts an attachment or execution of any substantial part of his or her assets that is not released within _____ days.

From the date of any of the preceding events, he or she shall be considered as a seller to the partnership of his or her interest in the partnership as set forth in this Agreement.

If a partner is expelled for one of the above reasons, the partnership shall not be dissolved, but shall continue to function without interruption.

2. Expulsion and Arbitration

Expulsions are one area where you may well not want to allow the possibility of arbitration. It can be wiser to prohibit any risk that an arbitrator will decide you can't expel a partner after you said you did. What a mess that would be! So, if you have an arbitration clause in your contract, as we urge (see Chapter 6), you may want to restrict it from applying to expulsions, and declare any expulsion decision absolutely final. There can be a slight risk in this approach, though. A court may be more likely to review an expulsion decision subject to no other review than it would be if the expulsion were subject to arbitration.

If you want to do the best you can to eliminate review of an expulsion decision, use or adapt the following clause.

 The following clause is in the file **EXPARB**, *in directory* **Clause09**.

Expulsion and Arbitration

☐ Any decision of expulsion made by the partners pursuant to this Agreement shall be final and shall not be subject to arbitration or other review, including review by any court.

As you'll see in Chapter 6, our arbitration clause starts with the phrase "Except as otherwise provided in this Agreement." Thus, the above clause is expressly exempted from the general arbitration clause.

E. Continuing the Partnership

If a partnership has more than two members, the remaining partners often—indeed, usually—want to continue the business in the partnership form, uninterrupted when a partner leaves. (If there is only one partner left, he may desire to continue the business, but by definition he won't continue it as a partnership.) Partners who want to continue to operate the business in the partnership form certainly do not want, or need, a formal dissolution and winding up of the old partnership. Indeed, whatever eventually happens to a partnership business, it's undesirable to wind up the old partnership soon after a partner leaves.

If the business is to continue as a partnership, a technical, formal dissolution of the old one can lead to unpleasant tax consequences. This can include the IRS regarding (old) partnership property as distributed to partners and therefore subject to tax. Even if the business will eventually be disbanded and sold, all interested persons (including the inheritors of a deceased partner) probably want the business to continue at least long enough so that it can be sold in an orderly fashion and not at a fire sale price.

To provide that your partnership continues after a partner leaves, use the following clause:

 The following clause is in the file **CONTINUE**, *in directory* **Clause09**.

Partnership Continues

☐ In the case of a partner's death, permanent disability, retirement, voluntary withdrawal or expulsion from the partnership, the partnership shall not dissolve or terminate, but its business shall continue without interruption and without any break in continuity. On the disability, retirement, withdrawal, expulsion or death of any partner, the others shall not liquidate or wind up the affairs of the partnership, but shall continue to conduct a partnership under the terms of this Agreement.

1. Protections Against a Departing Partner

Many business partners decide they want to prohibit a departing or expelled partner from directly competing against the partnership if she withdraws from the partnership. As many business partners have learned from painful experience, even when a partner leaves under friendly circumstances, he or she can easily start up a competing business and drain away a good deal of income from the partnership. So, although you may not want to think about it right now, there's a very real possibility that one or more partners will leave and that one of them will open a competing business when they're gone. As depressing as it sounds, you and your partners should decide now what a departing partner may (and may not) do upon her departure from the partnership.

> **EXAMPLE:** Paula and Ann open a dry cleaner, Le Chemise, in an upscale, wealthy neighborhood. Their quick, friendly service and specialized methods of getting hard-to-remove stains out of delicate women's clothing earn them a loyal following in the community. Eventually, however, Paula and Ann's views on how to run the business diverge. After some serious managerial skirmishes, Paula announces she is leaving the partnership, but is quiet about her future plans. Ann buys out Paula's share of the business at the buy-out price they arranged for in their agreement and bids Paula a not-so-fond farewell. Out for a walk a week later, however, Ann discovers that Paula has opened up her own dry cleaning service a few blocks away. When Ann sees some of Le Chemise's best customers in Paula's new store, she seethes and wonders if there is anything she can do to shut Paula down.

Although it isn't foolproof, one way to prevent this from happening is to include a noncompetition clause in your partnership agreement. A noncompetition clause prevents a departing partner from competing against the partnership for a specified period of time within a specific geographic area after he or she leaves the partnership.

Including this clause in your partnership agreement can help protect your trade secrets, as well as your client and customer lists. However, if you're contemplating including this clause in your agreement, you may wonder if perhaps you should question the advisability of going into business with your potential partners in the first place. Don't think that protecting yourself against future competition is necessarily a signal that you need to abandon your venture. Taking such measures can be simply an exercise of prudent paranoia that will prevent dire results and destructive conflicts if you do break up.

Forbidding a partner from engaging in his usual way of earning a living is obviously a drastic act. However, properly drafted noncompetition agreements, especially in the context of a departing partner, are legal in most states and can be enforced by court order if necessary. To be legal in most states, a noncompetition agreement must be reasonably limited in both time and geographical area, and be otherwise fair (that is, seem reasonable to a judge under the circumstances). For instance, an agreement that says a partner who voluntarily withdrew from a donut shop couldn't open up a competing business within one mile for a period of two years would probably be enforceable, but one that said he could not run a donut shop within 100 miles for ten years would almost certainly be thrown out by a judge.

While including this clause in your agreement might seem rather unfair to the departing partner, in some cases it may be warranted. For example, if a partner is taught some unique skill upon admission to the partnership (for example, rebuilding fireplaces or retrofitting houses to withstand earthquakes) and the local area can not support another enterprise selling that skill, a noncompetition agreement may be fair. By contrast, if the ex-partner has a general skill and no other way to make a living, a noncompetition clause might be struck down by a court. Note that since any noncompetition agreement must be reasonably limited in geographic scope to be legal, the worst that can happen is that the departing partner must run her business in another community.

 The following clause is in the file **NONCOMCL**, *in directory* **Clause09**.

Noncompetition Clause

☐ On the voluntary withdrawal, permanent disability, retirement or expulsion of any partner, that partner shall not carry on a business the same as or similar to the business of the partnership within the _[describe geographic area]_ for a period of _[time period you've agreed on]_ .

 Noncompetition law varies in all 50 states. *Whatever the specifics of your state's laws, these clauses are not favored by most judges. In legalese, noncompetition clauses are "strictly construed" (against the partnership) by a court. So, if this sort of clause is important to you, we advise you to see a lawyer in your area or do some of your own legal research to make sure your noncompetition clause will hold up in court. (See Chapter 10, Section C.)*

2. Control of the Business Name

In some businesses, the right to use a name has great value—a famous rock band's name is one obvious example. At the other extreme, Joe & Al's TV Repairs is unlikely to be more valuable than Joe's TV Repairs. If your business name could matter, you should decide who owns it and gets to keep it if someone leaves the partnership. If there are several partners, the usual solution is to let the ongoing partnership retain ownership of that name. However, if yours is an equal number partnership, you could face trouble with this situation; there could be

no majority. Also, it may be that one partner really coined the name and wants to be entitled to use it if he leaves the partnership or the business ends. And suppose the business uses one person's name—for example, The Toni Ihara Band and Toni decides to leave the band. Then what? When our friend John H. was thrown out of John H. Furniture, he attempted to open a new business using his name, John H. His old partnership agreement contained a clause granting the majority of remaining partners the sole rights to the name John H. Furniture. It took a lawsuit to convince John H., admittedly a bit of a wild man, that he couldn't use his own name any way he chose to. So he settled for John Studios.

It can also happen that one ex-partner doesn't want the name of the former business used at all. When a two-person partnership we know of split up, they agreed—at the insistence of one of them—that neither would use the old partnership name. The other partner then printed up letterhead with a new name but stating boldly, "Successor to…(the original name)." By this time, the objecting partner had had enough squabbling and merely shrugged her shoulders.

Here's another real life example:

EXAMPLE: BW opened a cleaner/laundry called BW Cleaners. When he wanted to do other things, he talked a friend, M, into going into partnership with him, with BW as the majority partner. M did, and the partnership continued still under the name BW Cleaners. The business became quite prosperous and well established. The name BW had acquired some "goodwill." Six years later, BW told M that he was going to dissolve the partnership and give the business to his son, which meant that M had to move on. M sued to keep the name BW Cleaners and won. He moved to another shop one block away from the old store and opened up BW Cleaners. BW's son had to get a new store name.

We tell you all this in order to help you evaluate how careful you need to be about control of your partnership business name. Following are four sample clauses defining who owns your business name if a partner leaves or the business dissolves.

 The following clause is in the file **NAMEOWN**, *in directory* **Clause09**.

Partnership Continues to Own Name

☐ The partnership business name of

_____ is owned by the

partnership. Should any partner cease to be a

member of the partnership, the partnership

shall continue to retain exclusive ownership

and right to use the partnership business name.

 The following clause is in the file **NAMEONE**, *in directory* **Clause09**.

One Partner Owns Name

☐ The partnership business name of

_____ shall be solely

owned by ____[person's name]____ if __[he/

she]__ ceases to be a partner.

 The following clause is in the file **NAMELATE**, *in directory* **Clause09**.

Control of Name to Be Decided at Later Date

☐ The partnership business name of

_____ is owned by the

partnership. Should any partner cease to be a

partner, and desire to use the partnership

business name, and the remaining partners

desire to continue the partnership and continue

use of the partnership business name, owner-

ship and control of the name shall be decided

[insert any method you choose, such a flipping

a coin, arbitration, etc.] .

 The following clause is in the file **NAMEMAJ**, *in directory* **Clause09**.

Dissolution: Majority Owns Name

☐ In the event of dissolution, the partnership

business name of _____

shall be owned by a majority of the former

partners. Any other former partner is not

entitled to ownership or use of the partnership

business name.

The business name may not be the only partnership asset you want to decide who controls if you split up. You can adapt the above clauses to cover copyrights, patents, trademarks, as well as your business telephone number, licenses, permits and similar assets.

3. Insurance and Partners' Estate Planning

Just because there's a provision in a partnership agreement that states that a departing partner will be paid off on a set schedule doesn't mean the business will actually earn sufficient money to make those payments. Sometimes the business can barely make the payments, and doing so imposes a serious, even grave, drain on cash necessary for other business purposes. So, many partnerships decide to protect themselves to some extent by purchasing insurance against each partner's serious illness, incapacity or death. Obviously, these kinds of insurance don't help you pay off a partner who just quit or who is expelled.

For many partnerships, life insurance can be a sensible way of obtaining the money needed to pay off a deceased partner's interest, especially by purchasing term insurance, the cheapest form of life insurance. If a partner dies, the partnership-financed insurance policy pays off his or her share, not partnership operating income. In *The Devil's Dictionary*, author Ambrose Bierce defined the business of life insurance as "An ingenious modern game of chance in which the player is permitted to enjoy the comfortable conviction that he is beating the man who keeps the table."

If you do decide to go the life insurance route, consider solving two problems at once by providing in your partnership agreement that the amount of the life insurance payout is also the value of the deceased partner's interest in the business. You don't have to tie them together this tightly, however. You can use any of the valuation methods discussed in Section B, above, and then make sure you buy enough life insurance to make any necessary payment if a partner dies.

Here are some useful points about using life insurance policies to finance a buy-out agreement:

- Partners have an "insurable interest" in the life of their partners, so they can buy policies on them directly. You can also purchase additional insurance to cover extra costs to the business caused by the death of a partner, such as hiring a new employee.

- There are two different methods of buying life insurance policies: Either the partners buy policies on each other (cross-purchase) or the partnership itself buys the policies. For small partnerships, a cross-purchase plan is usually more desirable. This is because if the partnership itself pays for and owns the policies on the partners, it has been held in some circumstances that the proceeds of the policy are partnership assets and are included in the value of the partnership, thus risking artificially increasing the worth of the deceased partner's share. In a cross-purchase agreement, each partner buys policies on the life of each other partner and this problem is avoided. The following is a provision for the cross-purchase of life insurance:

The following clause is in the file **LIFECROS**, *in directory* **Clause09**.

Cross-Purchase of Life Insurance

☐ Each partner shall purchase and maintain life insurance [and disability insurance] on the life of each other partner in the face value of $ _____.

In a larger partnership, a cross-purchase scheme is usually too cumbersome. If there are six partners, for example, each partner must buy five policies (one on each of the other partners' lives), which means a total of 30 policies. To avoid this much complexity and paperwork, it's probably better to have the partnership pay for a single policy on each partner's life, despite the problem mentioned above. If you do this, specify explicitly that only the cash surrender value of the life insurance policies before the insured's death is a partnership asset, whereas the proceeds themselves are not.

The following clause is in the file **LIFEPOL**, *in directory* **Clause09**.

Partnership Insurance Policies

☐ The life insurance policies owned by the partnership on the lives of each partner are assets of the partnership only in so far as they have cash surrender value preceding the death of a partner.

There's also the question of what happens to a life insurance policy if a partner quits or resigns. The usual solution is to allow the departing partner to purchase the policy, since the partnership no longer needs that protection. Here's a clause that covers this:

The following clause is in the file **LIFEDEP**, *in directory* **Clause09**.

Insurance Policies and Partner's Departure

☐ On the withdrawal or termination of any partner for any reason other than his or her death [add "or disability" if the partners purchase disability insurance on each other], any insurance policies on his or her life ["or health"], for which the partnership paid the premiums, shall be delivered to that partner and become his or her separate property. If the policy has a cash surrender value, that amount shall be paid to the partnership by the withdrawing partner, or offset against the partnership's obligations to him or her.

Here are some more facts you should know about life insurance:

- Insurance payments made by a partnership are normally not tax deductible. (Treasury Reg. 1.264-1; unless the policy is a condition for a bank loan with the policy assigned to the bank in case of death.)
- If a partner can't pass a life insurance physical, you have a problem. But unless you think this is reasonably likely, there's little reason to worry about it in the original partnership agreement; solve it when (and if) it arises.
- The partners will eventually want to do some estate planning. This isn't a book about estate planning, but we do want to alert you to the fact that buy-out agreements should be coordinated with each partner's individual estate plan. For example, if the proceeds of the insurance policy are payable to the deceased partner's estate, these proceeds are subject to probate and will increase probate fees. In order to avoid probate, someone other than the estate of the deceased partner should be specified as the beneficiary of each policy. For instance, if a partner intended to leave all her property to her spouse, that spouse could

be named as beneficiary of the policy. If the partner has a number of beneficiaries—say her spouse, several children and some friends—things get a little more complicated, but only a little. For example, by using a living trust, the spouse would name the other spouse, children and friends as beneficiaries of the trust, to receive the gifts specified in the trust. Then the trust is named as beneficiary of the life insurance policy.

 A living trust is a basic probate avoidance device that's normally quite easy to prepare. To create your own living trust, see Make Your Own Living Trust, *by Denis Clifford, or* Quicken WillMaker Plus *(software), both by Nolo.*

F. Terminating a Partnership

Let's imagine that you've prospered and all the partners decide to sell out and retire to Martinique, Marseille or Macon, Georgia, depending on each partner's dream. Or, contrary to all your hopes, your business just hasn't worked out, you're not making enough money, and you're tired of it all and want to move on and try something else. Or, perhaps, in a two-person partnership, one partner wants to leave and one wants to stay, terminating the partnership but carrying on the business. In short, for whatever reason your partnership is ending, and your concern becomes—what do you do now?

The legal terms for termination of a partnership business are "winding up" and "dissolution." This means that all partnership business is settled, the partnership books are closed and the partners go their separate ways. The former partners may continue the former partnership business in some other form, or the business may end altogether.

Do you need to cover termination in your partnership agreement? No, not beyond the clauses you'll use from this book to prepare your general agreement. This agreement will handle the basics of your termination—how the business is valued, who gets the business name, etc. Inevitably, though, there will be other details and fine points to be resolved, matters that haven't been foreseen. Who gets to keep that rocking chair? Who must cope with the hassle of a supplier pressing for a payment that all partners agree isn't owed? Who gets which customers? The sensible way to handle these details is to talk them over when termination occurs and resolve them between yourselves. Then, prepare a separate termination agreement apart from, and in addition to, the provision in your original partnership agreement.

This is a book about starting a partnership, not ending one. We do, however, include a sample termination notice in Appendix 3, and briefly discuss there what you'll need to do if your partnership business ends.

1. The Process of Termination

Once the decision has been made to end the partnership, existing partnership business should be completed as speedily as possible. Legally, ending a partnership business involves three stages:

1. First is the dissolution of the partnership—the decision to actually end it. Legally, no new partnership business can be undertaken after this time. If a partner is worried that another partner won't honor this rule, the worried partner can send formal written notices to business contacts that the partnership has been dissolved and cannot undertake new business. (See the sample letter, below.) There is no official or government office where you must record notice that the partnership has dissolved. You can record such a notice at your local county recorder's office, for whatever protection that can provide. (Not much.)

2. Next is winding up of the existing partnership business. Partners in a dissolved partnership do retain the authority to do those things necessary to close down the existing partnership business. Under UPA Section 34, each partner is liable for her share of any liability created by partners in the course of closing down partnership business, just as if the partnership had not been dissolved.

3. Finally, there is actual termination of the business. Once the partnership has ended, no partnership business of any kind is legally authorized. If, after your partnership is dissolved, you have any doubts at all about the honesty of any of your partners, play it safe and notify all possible creditors. Just because you know that your partnership has been dissolved and your business wound up doesn't mean your creditors know it. If a creditor, acting in good faith and without knowledge of the dissolution of a partnership, extends credit to a partner, for matters that the partner represents as being partnership business, but which in reality aren't (because that business is over), all the partners may be liable for that bill. Likewise, if a creditor extends credit to what he believes is the partnership, even after termination, you can be stuck for that bill. UPA Section 35 effectively requires that to relieve partners of this liability, the partners must actually deliver notice of dissolution to all individuals or businesses who have previously extended credit to the partnership. A simple written letter, as given in the following example, is sufficient notice:

To Whom It May Concern, and All Creditors of the Partnership:

This is to inform you that the partnership was dissolved by a decision of the partners on _____ and no new partnership business is authorized after that date.

Sincerely,

_____

2. Termination Agreements

Commonly, when partnerships end—especially when they do so with the partners on reasonably good terms, and when partners have a good partnership agreement—things go easily as to major matters, such as the division of partnership assets. But as we've said, even in the best terminations, there are bound to be some things that you didn't foresee when you drafted your partnership agreement. To handle loose ends, prepare a separate termination agreement covering, in specific detail, all matters in the breakup of the partnership. Be precise here. This is your final partnership document, and it's safer to pin everything down. (You'll find a sample termination agreement in Appendix 3.)

If the partnership is broke and can't pay its bills, and at least one, but not all, of the partners is insolvent, the solvent partners must contribute additional amounts to cover all liabilities. If more than one partner is solvent, the solvent ones must contribute in the proportion that those partners shared in the partnership profits.

3. Dissolution of a Partnership by Court Action

Under UPA Section 32, the courts have the power to order a dissolution leading to termination of a partnership for any of the reasons listed below, no matter what the partnership agreement provides:

- a partner has been declared mentally incompetent by judicial proceedings
- a partner is incapable of performing his part of the partnership agreement
- a partner has been guilty of conduct that prejudicially affects the carrying on of the business
- a partner willfully or persistently commits a breach of the partnership agreement (or is generally a bad egg)
- the business can only be carried on at a continuing loss, or
- any other equitable reasons.

(Note that if you have an expulsion clause, you shouldn't have to worry about a court kicking out a bad partner; you can do it yourselves.)

Here are examples of some of the types of misconduct that the courts consider justifiable grounds upon which to dissolve a partnership:

- failure to contribute initial capital funds urgently required by the business
- failure to account for proceeds of sales
- appropriation of partnership property to pay personal debts. or
- constant quarrels, irreconcilable differences, intoxication or gambling.

A lawsuit over a partner's asserted misconduct will be disastrous (really—take our word for it). First of all, these aren't easy matters for the remaining partners to prove. The courts usually require a strong case for dissolving a partnership on grounds of the misconduct of a partner. They greatly dislike dealing with what they feel are "trifling causes or temporary grievances." In any case, as we've urged before, lawsuits are generally horrendous. This situation should be unnecessary if you've provided for the expulsion of a partner. ■

Partnership Disputes: Mediation and Arbitration

If there's a serious disagreement between partners that can't be resolved by personal discussions and negotiations, you need a method in your partnership agreement for resolving the conflict. The basic dispute resolution methods are mediation, arbitration, some combination of the two or litigation.

Litigation should not merely be a last resort. It should, to the extent possible, be excluded as a resort at all. Lawsuits, as you may well already know, are expensive, tedious and emotionally draining, and rarely produce results in proportion to their cost. As Judge Learned Hand put it: "As a litigant, I should dread a lawsuit beyond almost anything short of sickness and death." Ambrose Bierce aptly defined a litigant as "a person prepared to give up his skin in the hopes of retaining his bones."

In your partnership agreement, you need a binding method for resolving disputes that you can't work out for yourselves. You thereby ensure that you don't become trapped in the horrors of partners versus partners litigation. The two major methods of dispute resolution are mediation and arbitration. Now let's examine how each process works and how they can sensibly be used in tandem in your agreement.

A. Mediation

Mediation is a process where an outside person—the mediator—attempts to assist two (or more) partners to solve their dispute themselves, by reaching a mutually satisfactory resolution. Unlike an arbitrator, a mediator has no power to impose a decision. Many people feel that mediation is the best way to resolve disputes because it's nonadversarial and encourages antagonists to arrive at their own compromise solution. Mediation's strength is that no partner feels that he or she wasn't treated fairly because the partners discuss, negotiate and reach an agreement voluntarily. Mediation can be especially valuable where the people involved in a dispute will necessarily have some form of continuing relation-

ship, as is often the case for partners or even ex-partners. This will clearly be the case if ex-partners are also relatives or members of a fairly small geographical or professional community.

Should Your Partnership Agreement Require Counseling?

You can also include, in your agreement, a clause requiring counseling, good faith discussions or other therapies aimed at resolving disputes. Personally, we're sympathetic to the motives partners have in including these provisions in their agreements, and are optimistic that, in some situations, they may serve to remind the partners of their commitments to one another if a dispute arises. However, we must also say that we're skeptical about the value of requiring these methods in addition to or (worse) as a substitute for a good, tight mediation/arbitration clause. Why? Because, obviously, if all partners voluntarily want to use therapeutic means to resolve a conflict, they'll go ahead and do it. But if feelings get truly ruffled and one or more partners refuses to be reasonable, you'll need more than a vague statement about good faith discussion to achieve a settlement.

The mediator's job is to assist the parties in communicating with each other, seeing the other's side and, hopefully, helping them to reach a compromise. By its very nature, mediation is an informal process, without formal rules of evidence and other court-like protocols. Normally, if one person thinks something should be discussed, it is. Though mediation is informal, that does not mean it is totally unstructured. Normally, the process follows several stages: The mediator's opening statement, explaining the process; the disputants' opening statements; joint discussion; private meetings with the mediator (often called "caucuses"); joint negotiation; and finally—closure.

Once the parties arrive at their own solution through mediation, the agreement is normally put in writing, and it becomes a legally binding contract.

Mediation has become widely used throughout the business world. Many business people have seen it work, and learned that it helps to avoid the pains that an externally-imposed solution may create.

The most important decision you'll make when including a mediation clause in your partnership agreement is deciding on the mediator. You can postpone this decision until a dispute actually occurs, but we feel it's usually better to decide who you'll have as a mediator at the beginning. You can always change your mediator later on, if all agree to. But if you do fall into a dispute you can't resolve yourselves, you don't want to fight over who your mediator shall be. But before you try and decide who to name as your mediator, read the next two sections covering arbitration and combining arbitration with mediation.

Be aware that being a good mediator takes skill—just being a decent, fair human being isn't always enough to qualify one for the job. If there's a person you know and trust who's served others as a mediator, he is likely to be a wise choice for you. Some lawyers who have been repelled by the hostility and craziness of the adversary court system have established legal practices devoted solely to mediating disputes and do an excellent job. Or, in some situations, you may want to designate a mediator with some technical expertise. For example, if your business involves complicated pieces of machinery, you may prefer a mediator who understands how these machines work.

If there is a dispute, the partners decide, along with the mediator, what issues need to be resolved. Together you and your partners also decide the rules of the proceeding. Generally, we don't believe it's sensible to set out details of a mediation proceeding in your partnership agreement. Since you ultimately will have to cooperate to resolve the dispute, the need to cooperate over procedural details can be a good place to start. But if you are comforted by pinning down some details now, we can't say that including them in your mediation clause will be fatal.

If you ever decide to mediate a dispute, here are some basic things you'll then need to resolve about the proceeding:

- When and where is the proceeding to take place?
- Will you limit or require the number of sessions?
- Will you be allowed to submit a written statement?
- Will attorneys or other representatives be allowed, or will each partner represent himself or herself?
- Is cross-examination allowed?

Following is a clause you can use or adapt if you decide you want mediation of disputes you can't resolve privately:

*The following clause is in the file **MEDIATE**, in directory **Clause10**.*

Mediation

1. The partners agree that, except as otherwise provided in this Agreement, any dispute arising out of this Agreement or the partnership business shall first be resolved by mediation, if possible. The partners are aware that mediation is a voluntary process, and pledge to cooperate fully and fairly with the mediator in any attempt to reach a mutually satisfactory compromise to a dispute.

2. The mediator shall be

   _____.

3. If any partner to a dispute feels it cannot be resolved by the partners themselves after mediation has been affected, he or she shall so notify the other partners, and the mediator, in writing.

   [If you prefer, you can vary this to require there be a set number of mediation sessions, so the disgruntled partner must say to all, face-to-face, that he won't agree to a mediation solution.]

4. Mediation shall commence within _____ days of this notice of request for mediation.

   [Here, in #4, you can add any other details of the mediation process you've decided to include.

   _____

   _____

   _____

   _____

   _____.]*

5. Any decision reached by mediation shall be reduced to writing, signed by all partners, and be binding on them.

6. The costs of mediation shall be shared equally by all partners to the dispute.

 For an excellent resource on mediation, see How to Mediate Your Dispute, *by Peter Lovenheim (Nolo).*

B. Arbitration

We believe that it's essential to include an arbitration clause in all partnership agreements. The basics of the arbitration process should be set out in your arbitration clause. If arbitration is ever called for, the arbitrator determines any other specifics of the process that all partners can't voluntarily agree on.

In an arbitration proceeding, each side presents their version of the dispute to the arbitrator. After the presentation, the arbitrator later makes a decision, normally in writing, which ends the dispute. All partners are bound by the arbitrator's decision, with very rare exceptions. If the losing partners decide to sue in court to overturn the arbitrator's decision (which seldom happens), the court usually will enforce the arbitrator's decision, unless the arbitrator was blatantly biased or crazy. In other words, once the arbitrator decides, that's it. The fight is settled, period.

Business and labor have used arbitration for years. They've learned arbitration usually leads to fair results, or a least results they can live with. Also, they realize that getting a dispute settled quickly, in a cost-effective manner, is often as important as who wins and who loses.

Below are two arbitration clauses. In the first, there's a single arbitrator. In the second, there are three arbitrators: Each side selects one arbitrator and then those two select a third. All three hear the matter and decide it by majority vote.

Our preference is to use the first clause and one arbitrator. It's much simpler and cheaper. On the other hand, with three arbitrators, each side has chosen one who, presumably, is "on his side."

If you decide to select the clause using three arbitrators, you can't name the three arbitrators now, because, obviously, you can't predict which partners will be on what side. (Except in a two-person partnership. Since there can only be one versus the other, each partner could, in theory, name "his" arbitrator now. But this is an odd way to begin a partnership, each thinking about who would serve on his side in the event of a dispute they can't resolve themselves.) However, you do need to decide now what would happen if the two arbitrators cannot agree on a third. So think of some method to handle that problem—like naming someone now all partners trust to make the decision.

If you select the clause using one arbitrator, you can either name that person now, or wait. We suggest it's preferable to name one now, for the persuasive reason that you should all be able to agree on whom to select. If the need for arbitration ever actually arises, that agreement is likely to be more difficult, or even impossible, to obtain.

Just because you name an arbitrator now does not, of course, mean you'll ever have to use her. After all, most partnerships don't fall so far apart that they can't resolve problems by themselves. Nor does it mean you must use that particular arbitrator, if you later decide on someone else. Years from now, if a dispute you can't resolve yourselves arises, you may all agree that another arbitrator is preferable. But if you're so far apart you can't then agree on who is the best person to decide the conflict—and this has certainly been known to occur—

at least you've got a fallback position, an arbitrator already named.

Whom do you select as your arbitrator? There's no one way to go about this that's inherently better than all others. You can name an arbitrator who's a trusted friend. Selecting a friend can result in some problems, however, if the friend later rules against you. Or, you may know someone who, although not a close friend, seems fair and capable of judiciously deciding matters (and of course, is willing to take on the job). Another possibility is someone who has served as an arbitrator before. Many lawyers frequently serve as arbitrators, as do other professional dispute resolvers. Also, in many areas of the country, retired judges (colloquially called rent-a-judges) serve as arbitrators. One caveat about professional arbitrators: Some, such as those from the American Arbitration Association, are quite expensive. The American Arbitration Association is a nationwide institution which provides arbitrators, who are often lawyers. In the past, they have specialized in big-time disputes and charged hefty fees. Currently, they claim to have more cost-effective arbitration programs for smaller disputes. Check fees before you agree on any expert. If you require specific rules for the arbitration proceeding, be sure the arbitrator or arbitration organization you choose will accept your rules. For example, the American Arbitration Association requires the use of their own detailed rules.

If you choose a combined mediation-arbitration clause, as we urge, you need to decide if you want to name the same person as both your arbitrator and your mediator. That's very much up to you. Some people decide that giving the mediator the power to impose a decision if the partners can't agree is a bad idea. Others decide that this risk is more than offset by the fact that there can only be one proceeding, not two. (This question is discussed more in Section C.)

Here are two arbitration clauses. The first uses one arbitrator. The second uses three. (If there are more than two sides to the conflict, the appointment of arbitrators becomes difficult. If you can't later get at least two of the sides to agree on one arbitrator, you'll probably wind up in court.) We believe it's preferable not to be more specific about the arbitration process itself in this clause. Leave that up to the arbitrator and yourselves, if the need ever arises. But if you want more specifics now, you can modify either clause, and specify more details of the arbitration process, including:

- Can the arbitrator(s) order you to produce evidence? (Normally they have this power.)
- Does the arbitrator have to explain the decision (that is, how and why the arbitrator(s) reached it)?
- Is there a time limit within which the arbitrator(s) must render a decision?
- Will you be allowed to submit a written statement?
- Is cross-examination allowed?
- Will lawyers be allowed?

 The following clause is in the file **ARBONE**, *in directory* **Clause10**.

Arbitration With One Arbitrator

1. The partners agree that, except as otherwise provided in this Agreement, any dispute arising out of this Agreement, or the partnership business, shall be arbitrated under the terms of this clause. The arbitration shall be carried out by a single arbitrator [who shall be _____ name _____] [or, if you don't want to name the arbitrator now, delete the phrase "who shall be ," and type in: "who shall be agreed upon by the parties to the dispute. If the parties cannot agree on the arbitrator, the arbitrator shall be selected by ." Include the method you decide on, such as naming a person all agree now is fair to select the

arbitrator.]

Any arbitration shall be held as follows:

2. The partner(s) initiating the arbitration procedure shall inform the other partner(s) in writing of the nature of the dispute at the same time that he or she notifies the arbitrator.

3. Within _____ days from receipt of this notice, the other partners shall reply in writing, stating their view of the nature of the dispute.

4. The arbitrator shall hold a hearing on the dispute within seven days after the reply of the other partner(s). Each partner shall be entitled to present whatever oral or written statements he or she wishes and may present witnesses. No partner may be represented by a lawyer or any third party.

5. The arbitrator shall make his or her decision in writing.

6. If the partner(s) to whom the demand for arbitration is directed fails to respond within the proper time limit, the partner(s) initiating the arbitration must give the other an additional five days' written notice of "intention to proceed to arbitration." If there is still no response, the partner(s) initiating the arbitration may proceed with the arbitration before the arbitrator, and his or her award shall be binding.

7. The cost of arbitration shall be borne by the partners as the arbitrator shall direct.

8. The arbitration award shall be conclusive and binding on the partners and shall be

set forth in such a way that a formal judgment can be entered in the court having jurisdiction over the dispute if any partner so desires.

Now here's the clause where each side names his or her own arbitrator, and those two name a third.

 The following clause is in the file **ARBTHREE**, *in directory* **Clause10**.

Arbitration With Three Arbitrators

The partners agree that, except as otherwise provided in this Agreement, any dispute arising out of this Agreement or the partnership business shall be arbitrated under the terms of this clause. The arbitration shall be carried out by three arbitrators. Each partner or side to the dispute shall appoint one arbitrator. The two designated arbitrators shall appoint the third arbitrator.

The arbitration shall be carried out as follows:

1. The partner(s) initiating the arbitration procedure shall inform the other partner(s) in writing of the nature of the dispute at the same time that they designate one arbitrator.

2. Within ___ days from receipt of this notice, the other partners shall reply in writing naming the second arbitrator and stating their view of the nature of the dispute.

3. The two designated arbitrators shall name a third arbitrator within ten days from the date the second arbitrator is named. If they cannot agree *[insert whatever you've decided upon to resolve this dilemma]*.

4. An arbitration meeting shall be held within days after the third arbitrator is named.

5. Each partner shall be entitled to present whatever oral or written statements he or she wishes and may present witnesses. No partner may be represented by a lawyer or any third party.

6. The arbitrators shall make their decision in writing.

7. If the partner(s) to whom the demand for arbitration is directed fails to respond within the proper time limit, the partner(s) initiating the arbitration must give the other an additional five days' written notice of "intention to proceed to arbitration." If there is still no response, the partner(s) initiating the arbitration may proceed with the arbitration before the arbitrators, and their award shall be binding.

8. The cost of arbitration shall be borne by the partners as the arbitrators shall direct.

9. The arbitration award shall be conclusive and binding on the partners and shall be set forth in such a way that a formal judgment can be entered in the court having jurisdiction over the dispute if any partner so desires.

C. Combining Mediation With Arbitration

We believe it's usually desirable to have both a mediation and an arbitration clause in your agreement. That way, all partners know that they'll try mediation first. Only if that doesn't work out can an outside arbitrator impose a decision.

Some experienced lawyers feel it is unnecessary to bother with a compulsory mediation clause. They prefer to omit such a clause from the agreement, thus making mediation optional. The reason is as follows: If all partners want to mediate, they can, but if one of the partners isn't interested in mediating, why waste the time seeking a cooperative solution? Also, they believe that if mediation fails, things can be worse because tempers can become inflamed during mediation. We're not so pessimistic. We believe mediation can often work, and we think there is a greater possibility that it will if partners agree in advance to give it an honest chance. Of course, if you only want one dispute resolution method in your agreement, select arbitration, because it must lead to a binding decision.

As we've mentioned, if you do follow our advice and choose both mediation and arbitration, you have to resolve whether the mediator and arbitrator should be the same person. The obvious advantage to having the same person for both is that you don't run the risk of having to present the case twice—first to the mediator, then, if mediation fails, to the arbitrator. The other side of this coin is that a person who has ultimate power to make a decision as an arbitrator may be less effective as a mediator. Indeed, whether mediators should have the ultimate power to decide a dispute if the parties can't is an issue that divides many mediation professionals. Some feel that giving the mediator that much ultimate power destroys the voluntariness of the whole process. Others feel that a good dispute resolver can readily switch hats from mediator to arbitrator, and this is far preferable for all involved than risking a second go-round. Personally, we have no conclusive opinions here and leave the decision entirely up to you.

Here's a clause to bridge your mediation clause to your arbitration clause:

 The following clause is in the file **MEDARB**, *in directory* **Clause10**.

Combining Mediation With Arbitration

If the partners cannot resolve the dispute by mediation, the dispute shall be arbitrated as provided in the arbitration clause of this Agreement.

The above clause doesn't set any express time limit on the mediation process. One side could simply quit and end the process. To eliminate the possibility of stalling, bad-faith mediation to drag out the time, you can add the following clause:

 The following clause is in the file **MEDTIME**, *in directory* **Clause10**.

Time for Mediation

If the partners have not resolved their dispute within *[whatever time you choose]* of the commencement of mediation, the partners shall have failed to have resolved their dispute by mediation under this Agreement, and the dispute shall be arbitrated.

Proceeding to Complete Your Agreement

You've now covered every specific clause we present for you to consider in your partnership agreement. The next four chapters, Chapters 7 through 10, do not contain any sample clauses. These chapters discuss subjects of interest to many readers: partnership taxation, realities of starting a business, limited partnerships, and using lawyers and other experts or doing your own research. If you are sure that none of these issues concern you, you can proceed directly to Chapter 11 and begin the process of preparing your draft agreement now.

Partnership and Taxes

L et us say here at the beginning of this chapter that neither of us has been trained as a partnership tax specialist, nor does either of us remotely resemble one. We've had to develop a basic knowledge of the subject to survive in business and law, but we've done so out of necessity, not love. Generally, we've found tax law to be full of frustration and loaded with boring complexities. This is particularly true of partnership tax law, which at its more complicated levels is generally recognized as one of the most difficult areas of the Internal Revenue Code. Nevertheless, understanding the basics of partnership taxation has been important to us and this will be equally true for you. So please plug in and learn the rudiments. Do it with cheer if you can, or with gritted teeth if you must, but do hang in there or that old IRS bogeyman may get you.

A Judge's Lament

Here's one tax judge's description of partnership taxation: "The distressingly complex and confusing nature of the provisions of [federal partnership tax laws] present a formidable obstacle to the comprehension of these provisions without the expenditure of a disproportionate amount of time and effort even by one who is sophisticated in tax matters with many years of experience in the tax field." David A. Foxman, 41 T.C. 535 (1964); Judge Rauml. Reuschlein & Gregory, *Agency & Partnership* (West) 1979.

In putting this chapter together, we've made a lot of judgment calls as to how deeply we should go into different areas of partnership taxation. We're also not sure how much knowledge we should assume an average reader already has. However, we arrived at two conclusions. First, partnership taxation is so complex that we have to stick to the ba-

sics. (In Appendix 1, we list some treatises covering more complex questions on partnership taxation in case you want to do some research on your own.) Second, since the focus of this book is on starting a partnership, we concentrate on the likely tax problems faced by a new small business.

In the more complicated areas of partnership taxation, all we can safely do is alert you to warning signals and advise you to see a tax expert. We've often found, in our own businesses, that having access to a partnership tax expert is essential. Yes, this is a costly process—experts do not come cheap—but it is still cheaper and far less anxiety-ridden than risking a confrontation with the IRS.

A. Using Tax Experts

Talking about tax experts raises questions: What is one, anyway? Do you need one? And where do you find a person like that whom you can afford?

Let's start with what a tax expert is. For your purposes, a tax expert is someone experienced with and knowledgeable about IRS law and rules governing partnership taxation (and your state's partnership taxation rules, too). Realistically, this usually means a certified public accountant (CPA) with lots of small business experience, and more specifically, partnership tax experience.

Next question: Do you really need a tax expert? Yes. Most definitely. Unless your business is very simple, you should find a knowledgeable CPA and work out an arrangement with her to give you the periodic help you'll need. In many—if not most—partnerships, it's beneficial to start a relationship with a tax expert as soon as you can. However, some truly uncomplicated partnerships might well not need a tax expert's services immediately. For instance, a service business with very little in the way of inventory costs, in which all the partners contribute the same amount of start-up cash, might not need one immediately. But change a few facts—such as some partners contributing property that's appreciated in value since they bought it, or the necessity for a modest inventory—and you'll quickly find yourself in a situation where you'll need expert advice.

Third question: Where do you find a high quality, affordable partnership tax expert? If you happen to know one you trust, fine. If not, you will want to check with small business people in your area and see who they use. (Also, in Chapter 10, we make a number of suggestions on how to find a reliable tax expert.) When it comes to expense, don't focus exclusively on how much the expert costs per hour. The key is to find an expert who will help you help yourself with routine matters, like establishing a good bookkeeping system. Once good systems are in place, you may only need to have them reviewed by your expert a few times a year.

We realize our recommendation that you use a partnership tax expert is at variance from our usual position that you can handle most matters yourself. The reason for our switch in position is simple. The tax code is so complicated, especially for partnerships, that unless you want to make understanding it your hobby, you'll be better off allocating money for expert help. This shouldn't be enormously expensive at the beginning, especially since many small business partnerships don't initially have tax problems that will cost a great deal in tax expert's fees. Also, remember that you're becoming involved with a tax system that rewards people in business with all sorts of perfectly legal loopholes. This often means a good tax advisor can make legitimate suggestions that will save you more than her fee.

B. Partnership Business and Personal Income Taxes

Before we review the various tax rules applicable to partnerships, you might be wondering if you're likely to pay more or less tax as a partner in a business than you would as a salaried employee working for someone else. Assuming your business does well enough so that your gross income is roughly the same as before, the answer is that as a partner

in a business you'll very likely pay less. Why? Because by opening your own business, you move from the ranks of the salaried and rigidly taxed to the land of free enterprise and business tax deductions. The American tax structure, as a whole, is sympathetic to business activity and money spent for business purposes. Or, as Calvin Coolidge said in the early 1920s, "The business of America is business"—and in the 21st century, it still is.

But it's also important for prospective partners to be realistic about taxes. Some people unfamiliar with the realities of small businesses occasionally fantasize that they are passports to a tax-free land. Not so. If your business is successful, you'll pay taxes. Still, you'll probably find you're better off than if you remained a salaried employee.

For starters, business expenses are generally deductible. Yes, Congress has made a few token restrictions in an attempt to cut back on the infamous three martini lunch, but still, the great majority of valid business expenses remain deductible.

Here are some legitimate deductions:

- fifty percent of business entertainment, as long as the meeting involved, or furthered, your business
- business travel
- automobile expenses (except travel to or from home)
- classes you take to improve skills you need in your business (for instance, a commercial illustrator could deduct the cost of a drawing class, but a dentist couldn't), and
- child care expenses necessary to permit a parent to work, but only according to a complex formula that allows you to deduct far less than you actually spend.

For more in-depth information on how to make the most of these business deductions, see Tax Savvy for Small Business, *by Frederick W. Daily (Nolo).*

C. Taxation of Partnerships

The most basic tax rule on partnerships is that the partnership itself is not subject to taxation. (As with any statement about partnership taxation, there are exceptions to this rule—particularly in certain complex partnership situations that rarely, if ever, apply to a small start-up business.) The partnership's profits (and losses) simply flow through to the individual partners. Each partner is taxed on his distributive share of partnership income. This can be more than profits or payments a partner actually receives, particularly if any profits are retained in the business.

What is a "distributive share"? It's the amount of money a partner is deemed to have received as income under IRS rules. Yes, this sort of begs the question. In other words, you need to know what income the IRS will deem you to have received in order to know your tax liability.

Let's take an extreme example of distributive income. Suppose a two-person partnership in the direct mail advertising business lands some very lucrative work. At the end of the tax year, after paying all of their overhead, including employee expenses, the partnership has $1.5 million in the bank. The partners cannot simply say, "Okay, none of that $1.5 million is profit to us. We're setting it all aside for a rainy day." Even if the $1.5 million is left in a partnership bank account and never paid out to the partners, the IRS will deem that almost all of it (less what IRS rules permit to be withheld for a business reserve) was distributed to the partners and is treated as taxable income to the partners.

The IRS distributive share rules generally mean that the partnership business can't retain significant earnings for the future expansion of the business without the partners having to pay tax on that money. Indeed, the rules on distributive shares are so strict that a partner will be taxed on her distributive share even though a dispute among the partners prevents any actual distribution of partnership profits..

Once your business is underway, determining the partners' distributive share of partnership income can be quite complex. One of the many reasons you will want a partnership tax expert is to minimize the chance the IRS will tax you for some distributive share of money you didn't really get.

D. Family Partnerships for Tax Savings

When the highest income tax rates were 80% or 90%, some families attempted to lower their tax burden by creating family partnerships and shifting some income to members in a lower tax bracket. Because the maximum tax rates have been so drastically reduced (the highest tab is roughly 38.6%), there's less incentive to do this now than previously. Also, federal tax law imposes stringent rules on family partnerships, making it very difficult to shift income to members who are not currently economically productive. For example, under the kiddie tax, all income of a child under 14 is attributable to a parent—that is, included in that parent's income for tax purposes. If you want to try to create a family partnership to save on income taxes, you definitely need to see a tax expert. And even then, be wary—try to make sure you don't risk winding up acquiring only costly IRS penalties for your efforts.

E. Tax Consequences of Contributions to a Partnership

The tax area that is usually of most concern to new partners involves contributions partners make when the business is just getting started. There are no tax problems if all partners contribute only cash—it's pretty clear how much each one contributed. No taxable gain or loss occurs simply because money is transferred from a partner to the partnership. Similarly, there's no taxable gain or loss if a partner withdraws some or all of the money he's contributed to the partnership. (Note that withdrawing contributed capital is most definitely not the same as a partner's distributive share of partnership profits, which is taxable income to the partner who receives it.) But if a partner contributes property, especially property that has increased (or decreased) in value since he bought it, the tax consequences of these transactions can become complicated. Likewise, there are complexities, although different ones, if a partner receives her partnership interest in exchange for a pledge of future services.

1. Contribution of Property

If a partner contributes property whose current market value is the same as the partner originally paid for it, there's no tax problem. As with cash, no taxable transaction occurs merely because property is transferred from an individual owner to the partnership. But the tax situation is more complex if the property has gone up or down in value since the partner bought it.

> **EXAMPLE:** Suppose Harry contributes a building he owns to a new partnership in exchange for a one-half partnership ownership share valued at $120,000. Jennifer, the other partner, contributes $120,000 in cash. If Harry recently bought the building for $120,000, there won't be any tax consequences. But suppose Harry bought the building years ago for $20,000. (The tax basis of a building to the owner is normally his acquisition cost, plus the cost of capital improvements, less any depreciation taken. Here we're assuming, for the sake of simplicity, that the original cost alone remained Harry's basis.) Since the building's market value is now $120,000, his partnership share is based on this amount. Does this mean that Harry has now realized a gain, for tax purposes, of $100,000, as

if he'd "sold" the building in exchange for his partnership share? The answer is no. The tax code provides that when a partner contributes property to a partnership that's worth more than he paid for it, no immediate gain or loss is recognized to the individual. (IRC Section 721.) This also applies to a contribution of goods to be given to the contributor over time, called "installment receivables," although normally a gain is recognized when installment receivables are disposed of. (Treasury Reg. Section 1.453-9(c)(2).)

This sounds fine so far, but as you might expect, tax situations don't always stay so simple. To continue the above example, there can still be eventual tax consequences because the building was transferred to the partnership. For instance, since no taxable gain or loss is recognized on the transfer from Harry to the partnership, it follows that the tax basis of the building to the partnership must be the same amount as Harry's basis for it, that is, $20,000. Now, let's suppose that the partnership decides to sell the building for its market value of $120,000. As far as the tax man counts, the partners have realized a taxable gain of $100,000. After all, the building was purchased for $20,000. But for purposes of partnership bookkeeping, there's been no gain or loss because a $120,000 partnership asset has been traded for a like amount of cash.

Now (if you've been willing to follow closely) you should begin to see a problem. If the taxable gain (the $100,000 profit) is divided equally between the two partners, this would mean that Jennifer will have to pay tax on a gain of $50,000 (one-half of the $100,000 gain) although in fact she hasn't received income (remember the property was valued at $120,000 for general partnership contribution purposes but at $20,000 for partnership tax purposes). So the tax code now provides that the partner who contributed the appreciated property is regarded as receiving all of that built-in profit from a subsequent sale. This issue can get very complex, especially if the partnership held the property for a time and there was further appreciation. It's yet an-other area where you need to see a tax expert.

a. Contribution of Mortgaged Property

Potentially there are many other complex tax prob-lems involving contributed property. We don't go into these in depth because we doubt if many people establishing new partnerships will face them. Nevertheless, it makes sense to highlight a few areas that may affect you. In particular, issues are raised by the contribution of real estate with an outstanding mortgage or any encumbered property, such as a car with a loan balance owed. If mort-gaged or encumbered property is contributed to a partnership, the partnership's liabilities are in-creased by the amount of the debt. (Technically, the property can be transferred subject to the mortgage, or the partnership can, actually, formally assume the mortgage. In either case, the tax reality is the same.)

EXAMPLE: Juanita contributes real estate with a market value of $210,000 and a mortgage of $150,000 into her partnership with Ricardo and Carlita, who each contribute $210,000 cash. Juanita just bought the real estate, so her basis in it is the purchase price, $210,000. For tax purposes, Ricardo and Carlita have each taken on, through the partnership, $50,000 of the mortgage. (Of course, each has also received, as members of the partnership, real estate worth $70,000.)

Now, watch things get tricky. Because Juanita contributed the real estate with the mar-ket value of $210,000, she has initially contrib-uted the same amount. But because the two other partners have assumed $100,000 of her mortgage, the tax code treats this as a money distribution to Juanita of that amount. (See IRC Section 752.) Thus, for tax basis purposes, her

interest in the partnership is reduced from $210,000 to $110,000.

If the contributing partner's tax basis in the mortgaged property is lower than current mar-ket value, as it would be if she had purchased it some time ago, and it has gone up in value, matters get more complicated. And if the mort-gage or encumbrance actually exceeds the con-tributing partner's tax basis, matters are yet more complicated.

EXAMPLE: Jennifer contributes her mint condi-tion, lemon-yellow, 1970 Jaguar XKE to the partnership. She bought it for $2,000 (call that her basis). It's now worth $30,000. She has used the car as security for a $20,000 loan. The en-cumbrance on the car ($20,000 lien on the loan) far exceeds her basis of $2,000.

We won't even try to go through the possible tax permutations here. (See IRC Section 752.) Simply put, if a partner is contributing mortgaged or en-cumbered property, see a partnership tax expert.

b. Alternatives to Contributing Property

For a variety of reasons, partners may desire to have their partnership acquire property from a part-ner by another method than contribution. For ex-ample, a partner may be willing to allow the part-nership to use valuable property that partner owns, such as a patent, but be unwilling to contribute that property outright to the partnership. Or the partner-ship may want to use real estate a partner owns without having to acquire that property by contribu-tion.

A partner can legally engage in all legitimate property transactions with the partnership, such as sale, lease or loan.

EXAMPLE: Kim, Lee and Hung all want to be equal partners in the KLH Burglar Alarm Installation and Service business. Their main asset, initially, will be equipment of Lee's, worth $60,000 (which he bought for $50,000). Kim and Hung do not have enough money to contribute $60,000 cash each to the partnership; the most each can each pay is $20,000. So all three partners contribute $20,000—a total of $60,000—and the partnership buys Lee's equipment. (If Lee makes any profit on the sale, he must pay taxes on the profits.) If they don't want to use most or all of their cash to do this, the partnership could give Lee a promissory note to be paid off over time.

Business transactions such as this between a partner and the partnership can get much more complicated. For example, a partner can sell a partial interest to other partners, and then each partner can contribute his or her interest to the partnership. A partner can lease, rent or loan property to the partnership, or combine these methods. When contemplating any of these types of transactions, see a partnership tax expert.

c. Real Estate Exchanges

Here's one more potential partnership trap for real estate owners. The tax code permits, as most real estate investors know, tax-free exchanges of real estate. (See IRC Section 103.) You can sell one parcel, buy another for what you sold the first parcel for (or more), and not be subject to any tax. In other words, you're allowed to roll over any profits from sale of the first property into the second.

However, IRS rules require that the same type of legal entity be both the seller of the first property and the buyer of the second. If a partnership sells the first property, but a partner individually buys the second, that doesn't qualify. Likewise, if a part-ner as a separate individual buys one property, but a partnership sells another, that doesn't qualify. So you have to think through how you are going to handle both transactions before engaging in a tax-free real estate exchange, and be sure it's the same legal entity that engages in both deals.

2. Contribution of Services

Okay, so much for property. Now let's look at the tax consequences if a person receives an interest in a partnership in return for the contribution of services. Under the tax laws, services aren't regarded as property. If the contributing partner receives a capital (ownership) interest in the partnership in exchange for (the promise of her) services, she has received taxable income.

EXAMPLE: Alicia, Rose and Ruby form a partnership to operate a hair salon. Alicia and Ruby each contribute $15,000 for start-up capital and plan to work part-time in the business. Rose has no cash to contribute, but she receives a one-third ownership of the partnership in exchange for promising to work full-time for a year. As far as the tax laws are concerned, Rose has received present taxable income by this agreement. The cash contributions to the business total $30,000; Rose owns one-third of the business. According to tax law, Rose has received taxable income of $10,000.

Unfortunately, Rose hasn't really received any money. If the business was sold, and she got one-third of the cash for the sale, it would clearly be okay to tax her. But what the tax code says here is that a promise to work isn't equal to property. It may seem unfair—but it is the law.

Now, suppose the partnership agreement doesn't give Rose a present ownership (capital) interest in the partnership but only the right to receive one-

MY JOB IS TO CREATE THE ILLUSION THE HAVES AND THE HAVE-NOTS ARE THE SAME PEOPLE.

third of the future profits in return for her services. In other words, if the business is sold, Rose gets nothing. But as long as the business continues, she gets one-third of the profits. Until a few years ago, tax experts believed there were no tax consequences if only future profits were involved. However, in a case that involved receipt of future profits in a partnership in exchange for the promise of future services, the tax court held that this amounted to a cash depreciation, and the present value of this right to receive future profits was taxable income to the services-contributing partner. (*Sol Diamond, 56 T.C. 530 (1971), aff'd 492 F.2d 286 (7th Cir. 1974). Questioned and narrowed in Campbell v. Commissioner, 943 F.2d 815 (9th Cir. 1991).*)

Many tax practitioners believe that the *Sol Diamond* case is an aberration—or explainable by, and limited to, its peculiar facts. Among these was the fact that there was an admitted dollar worth to the present value of the right to receive future profits, which was readily calculable and, indeed, had actually been determined because the right to receive

future profits had been sold—which is an unintelligible way of saying that Sol's idea was a tax scam, disguising a present ownership interest by calling it "the right to receive future profits."

Returning to our example of Alicia, Rose and Ruby, it's quite possible that Rose will have no tax liability if all she receives is a right to share in future profits. After all, who can tell if there will be any profits? However, if the partnership had existed for a while when Rose was invited to join in exchange for her promise to work full-time, and the partnership has been profitable, Rose might have incurred a tax liability. Why? Because the track record of the business profitability might establish a basis upon which to value Rose's present right to receive future income.

If you're considering giving a partner an ownership interest, or even the right to receive future profits in exchange for services, see a CPA. One possibility to evaluate is hiring the would-be partner as an employee and paying her enough so she can save up and buy a partnership interest outright for cash.

In more involved service-contribution situations, the tax rules can become extremely complicated. If your partnership profits will involve this kind of problem, it's essential that you see a tax expert. Here are some examples of complicated situations:

Appreciated Partnership Property: In exchange for services to be rendered, a partner receives an interest in partnership property that has appreciated in value since being acquired by the partnership.

Restrictions on Transfers of a Partnership Interest: Special tax rules govern partnership interests exchanged for promised services if there are certain types of restrictions on the service partner, such as an agreement to sell her interest to the other partners for less than market value if she ceases performing the services.

3. Expenses Paid to Organize the Partnership

Here's one piece of tax law that might surprise you. Money spent to organize the partnership (that is, spent before you finalize your agreement) cannot simply be deducted as a business expense in the first year you are in business. These expenses can include lawyer's fees, accountant's fees or—in your case—the cost of this book. These expenses must be capitalized. Capital expenditures are ones that you can't deduct fully in one year, but must spread out over however long a time period the IRS decrees. With a partnership, you must amortize these costs over at least 60 months from the month you actually begin business.

F. Management of the Partnership Business

As anyone in business soon learns, taxes, tax problems and tax concerns are part of your life. Aside from ongoing tax matters, there are some initial op-

erating tax issues you'll need to discuss and review with your tax expert. These include:

- deciding what accounting method you'll use (accrual, cash or other permitted methods)
- deciding the depreciation method you'll use for partnership property, and
- choosing the partnership's tax year.

As your business grows, it can be particularly important to determine whether there are tax or financial reasons for varying the way partnership income is distributed to partners. Specifically, tax laws allow any particular partnership income, profit, loss or deduction to be distributed between partners in a way that is different from their standard division: (1) if that's permitted in the partnership agreement, and (2) if this particular distribution has "substantial economic effect." (See IRC Section 704(b)(2).) It takes an expert to figure out if varying your income or profits figures is going to be beneficial for all involved (or, at least, overall). This type of sophisticated maneuvering of partnership taxes is beyond what's possible, or needed, for beginning businesses, so we don't delve into it here. Nor do the partnership agreements we provide have clauses covering ways in which to vary the normal distribution of profits, income, etc., for tax purposes. If this proves advantageous years down the road, you can always amend your partnership agreement to include exactly the magic words tax law then requires. It's fully legal and acceptable to the IRS to make such later amendments if you decide to.

G. Tax Returns

Before finishing up on partnership taxation, we'll cover what you'll definitely have to do:

1. The partnership must file an informational partnership tax return (Form 1065);
2. The partnership must provide each partner with a Schedule K-1 which breaks down each partner's share of partnership profits and losses; and

3. Each partner must report her share of partnership income on her individual tax return.

1. The Partnership Tax Return

As we've discussed before, a partnership itself isn't subject to income tax. Income and profits generated by a partnership business flow through the partnership and are taxed to the individual partners. Nevertheless, a partnership must file an "informational" federal tax return, called IRS Form 1065. This return lists the partnership income, expenses and other required financial data, many of which must be separately identified. This way, you report all the basic economic facts about your partnership, in addition to the net income reported on each partner's individual return. The Internal Revenue Service publishes free aids to completing a partnership tax return, including Publication 541, *Tax Information on Partnership*, and Publication 334, *Tax Guide for Small Business.*

The yearly federal IRS partnership return must be filed by the fifteenth day of the fourth month following the close of the partnership tax year.

Most states also require an informational partnership return to be filed. Like the federal government, the states don't tax partnership income per se.

2. The Partner's Individual Tax Return

We don't have the space to provide a thorough explanation of the intricacies that can be involved in reporting your share of partnership income in your individual tax return. However, there are a few points worth mentioning.

a. Self-Employment Taxes

First and foremost, the federal government, and most states, consider most partners of a partnership to be "self-employed." Since self-employed people like partners don't have an employer to withhold income taxes from each paycheck, partners must file quarterly estimates of their taxable income on Form 1040-ES, along with the appropriate tax payments. Generally, you must make estimated tax payments if you owe at least $1,000 and any tax withheld will be less than 90% of the tax you'll owe or 100% of last year's tax bill. If you don't make these quarterly payments (in April, June, September and January), you can be subject to fines and penalties. While it can be difficult to figure out ahead of time how much tax you'll owe, as a general rule, you can make payments equal to your tax liability for the previous year. You can also purchase tax preparation software, such as Intuit's *TurboTax* program, to help you estimate these amounts.

In addition, each partner must also make quarterly estimated payments of his own self-employment taxes, which includes Social Security and Medicare. Right now, these amount to 15.3% of the first $72,600 of income, and 2.9% of the remaining income. Fortunately, a portion of these self-employment taxes is deductible, so this relieves some of the tax bite. As with the estimated income tax payments discussed above, the main thing to keep in mind is that you'll have to pay these taxes whether the partnership actually distributes this money to you or not, so plan ahead.

b. Other Income Tax Considerations

On top of self-employment taxes, here are some more basic partnership tax points which affect your individual income taxes.

- As we've said, an individual partner's yearly tax return must report a partner's distributive share of the taxable income or loss of the partnership.
- A partner's distributive share of partnership profits is, in part, determined by the partnership agreement. If the agreement makes no specific mention of the manner of sharing

particular income, gains, losses, depreciation or credits to be allocated, a partner's distributive share is determined by the IRS in accordance with the provision of the partnership agreement for division of general profits or losses.

- As noted, the IRS will disregard special provisions as to distributive shares of partnership profits if it determines that the provision lacks "substantial economic effect," that is, has been adopted for the sole purpose of dodging taxes by shifting tax liability to partners in a lower tax bracket. In that case, the IRS will reallocate distributive shares according to the partners' ownership interest in the partnership. If you are interested in making special allocations, consult a partnership tax expert.

- There are special income tax rules governing allocations of partnership interest to individual partners to or with whom one partner sells or exchanges his partnership interest (see IRC Section 706(c)), or where there's a shift of the percentage of ownership interest (or sharing of profits and losses) during the year. If this happens to you, you'll certainly need tax assistance.

- Each partner also takes his share of any loss into account each year. It may become part of his carry-back or carry-forward for tax purposes (see IRC Section 172), used to offset positive income in other years.

- If a partner has a "subpartnership" contract, sharing her partnership profits with someone not a member of the partnership, the partner is still required to report as income the entire amount of the profits she was entitled to receive from the partnership, with a subsequent deduction for the share allocated to the subpartner.

- Tax law provides different tax treatment for earned, investment and passive income. If you plan to actively participate in your business, there is no need to worry about this. However, if you will be an investor only, see Section I of this chapter for more on these legal distinctions. If you have any doubts or questions concerning these types of income, see a tax expert. And, if you're looking for tax shelters, be wary. We certainly know people who invested in so-called tax shelters that eventually backfired and cost them a lot of money.

3. The Partnership as a Separate Tax Entity

Okay, we've established that for income tax purposes, a partnership is basically a conduit allowing income to pass through to the individual partners. However, as is so common in the tax field, no sooner do we learn something than we have to deal with qualifications, exceptions, and but ifs. To be more specific, for certain purposes, a partnership isn't treated as a conduit but is viewed as a distinct entity by the IRS. For example:

- For computation of partnership income— profits and losses—a partnership is regarded as a unified enterprise. In other words, whether a profit or loss has been made is determined by looking to the partnership as a whole, not to any individual partner.

- The partnership itself, not the partners, must make certain tax elections, such as the choice of the method of accounting.

- In the unusual instance in which a partner has a different tax year than the partnership, the time for inclusion of an item or distributive share of income or loss in a partner's tax return will depend on the tax year of the partnership itself.

- The characterization of business income, whether in tax terms that income is earned or passive (see Section I), is made at the partnership level, not at each partner's level.

H. Taxation and Sale of a Partnership Interest

Clearly, the sale of a partnership interest has tax consequences. On the simplest level, a partner who sells a partnership interest will receive income from the sale and be subject to tax on that income. However, tax problems related to the disposition of a partnership interest can become much more complex. Since this is a book designed for those beginning a partnership, we don't go into these possible complexities in detail. You should know that if your business is successful and some time in the future a partner wants to sell, retire or dies, you can avail yourself of any tax options permitted to you within that year of sale. In other words, you're not now locked into anything that could have adverse tax consequences later.

1. Termination of a Partnership on Transfer of a Partnership Interest

As noted, you do not want your partnership considered legally terminated unless in fact it truly is—that is, the business is over and all partners are out of it. (Special rules apply to two-person partnerships—see Section 2, below.) If only one or some partners leave the partnership, tax reasons alone make it desirable to have the partnership continue, rather than terminate it and commence a new partnership. If the partnership is formally terminated, all partnership properties are considered distributed to the partners. Distributed, as you know by now, means that the IRS regards the property as received as income by the partners, so any gain received by the partners will be taxed. This can be very undesirable for property that has increased in value since acquisition by the partnership.

> **EXAMPLE:** A four-person partnership buys a piece of real estate for $160,000. Ten years later,

the market value of the real estate is $480,000. The partnership has made a paper profit of $320,000, or $80,000 per partner. One party leaves, selling his interest to a new person. The other partners remain, continuing the business. They do not want to sell the real estate, which they use in the business. Unfortunately, the partnership agreement provides that the partnership is terminated if any partner leaves. Because the old partnership has technically been terminated, the IRS considers all the profits on the real estate as having been distributed to the partners. Each partner's profit is $80,000. If they don't want to sell the real estate, they must each come up with the cash from somewhere else to pay taxes due on their $80,000.

Because of this risk, we've provided you a clause, which we urge you to include in your agreement, which states that the partnership continues and is not dissolved or terminated if a partner, or partners, leaves the business. (See Chapter 5, Section E.)

2. Sale of Fifty Percent or More of a Partnership

The sale of an interest in 50% or more of a partnership capital or the right to receive profits raises immediate tax problems. No matter what the partnership agreement says, tax law provides that such a sale results in the distribution of all partnership property to the partners. There's no easy way to escape this rule, though tax experts surely try.

This rule can create hardships for a two-person partnership. In a two-person, 50-50 partnership, sale of either partner's interest obviously terminates the partnership. But if one partner buys out the other, the rule that all partnership property is distributed can lead to very unfair results. It can be difficult enough for the buying partner to pay for the other's share, without also having to pay tax on the distributive share of the buying partner's own share if that share will actually be left in the business. Happily, tax law recognizes this reality, so the tax rule is different if one partner buys out another. In that case, the partnership can, if the remaining partner so desires, be regarded as continuing. The Internal Revenue Code provides that when payments are made by a remaining partner to a retiring partner of a two-person 50-50 partnership, that partner will be regarded as remaining in the partnership until her entire interest is liquidated. (See IRC Section 736.) This rule applies even if state law specifically provides that the partnership has been terminated on sale. Without this federal tax law, the partner continuing the business would also have to pay income taxes on her interest in the business when the other partner retired—an unfair burden to impose on one who wants to continue an existing business, not cash it out.

3. Sale or Buy-Out of a Partner's Interest

As we said, the details of an actual sale or purchase of a partner's interest should not be finalized without consulting a tax expert. There are a number of tax options you need to consider. And as we also told you, you can handle these problems at the time—or near the time—of the transaction. For example, IRC Section 754 permits the partnership to adjust the basis of certain partnership assets when a new partner buys into the partnership. The partnership must make the election to adjust the basis of these assets in the year in which the sale occurs. The tax code doesn't require you to make an election about partnership assets now that you have no idea if you'll ever need.

The partnership tax year for the selling partner (only) closes on the date of the sale. The selling partner's share in net partnership income or loss for that period must be reported on her tax return for that tax year. The IRS permits the use of "reasonable" estimates by the partners to determine that

income. This reasonable estimate can be made by agreement of the partners in the year of the sale.

EXAMPLE: John sells his one-third interest in the Alice-John-Joan partnership on March 1. The partnership is on a January 1 to January 1 fiscal year, and profits are determined quarterly. Under the IRS rules, John's tax year for his partnership interest closes on the date of sale—March 1. But what is his portion of partnership profits for the two months he was a partner that year? Since they haven't yet been calculated, the partners can make a reasonable estimate of the profits to which John is entitled.

4. Retirement or Death of a Partner

Finally, a few points regarding the retirement or death of a partner:

- Payments made in exchange for a partner's partnership interest that are considered a distribution of partnership profits are not deductible to the partnership as a business expense. They are, of course, taxable income to the partner.
- The valuation placed on a retiring partner's interest in an arm's length, or bona fide, transaction will normally be accepted by the IRS.
- If a partnership business is to be terminated completely, with all assets sold and the enterprise liquidated, complex tax rules are involved, and (we'll say it one more time) you should see a partnership tax expert.

I. A Few Additional Tax Concepts

Before we bid a gleeful good-bye to partnership taxes, let's discuss a few more tax concepts that may come in handy as you run your business. They may at least enable you to sound like a tax-hip grown-up when talking, say, to a banker or loan officer.

Earned Income: This is income you receive as the result of your own efforts (and your partners' too). For federal tax purposes, earned income and losses are taxed separately from passive income and losses. A partner's income is earned if she materially participates in partnership business, which is defined as "regular, continuous, and substantial involvement" in partnership business operations.

Passive Income: Income received from businesses in which you don't materially participate. Tempting as it might be, you cannot use a passive income loss to offset profits from earned income in figuring your tax bill. You can only use losses from passive partnership activities—such as real estate investments (without a management role) to offset gains from other passive activities. (See IRS Publication 925.)

Investment income is essentially certain types of passive income, such as stock dividends or profit from stock sales.

You generally want to have partnership income treated as earned income. Why? Because if it is, and the partnership suffers a loss, you can use that loss to offset other earned income, such as other employment income. This reduces the amount of income subject to taxation. By comparison, losses that result from passive or investment income cannot be offset against income actively earned. They can only be used to offset passive income from profitable investments.

EXAMPLE: Manuel has a loss of $8,000 from his first year in the DPT Partnership, in which he works part time. In the same year, Manuel earns $48,000 working as a disk jockey and receives $16,000 in dividends on stock investments. For tax purposes, Manuel can subtract his $8,000 loss from his other active income, the $48,000 he made as a disk jockey. However, if Manuel

hasn't worked for DPT, and his partnership income was solely the result of dividends on the money he invested, which is passive (investment) income, he could not subtract his $8,000 loss.

For most readers of this book who are involved in the day-to-day operations of their businesses, there's absolutely no need to worry about this earned/passive income distinction. You are active in your business, sometimes too active, and should your partnership suffer a loss, there's no question but that it will be an earned income loss.

Earned Passive Income and Rental Real Estate: Real estate partnerships are an area in which income is generally treated as passive income. However, there's a special exception for individual owners, allowing them to offset up to $25,000 of losses from passive real estate income against earned income if the owner "actively participates" in the real estate business. Active participation is a lesser standard than is material participation, which we discussed above. (They may sound about the same to you, but not to the IRS.) To actively participate, an owner must be involved in management decisions, such as approving new tenants, making repairs and deciding on new capital expenditures and rental terms.

Basis: In order to determine your profit or loss on the sale of an asset, you have to know what you originally paid for it. "Basis" is a tax term that means, very roughly, your purchase price.

Net Adjusted Basis: Often your profit on a sale cannot simply be determined by deducting your original purchase price from the sale price. To determine the real basis of the property, you need to include other factors, such as subsequent capital improvements or additions to the property that you paid for, or depreciation, other tax credits or other expenses. Net adjusted basis means the figure you or your accountant use as your basic cost figure for an item of property when you sell it. Sale price minus net adjusted basis equals profit (or loss).

Depreciation: Some types of property wear out gradually. A typewriter may last ten years, a building 30, a car 15. Eventually, when the item is completely worn out, it's worthless. Depreciation is a system that the IRS and state tax authorities allow you to use to allocate the loss caused by the decrease in value of your property over a certain period of time and to enable you to deduct the amount from your income for tax purposes. Another way to look at depreciation is that it's a system whereby the IRS requires you to spread out (or deduct) the cost of a capital asset over so many years, regardless of whether or when the asset actually wears out.

Accelerated Depreciation: Depreciation for tax purposes used to be a more treacherous game than it is now. Until recent tax law changes, there were a number of ways of calculating depreciation on the same item of property. Rapid (that is, accelerated) depreciation was a centerpiece of many tax scams, particularly in real estate. Accelerated depreciation has largely been eliminated (at least for a while).

Depreciation Recapture: Suppose a building is purchased for $100,000. The owner depreciates the property at the legal rate over the next 20 years. The owner then sells the building for $1 million. Did the building depreciate? No. So isn't it now unfair that the seller took depreciation on it all those years? Yes. So there are tax law provisions for recapturing (that is, retroactively disallowing) that depreciation. ■

Getting Your Business Started

Now that you've been through the basic elements of a partnership agreement, we want to switch gears before you actually prepare your own. Obviously, there is a lot more required to establish a successful business than just working out that agreement. This chapter provides an overview of practical matters and discusses some of the realities we've learned about running a small business.

Those of you who have already lived through the excitement and intensity of starting a new enterprise may prefer to skip ahead to the next chapter. Those of you for whom this material is new may wonder why it isn't in one of the early chapters of the book. After all, what good is a solid partnership agreement if you can't cope with the practical realities of running a business? The truth is you need both a sound partnership agreement *and* a sensible grasp of business fundamentals to succeed. Since the primary purpose of this book is to assist you in drafting your partnership agreement, we've given that precedence.

Let's start with the most important aspect of running a business—keeping good financial records. Not only is establishing and maintaining an excellent bookkeeping system important for dealing with the tax and license authorities, lenders and others in the outside world, they're absolutely essential to running your business. Without a simple, efficient accounting system, even the most basic information may be difficult to come by, such as whether or not you are making a profit. (See Section C, below, for more on how to set up a good bookkeeping system.)

For example, our friend Annalise, a partner in a small consulting firm, realized after many months in business that employing a bookkeeper with marginal skills was a big mistake. The record keeping was so haphazard that the partners found themselves unable to allocate overhead to their different projects because they had no solid facts at their disposal on which to base estimates. Since their bidding on various projects depended in part on

knowing their own overhead and administrative costs, and they didn't, they were at times unable to determine how much they should bid to ensure that a job would be profitable.

Good Records Are Important

Establishing and maintaining good financial records requires a little initial research which is well worth the effort. You should not be a slave to your accounting system, but rather your accounting should be a personalized tool, assisting you in the efficient management of your business.

WELL MATILDA, WE'VE GOT TO BE NICE AND TIDY WITH THESE WORKSHEETS.

Business Resources

Thorough discussions of different aspects of starting and maintaining a small business can be found in the following books:

Small Time Operator, by Bernard Kamoroff (Bell Springs). Updated yearly, this book has been popular for decades for excellent reasons. It gives you the essentials of the paperwork you'll have to deal with, including keeping books, paying taxes, becoming an employer, etc. The book also contains an excellent synopsis of the basics of computerizing your record keeping. If you have a cash register in your business, you must have this book.

The Legal Guide for Starting & Running a Small Business, by Fred S. Steingold (Nolo). A nuts-and-bolts guide of the laws that affect small businesses every day. The book covers a wide range of important subjects, including leases, trademarks, contracts, franchises, insurance, hiring and firing and independent contractors.

Legal Forms for Starting & Running a Small Business, by Fred S. Steingold (Nolo). All the forms, both on CD-ROM and as tear-outs, that small business owners need to handle practical legal problems, from dealing with the IRS to hiring employees and much more.

The Small Business Start-Up Kit, by Peri Pakroo (Nolo). A user-friendly guide to all major steps involved in launching a new business.

Tax Savvy for Small Business, by Frederick W. Daily (Nolo). To run a successful small business, you have to have a good grasp of tax law. This book tells business owners what they need to know about federal taxes and shows them how to make the best tax decisions for their business, maximize profits and stay out of trouble with the IRS.

Quicken Lawyer 2003 Business Deluxe (Nolo). A complete software legal reference for small business owners.

Drive a Modest Car & 16 Other Keys to Small Business Success, by Jake Warner (Nolo). A founder and continuing leader of Nolo provides his business insights and philosophy; a perfect read for anyone interested in starting a new business.

How to Write a Business Plan, by Mike McKeever (Nolo). This book shows you how to raise money for your new business, including methods for estimating income and raising outside capital by loans or other means. As part of doing this, it forces you to do a thorough financial plan for your proposed business. In our experience, such a plan may demonstrate that even using your best case assumptions, your proposed business won't produce the financial rewards you expect. In short, this book gives you the tools to reject bad business ideas and refocus on those likely to be profitable.

The Employer's Legal Handbook, by Fred S. Steingold (Nolo). A comprehensive resource that employers can use for all major employment law concerns, from hiring to firing to everything in between.

Create Your Own Employee Handbook: a Legal and Practical Guide, by Lisa Guerin and Amy DelPo (Nolo). A thorough presentation of how you can create an employee handbook—quickly, easily and professionally.

Finally, the U.S. Small Business Administration publishes a good many useful books and pamphlets covering everything from finance to insurance to exporting and franchising. You can download many free publications from the SBA's website at www.sba.gov. If you don't have access to a computer, most SBA pamphlets are available in the reference section of your library, or you can get a list from Superintendent of Documents, U.S. Government Printing Office, P.O. Box 371954, Pittsburgh, PA 15250-7954 or by calling 202-512-1800 (Website:www.bookstore.gpo.gov).

A. Permits and Licenses

Many businesses require one or more state and/or local permits and licenses. Sometimes the individual members of the partnership must be licensed in order to practice their profession (for example, lawyers, doctors and architects), while in other situations the business itself must be licensed (restaurants, bars, massage parlors, movie theaters). Individual licenses and permits are normally related to registration, experience, education, equipment, cleanliness, safety and posting an adequate bond.

You'll probably know whether the individuals in your business must be licensed, but you may not be so sure what sort of other "permission slips" your business might require. If you have doubts, check with the appropriate state agency (often the Department of Commerce) to see if they have a general publication on state licensing requirements. For example, the *California License Handbook* is a comprehensive guide to California license requirements, as well as a thorough sourcebook listing California's regulatory agencies and the red tape involved in doing business in the state. It is published by the Office of Small Business Development, California Department of Commerce, Sacramento, California. You can download it for free by visiting the Department of Commerce's website at http://commerce.ca.gov and clicking on "Permits and Licenses" and then on "License Handbook."

In addition, it is always helpful to talk to others in the same field to get some feedback on their personal experiences. City and county authorities can also be helpful with regard to local requirements and may even be able to steer you in the right direction where state agencies are concerned. Use your common sense. If you're in the food business, be sure you know all federal, state and local health rules. If your business makes noise, find out about local noise abatement ordinances. Whatever your business, make sure you understand how local zoning ordinances apply to any location you are considering. The fact that you find a commercial location for your business doesn't mean that you can carry on any sort of commerce there. For example, you may be too close to a school to sell liquor, or your type of business may require more parking than is available.

1. Business Licenses

Most cities and counties require one or more types of business licenses. We'll discuss the different types of licenses in more depth, below.

a. Local Tax Registration Certificate

Most cities (or, if your business is located outside of the city limits, counties) require every business to register with the city's (or county's) tax collector. Although some people refer to this as a business license, its purpose is really to collect taxes (true business licenses are discussed in Subsection b, below), so it's more appropriate to call it a tax registration certificate or permit. The fees your business must pay, usually on a yearly basis, are often graduated, based on the gross receipts of the business. However the fees are calculated, it's really just one more tax. To find out how to register, call your city or county tax collector.

b. Specialized Business Licenses and Permits

Unfortunately, this is such a varied area it's difficult for us to give any specific advice on how to go about obtaining any specialized business licenses or permits your business might need. However, we can give you a few pointers:

- If your business is highly specialized, or is typically regulated by the state (such as hairdressers, morticians and chiropractors), check with your state's commerce or trade department about any licensing or permit requirements. However basic you might think your business is, it could very well be regulated—California, for instance, regulates everything from locksmiths to tanning salons. And don't forget the federal government, which gets involved in things like trucking, meat manufacturing and operating a radio or television station.

- Your business will also have to comply with local zoning ordinances. If you lease space, your landlord may be able to help you get information on complying with zoning laws, but don't rely solely on her information. Contact your city or county planning department for information on compliance with zoning laws in your area.

- Finally, don't forget the health department, the fire department, the building inspector and the myriad other state or local agencies who may need to sign off on your new business. Fortunately, when you register with the local tax collector, you'll often receive helpful information on complying with these requirements.

Get Permits and Licenses in Your Partnership Name

In most situations, you'll want to get any required licenses and permits in the name of your new partnership. If the business will operate with a different name than the partnership itself, you can obtain the licenses and permits in both names: "X partnership doing business as Y name...." (See Section 3, immediately below, and Chapter 3, Section A.) Using the partnership name (rather than one individual partner's name) reduces the possibility of any conflict later should you and your partners get into a spat. We know of nasty situations where one partner got all permits and licenses in her name, and then later—after a falling out with the other partners—refused to execute documents so that the partnership business could operate. In another situation, we witnessed a partner trying to use her supposed control of the licenses and permits as leverage to take over the business and drive the other partners out. As we've already suggested, the partnership agreement should define who controls these licenses in the event the partnership breaks up. Still, it's best to have these licenses in the partnership name from the start.

The preceding discussion of business licenses and permits is adapted from The Small Business Start-Up Kit, *by Peri Pakroo (Nolo). This is an invaluable resource, which contains much more detailed, step-by-step information on obtaining licenses and permits as well as other important tips on starting your new business.*

2. Fictitious Business Name Statements

If your partnership will conduct business under a name other than that of the partners, you must file and publish what is called a "fictitious name statement" (sometimes referred to as a dba—"doing business as"). We also discussed this in Chapter 3, Section A. This must be done in the county of the partnership's principal place of business. (Remember, a fictitious name is simply any business name that is not the name of the partners.) First, pay a visit to your county clerk's office where information of this nature is a matter of public record. Be sure the name you have chosen is not already in use. Then proceed by completing the appropriate forms and filing them with the requisite local governing agency. They will alert you to any publication requirements.

Publishing your fictitious name statement as well as the real names of the partners in a local newspaper is a standard procedure—it alerts anyone who might wish to know that you and your partners are operating a business and the name you are using. It's common practice to publish these statements in the back pages of an obscure newspaper because their ad rate is relatively low. This gives some people the impression that the fictitious name filing is somehow fishy or sleazy. Be assured that it is a serious requirement that can help keep you from legal entanglements at a later date.

3. Transferring an Existing Business to Partnership

If you're transferring an existing business, normally a sole proprietorship to a partnership, the previous owner must file all documents needed to terminate this prior business (including final sales tax and employment tax returns, if appropriate). Chances are you will want to open a bank account in the name of the partnership long before you can close the last account from the prior business. In addition, if the prior business holds licenses or permits, these should, if feasible, be canceled and new licenses or permits taken out in the name of the partnership.

If you transfer inventory of the prior business to the partnership, you must comply with your state's bulk sales transfer law. Essentially, this law requires you to notify the creditors of the prior business and other interested parties (for example, suppliers, others with whom you have open book accounts or lines of credit, etc.), in writing, of the termination of the prior business entity and the fact that its business assets have been transferred to a partnership.

4. Sales Tax or Sellers' Permits

Most states impose a sales tax. In the states that do, any business, whether it's a sole proprietorship, partnership or corporation, that collects money in exchange for most types of goods must obtain a tax permit or license to sell that merchandise. When the business makes retail sales, the business must collect state sales tax and periodically reimburse the state. One of the partners must present herself in person at the appropriate state agency to make application for a license to resell or resale license. Often, you must post a refundable bond or deposit, which is normally based on your estimated sales volume—so it pays to make a conservative one. You can request a refund of the bond at a later date, usually after you have demonstrated your ability to comply with the sales tax rules and regulations. Your partnership must, of course, keep complete and accurate records of your purchases and sales. These records must be made available to the licensing board of your state upon request.

B. Federal and State Tax Requirements

Everyone who conducts business has inescapable obligations to the IRS and one's state tax board. We discuss the partners' obligations in Chapter 7. This section is concerned with the routine requirements imposed by tax agencies on small businesses. *Tax Savvy for Small Business,* which we cited in the "Business Resources" box at the beginning of this chapter, is extremely helpful here. Also, the IRS publishes a pamphlet (IRS Publication 454) entitled *Your Business Tax Kit,* which contains a lot of solid information. Since your sales and profit are what interests these agencies, a sound accounting system will also serve you well here. The forms you must file and your tax obligations will vary depending upon where you live and the location and type of business in which you are engaged. For example, some states have special taxes for certain types of businesses such as hotels and logging companies. Some states impose a gross receipts tax (Washington), while others have a business income tax (Michigan). Be sure to contact state tax authorities for details when setting up your business. If you "inadvertently" overlook any tax requirement, they

are sure to eventually find you, because you've obtained a tax registration certificate from your city or county or a seller's permit from the state.

1. Federal and State Employer Identification Numbers

Your first order of business is to apply for both state and federal employer identification numbers. Don't be misled by the word "employer." All businesses must obtain these. For tax purposes, these numbers function for the partnership like your individual Social Security number functions for you. In short, the number identifies the entity that is your business partnership. To get a federal Employer Identification Number (EIN), obtain and fill out Form SS-4 and send it to the IRS. Better yet, call the IRS's free Tele-TIN number on the form (make sure to call the office designated for your location) and get your EIN over the phone. Once you receive your EIN, you will also begin to receive annual *Employer Tax Guides* from the IRS (IRS Publication 15, Circular E, *Employer's Tax Guide*) and your state tax agency.

Your state may have a similar form you must fill out to obtain a state employer identification number. This is the number you will use on state forms you file with your state's employment agency. Contact your Secretary or Department of State, or Department of Employment, for more information.

Obtaining IRS forms is easy. *Most IRS forms are available for free from the IRS's website at www.irs.gov. If you don't have access to a computer, you can pick up IRS forms at your local IRS office or order them by calling 800-TAX-FORM.*

2. Employee Tax Forms and Rules

The term "employee" refers to anyone to whom the partnership pays wages. All employees are treated the same with regard to the rules and regulations of payroll taxes. All employees must, of course, be paid at least the minimum wage. Other legal requirements apply as well. The U.S. Department of Labor provides posters that you must display which give all the details regarding hours, safety and discrimination prevention (Occupational Safety and Health; Equal Employment Opportunity Commission). You can get all this information, plus these mandatory posters, by downloading them directly from the Department of Labor's website at www.dol.gov (click on "Workplace Posters") or by writing to the U.S. Department of Labor, Employment Standards Administration, Washington D.C. 20210. The corresponding department in your state will provide you with similar information regarding your state laws. Some states have established higher standards than the federal ones, and you are required to adhere to the higher. (For example, several, including California, have established a higher minimum wage.)

The tax requirements of being an employer may be a little intimidating at first, but here again, organization is the key. Also, if you have five or more employees, consider hiring one of the many payroll services that have sprouted up in recent years. Typi-

cally, for businesses with five or more employees, they can prepare your payroll, alert you to the amount and due dates of all your payroll tax obligations, produce all your payroll tax returns and handle all your year-end requirements (including W-2 forms and 1099s), for less than the cost of doing it in-house. Do shop around! Most of the payroll services offer much the same thing, but they are not all competitively priced. Be wary of services that charge a setup fee, charge you for checks and/or charge you extra for year-end work. Also, ask for references and check them out.

Here is a summary of what an employer must do regarding employee taxes:

Have each employee fill out IRS Form W-4 or W-4E. This form must be updated at least once a year, but the employee is entitled to change it whenever his circumstances change. He is also required to update it if his legal status changes (such as he gets married). Many states have a corresponding form which you should make available to your employees upon request. These forms are used to determine the amount of income taxes to be withheld from employees' wages. In addition, the Immigration and Naturalization Service requires all employees to fill out Form I-9, Employment Eligibility Verification. This form need only be completed at the time an employee is hired, but the employer is obliged to keep that form on file indefinitely.

Each payroll you are required to withhold for each employee: federal income tax, Social Security (FICA), state income tax (where applicable), and any other state imposed taxes. (In some states, you are also required to withhold for state disability insurance.) The amount of federal and state income tax withheld from each employee's earnings depends upon how the employee completed his W-4 or W-4E and/or its state equivalent. Social Security and state disability withholding are based on a certain percentage of the employee's gross earnings. The partnership is required to make matching Social Security tax contributions for each employee. There are annual maximums on these particular taxes. IRS Circular E (mentioned earlier in this section) and the corresponding state publication will tell you what you need to know here. As a rule, you will transmit these funds to the IRS or the appropriate state agency via a deposit to a banking institution qualified as a depository for federal taxes.

Depending upon how large your payroll is, the deadlines for making these payments to the federal and state governments vary. Minimally, you will be required to file quarterly returns.

The federal government requires:

- Form 941—Employer's Quarterly Federal Tax Return—to report and/or remit the amount of federal income tax and Social Security withheld and the partnership's share of the Social Security tax due or deposited for payroll within the quarter. You must file this return on a quarterly basis.
- Form 940—Employer's Annual Federal Unemployment Tax Return (FUTA)—to report the quarterly deposits made based on the gross amount of payroll. This tax is paid by the partnership and is not withheld from earnings. This tax return is required annually.

In addition, most state governments require:

- At least quarterly payment of any state income tax and/or disability withheld from earnings. Payment of state unemployment insurance is also required in most states.
- Both state and federal governments require the partnership to furnish each employee with three copies of IRS Form W-2, Wage and Tax Statement. All earnings and withholdings appear on this statement and, as most people know, one copy is used to prepare the individual's federal income tax return, one copy is used to prepare his state income tax return and one copy is for the individual's tax records.
- In addition, the partnership must inform the federal and some state governments of the W-2 forms furnished. Therefore, one copy of all

the W-2 forms furnished must go the IRS with federal Form W-3, Transmittal of Income and Tax Statements. The corresponding state transmittal form will require copies of the W-2 forms, as well.

Even if your partnership does not have employees, you are still not completely off the hook. You need to keep track of the total amounts paid to any outside contractors or consultants. You must file IRS Form 1099, Statement for Recipients, for each contractor at the end of each calendar year. When you hire an independent contractor, have her fill out IRS Form W-9, Request for Taxpayer Identification Number and Certification. This gives you her correct name, address and taxpayer ID number. Also, be careful that when you use contract labor that you are in compliance with IRS rules which differentiate independent contractors from employees. If the IRS or a state tax or employment agency determines in an audit that those contractors should have actually been classified as employees of the partnership, the partnership may have to pay back taxes and associated payments, plus penalties and interest.

You are not required to furnish Form 1099 to corporations, but you must furnish one to anyone who is not incorporated to whom you pay non-employee compensation of $600 or more per year (or $10 per year or more in royalties). There are 14 different types of recipient statements, so be sure you are using the correct one for the type of compensation being paid by the partnership.

Like the W-2 Form, the 1099 has its own transmittal form—IRS Form 1096. Some states will have a corresponding one as well, which you must file with copies of the 1099s you produce.

 To learn more about how to properly classify workers and safely hire independent contractors, see Hiring Independent Contractors: The Employer's Legal Guide, *by Stephen Fishman (Nolo).*

C. Bookkeeping and Accounting

If this is your first venture into business, it may seem that accounting, taxes and insurance require such an overwhelming amount of work as to be nearly insurmountable. This is not true. What you do need are a reasonable amount of intelligence, good organizational skills and a commitment to meeting your obligations in a timely fashion. While we recommend that you work with a competent bookkeeper from the start (see Chapter 10, Section B), you do need to know enough about the subject to understand the basics involved. After all, you don't want to be out-of-touch financially with what's going on with your own business and not know how your own bottom line is determined. We also want to remind you that the most important financial aspect of any business is income. We know small businesses that have been successfully run, in their beginning stages, with no more than a checkbook for financial structure.

There are many choices your partnership can make regarding bookkeeping methods. But the primary concern should be that whatever methods you use, your system should be simple, accurate and provide you with the information you need to facilitate good decision-making. It goes without saying that your bookkeeping and accounting should be scrupulously honest.

1. Bookkeeping

Start by understanding the basics of how business records are kept and what that information can do for you. If you and your partners don't know, learn. Then adopt a bookkeeping plan and stick to it. Your CPA can be helpful in making this plan and guiding you in its implementation. Your bookkeeping records are what your CPA will use to produce your tax returns and financial statements, so some team work is called for here. This initial team work can save you time and money later, because your

CPA can have all the information she needs at her fingertips.

Consider using computers for financial record-keeping right from the start. While it is possible to convert to a computerized system at a later date, setting up everything on computers to begin with is far more cost-effective. There are many financial record software programs for small- and medium-sized businesses. If you have already chosen your computer hardware, check the computer magazines that review software for your type of computer, and contact software publishers. Usually for a small fee they will send you information and/or a demonstration disk that will give you some idea of how their program works. Most of all, ask others in your type of business what systems they have been most satisfied with and why. Often you'll find that small companies sell customized accounting products designed specifically for use in your particular type of business. Taking your time in this search is more than worth it. Especially at first, avoid the temptation to set up overly complicated or sophisticated books. If your business is small and simple, so too should be your accounting system.

IRS Publication 538, Accounting Period and Methods, *and Publication 583,* Information for Business Taxpayers, *contain helpful information on accounting methods and bookkeeping procedures.*

2. Partnership Accounting

There are two commonly used accounting methods: the accrual method and the cash method.

Manufacturing businesses and businesses with inventories generally find it necessary to use the accrual method. For some, this method is required for income tax purposes. Accrual accounting means the partnership recognizes income when you send a bill to a customer, not when they pay you (you have reason to believe you will be paid, of course, or you wouldn't have given the customer credit terms in the first place). Likewise, you recognize expenses when you receive what you have ordered, not when you pay for them (since you have every intention of paying for your supplies, barring any problems with your orders, or you would not have ordered them in the first place).

Retail businesses such as dress shops and restaurants often use the cash method of accounting: This means income is recognized when you actually receive it, and expenses are recognized when the check is cut.

In many cases, your business may choose the method that is most advantageous to you. However, it's important to understand that neither of these methods will give you a complete picture of your financial situation. Advice from your CPA is necessary here.

D. Budgeting

During the planning stages of any new venture, discussion inevitably turns to finances. To determine the amount for yourself, it's imperative that you carefully examine your projected expenses and income. Below we give you some worksheets you can use to make estimates of your budget and profits (or losses, God forbid!).

1. Projecting a Budget

This projection gives you an idea of what it will cost to set up shop. Initial expenses include:

- down payment on purchase of business property, or a deposit on a lease
- essential furniture and fixtures, and any required remodeling (it's easy to spend too much in this area, so be frugal)
- purchase or lease of necessary machinery and equipment
- opening inventory and enough money to replace what sells, especially if you offer credit

terms (some suppliers will eventually allow you 30 to 60 days to pay, but typically suppliers do not give much credit to a new business with no established credit history)

- installation fees and deposit for telephone and utility services
- office supplies (including stationery, receipt books, pens and paper clips)
- taxes and license fees
- professional fees (architects, designers, business consultants, attorneys, accountants)
- initial advertising and promotion, and
- other: Depending on your business, you may need to license patents, or copyrights, or spend money on other items; if so, be sure you include it.

A sample budget worksheet is shown below.

Open Books: The Hallmark of an Honest Business

We suggest that you agree to a policy of open financial books. No money secrets; let the world know how you're doing (you may be surprised how little it is interested). Here are some excellent thoughts on open books from *Honest Business*, by Michael Phillips and Salli Rasberry (Random House):

- No single element defines the distinction between an honest business and one that is not, more than the issue of open books... Yet 99% of the people in the general business world will have a reaction of total terror at the possibility of some outsider seeing their financial records.
- Having open books means letting anyone look at your business records, especially your financial statements, and the details necessary to understand them. Anyone includes employees, customers, suppliers and curious bystanders.

SAMPLE BUDGET WORKSHEET

Living expenses for partners for first three months
(including regular monthly payments, household
operating expenses, food, personal expenses, and
tax expenses based on average months)   _____

Deposits and prepayments—one month's business
rent or mortgage payment (the first three are in
operating costs, below)

    Telephone and utility deposits and installation   _____

    Sales tax deposit   _____

    Business license and permits   _____

    Insurance premiums   _____   _____

Real property improvements, remodeling expenses

    Furniture, fixtures and equipment, including
    signs (indoors and out)   _____

    Labor for installation of above   _____   _____

Inventory

    Service, delivery charges, supplies   _____

    Merchandise   _____   _____

Miscellaneous

    Professional fees   _____

    Advertising and promotion   _____

    Business travel expense   _____   _____

Total operating costs for three months
(from projection profit-and-loss statement)   _____

Reserve to carry credit accounts   _____

Cash on hand to set up cash register, petty cash, etc.   _____

Total   _____

Before we go on and examine an estimated profit-and-loss statement, let's take a moment to leaven our calculations with some common sense. It may seem obvious that partners starting a new enterprise need enough money to get it off the ground, but in our research, we've been struck by two phenomena:

- Many people have made a small business work with very little start-up money. Hard work, creative marketing and an excellent product or service are what's most important. We've found that lots of money, a flashy store or office, and high salaries are no guarantee of success. People who start small have one enormous advantage—low overhead. They are not burdened by the necessity of meeting huge fixed costs.

- People who invest a lot of money in a business to start with often seem to be trying to make up for their lack of business skill by throwing money at the problem. However, this approach is often counterproductive. Most small businesses go through an inevitable (and healthy) learning stage in which a number of business assumptions must be modified. If a business is overcapitalized it can be difficult to do this for several reasons, including the fact that the money may have already been spent in the wrong place. Put another way, it's fairly easy to recover from small, cheap mistakes, but can be impossible to climb out of a hole dug by spending large amounts on nonessential equipment, salaries, buildings, leases or promotion.

In *Honest Business*, Michael Phillips and Salli Rasberry have some wise words to say about the overcapitalization phenomenon:

"When you start and run a business with the primary goal of serving people, you will be more effective by starting with the minimum capital. Minimizing your capital requires maximizing other business components such as quick response to the market, attention to details, and innovation.

"The idea of starting with small capital is opposite from the prevailing view of most graduate schools of business, and from the advice almost universally given by small-business writers. The most commonly stated reason given for the failure of small businesses is that they're undercapitalized.

"Nonsense! Undercapitalization is the prevailing excuse for insensitivity to the real needs of the market. Too much capital is often a more serious problem than too little."

 We don't mean to suggest that you don't need money to get started. *As everyone will tell you, you do. But don't go overboard—a better mouse trap, a tastier brownie or more efficient bookkeeping service, and a lot of hard work, have launched many a successful partnership. The fact that they were launched from a garage, not a penthouse, probably had a lot to do with their eventual success.*

2. Profit-and-Loss Statement

Now, let's return to our forms. Here we provide a sample estimated monthly profit-and-loss worksheet.

MONTHLY PROFIT-AND-LOSS STATEMENT

Date: _____

Total sales during month

(excluding sales taxes)   _____

Cost of goods sold   (_____)

Gross profit   _____

Expenses:

    Operating Expenses

        Salaries   (_____)

        Payroll taxes   (_____)

        Advertising   (_____)

        Auto and travel   (_____)

        Supplies   (_____)

        Telephone and utilities   (_____)

        Other   (_____)   (_____)

    Fixed expenses

        Depreciation   (_____)

        Insurance   (_____)

        Rent   (_____)   (_____)

    Total Expenses   (_____)

Net Income (before taxes and partner draw)   ====================

A worksheet is only as accurate as the information the partners plug into it.

We've learned that it's wise to err on the conservative side. The art of drafting profit-and-loss statements is fully explained in How to Write a Business Plan, *by Mike McKeever (Nolo). (See box on "Business Resources" at the beginning of this chapter.) This book provides a far more detailed and sophisticated approach to financing a small business start-up than we have room for here. For example, it shows you how to do a cash flow analysis, an essential tool for retail and manufacturing businesses. It allows you to figure out whether you'll be paid fast enough by your debtors to keep your suppliers and other creditors from pulling the plug on you.*

3. Balance Sheet

This document is useful in answering two basic questions: Are you solvent and, if so, by how much? This is determined by subtracting what the business owes from what it owns, to determine net worth. Partners can use a beginning balance sheet as one tool to indicate the state of their business at the start. Subsequent balance sheets are useful to monitor business activity.

BALANCE SHEET

Date: _____

Current Assets:

    Cash   _____

    Accounts receivable   _____

    Inventory   _____   _____

Fixed Assets:

    Real estate   _____

    Furniture and equipment _____

     Less: accumulated depreciation _____   _____

Other Assets: _____

    Total Assets   _══════════════

Current Liabilities:

    Notes payable within one year _____

    Accounts Payable   _____

    Accrued expenses   _____

    Taxes payable   _____   _____

Long-term Liabilities:

    Notes payable after one year   _____

    Others   _____   _____

    Total Liabilities   _══════════════

    Net Worth (assets minus liabilities)   _══════════════

[Liabilities + Net Worth = Assets]

E. Insurance

We mentioned earlier that because partners do not enjoy limited liability, it is wise to purchase insurance against obvious business risks. If someone slips on your linoleum, swallows a bad oyster or walks under your ladder at the wrong moment, the partnership and all general partners can be sued.

If you're found to be at fault (you could be held liable by court decision made either by a judge or jury or you could even admit you were at fault, if you decided that was clearly true), a legal judgment for losses or damages can be entered against the partnership. And if the partnership assets are insufficient to pay the judgment, the partners can be made to pay out of their own pockets.

1. Liability and Risk Insurance

The type of insurance you should buy is directly related to the kind of risks typical of your business. In addition to normal fire and theft coverage, it's an excellent idea to get a general liability policy, which will cover normal sorts of accidents, such as someone slipping on your front step. In California, it's prudent for many businesses to carry earthquake insurance (although it's often very expensive; make sure you research your options thoroughly before you purchase any). And if your warehouse is located next to a river, flood insurance makes obvious sense as well. Beyond that, you'll have to think about the details and risks of your own business. An architectural firm will need professional liability insurance; a small business manufacturing children's swings will want product liability insurance.

Buying insurance to protect against predictable risks makes sense if you can purchase it at a cost that isn't prohibitive. Obviously there is a trade-off here—if you don't think the risk is severe enough to justify the cost of the insurance, you probably won't buy it. However, if your business uses ve-hicles, you'll want to be sure they're adequately insured, even if they belong to an employee. (This is required in most states.) If an employee driving her own car gets into an accident on partnership business, you are likely to be sued.

Who do you buy business insurance from? We haven't got any pearls of wisdom here, except to say you'll want a company that is solvent and will stay so. (Since some insurance companies bought large amounts of junk bonds, they may be at risk—don't gamble. A.M. Best Co. rates the financial health of insurance companies in a book available at most libraries. For a fee, you can even call A.M. Best, at 900-420-0400.) And you want an insurance broker with small business experience whom you both like and trust. We consciously use the word broker—not agent—because when it comes to business insurance, which commonly means insuring your business against a variety of risks, we believe it's better to work with a broker who typically works with a number of insurance companies rather than an agent who usually works with (and may even be employed by) a single company. Most ongoing businesses maintain a continuing relationship with their insurance broker, and if they're smart, they use their broker as an advisor on how to limit or avoid risks.

When Nolo first purchased business insurance, we started by getting leads from other small-business people about knowledgeable brokers. We called these people and asked each to stop by our office for a short talk. One person seemed to have a lot more knowledge and common sense about small business needs than the others. Nevertheless, we asked for bids. They varied considerably as to both amount and details of coverage. Not surprising, the best bid came from the most knowledgeable broker. Over the years, as our business has grown, we've changed the details of our coverage a number of times, and even switched insurance companies, but we still work with the same broker and are very glad we do.

2. Workers' Compensation Insurance

All businesses, including partnerships, are required to carry workers' compensation insurance coverage on all employees. (Generally, the partners themselves are not employees.) And in some instances, it is even necessary to cover subcontractors if they are working on the partnership's premises. Workers' compensation insurance rates are highly regulated, so it pays to find a company that has a good reputation for paying claims in a timely fashion and responding to your requests appropriately. Your insurance broker will be the expert in this case since he will have had some experience with this type of insurance with his other clients. The insurance rates are calculated on each $100 of payroll and are based on the type of work the employee does. Rates for types of work vary considerably based on the risk involved, so it is essential that you set up your payroll with these rates in mind. For more information check with your State Compensation Insurance Commission or your broker.

F. Rent and Lease Negotiations

Rent can be one of the larger expenses for many small businesses. While it's essential that you locate your new enterprise in an advantageous location, it's also important that you not obligate yourself for so much rent that you jeopardize the future of the business. Here are a few lessons that the small-business people who have helped us put this book together have learned:

- **Make sure your needs and your pocketbook match.** Figure out your minimum space requirements and then really shop around. For some people, even minimum needs will be fairly costly (for example, a specialty food shop that has to locate in an expensive neighborhood). For others, minimum needs can be truly bare bones—that is,

they can start their operation in a low-cost office setting or even a spare bedroom or garage. In the good old days, we ran Nolo out of an attic and used the rent savings to print more books.

- **Get the security you need.** If you do rent commercial or retail space, and location is important to you, as would be the case with a retail business or restaurant, be sure to get a lease that provides you with adequate security. You want to avoid the situation in which you rent a location fairly cheaply, on a short lease or month-to-month tenancy, only to have the landlord raise the rent as soon as you begin to prosper. Also, remember that real estate prices have a way of rising fast in neighborhoods that are in transition. You know the phenomenon: First artists and bohemians congregate, then come the first arty shops and hearty entrepreneurs, and then—shazaam—the media says it's chic, and you've got Soho, Manhattan or Venice Beach, California, or other similar success stories.

We recently spoke with some partners who had opened a restaurant in a rundown neighborhood in Philadelphia. The food was wonderful and people lined up to get in. Before long, two similar, equally interesting restaurants announced plans to open nearby. What happened next? You guessed it—the landlord tripled the rent. Of course, some small businesses aren't particularly sensitive to location, and others plan to move fairly quickly from the start. But if you have a business such as a restaurant in which you're making a real investment in having people know where you are, plan ahead.

Here are a few things to consider:

- Long-term leases can be less dangerous than you think if a location is very desirable, because it's often fairly easy for a tenant to end a lease. Why? Because of a legal doctrine known as "mitigation of damages." This bit of legal jargon means that if you do move out before the lease term is up, your landlord must try to rent the place to someone else. If he does so immediately (or often even if he could have), you're off the hook, and normally you won't owe any damages for moving early. (This is a brief summary of what can be a complicated subject. If you face this problem, check the laws in your state and the terms of your lease. Often you can find a new tenant for the landlord and ensure that he suffers little or no damage.) However, in a marginal or overbuilt area, the last thing you want is a long lease. If you want to leave early, it is likely to be tough to find someone to take over your legal obligation.

- An option or options to renew a lease can be desirable from a tenant's point of view. An option to renew enables you to keep the place when the original lease runs out by exercising your option but doesn't require that you do so. For example, you might get a lease for two years that contains options to renew for two additional three-year periods at a rent increase that reflects increases in the cost of living. In this situation, you would be free to stay (or not stay) at the end of the second and fifth years, depending on how things looked at the time, without the risk of drastically increased rent. In some circumstances, you will have to pay a fee for the option. As long as it's a reasonable amount, do it—after all, the landlord is giving you a valuable right.

- Landlords are sometimes reluctant to commit themselves to a long-term lease because they don't know how bad inflation will be, or how desirable the neighborhood will become. One way to mitigate their anxiety is to offer to tie automatic, yearly rent increases to the consumer price index (CPI). For example, it might be appropriate to have your rent automatically go up each year at the CPI increase. Better yet, persuade your landlord to accept a fraction of the CPI (for example, two-thirds). Thus, if the CPI went up at a yearly rate of 5%, your rent would go up about 3.5%. We suggest that you bargain for a rent increase of

less than the CPI increase because many of the landlord's costs will be fixed and are unlikely to be going up as much as the CPI.

- If the landlord promises to make improvements on the property to induce you to sign the original lease, make sure you get this in writing, with firm dates.

- If you need to modify the structure of your rented space in any way, be sure you have written permission to do so as part of the lease. This advice also applies if you plan to attach anything (called a "trade fixture" in lawyerese) to the building that you will want to take with you when you leave. Otherwise, legally, you've made your landlord an unintentional gift because a fixture becomes (for legal purposes, anyway) a part of the real property. A simple written statement from the landlord saying, that as part of the lease, you can detach your fixture when you leave is all you need.

- If you lease retail space in a shopping center, mall or certain other types of premium space, you may face a landlord's demand that you pay a basic rental amount plus a percentage of your receipts. Chain stores with lots of marketing clout, leasing experience and tough negotiators can often make these deals work to their advantage; most small businesses can't. Unless you thoroughly understand the shopping center environment, or hire a negotiator who does, stay away. In addition, if you must negotiate a shopping center lease, make sure you are clear on whether your landlord can lease space to one of your direct competitors. Depending on the type of enterprise you're engaged in, if a landlord allows a competitor to move in, this could wreak havoc on your business.

- Especially if you rent or lease in an area with lots of vacant rental space, be sure you understand the types of concessions landlords are offering to get good tenants. Often a savvy tenant who has checked out the local market carefully can bargain for free rent for an initial period, or for modifications to the building, or a lower rent.

⚠ Don't forget about zoning laws when you're choosing a location. *Be absolutely sure that the location you choose meets all the zoning and other permit requirements necessary for your business.*

💡 Be sure to deal with the lease in your partnership agreement. *If your lease will be a main asset of your business, it's important to define what happens to it if a partner leaves or the partnership dissolves. (See Chapter 5, Section E.)*

Sometimes partners will still be formulating the written agreement when they find the perfect location and want to sign a lease. Perhaps the best thing to do in this situation is to slow down—simply wait to make any formal commitments until the partnership agreement is signed. But this is an impatient society, and sometimes you do have to move quickly to be sure you get the right location. If this happens, you may want to sign a short-form partnership agreement like those set out in Chapter 2, Section K. This will formally establish your partnership and will provide a sound legal basis for leasing property in the partnership name.

📖 *For great information and tips on leasing commercial space, see* Leasing Space for Your Small Business, *by Janet Portman and Fred S. Steingold (Nolo).* ∎

Limited Partnerships

Limited partnerships are, essentially, money-raising or investment devices. They allow people operating or forming a partnership business to raise additional money without taking in new owners. Rather, the existing partners sell limited partnership shares in the business to investors, who are called limited partners. This can be less burdensome than having to sell shares in a corporation or borrow money from a bank.

> **EXAMPLE:** Je'rod and Ira form a 50-50 partnership to produce honey. After several years of small-scale success, they decide to triple the number of their hives. To do this, they need more capital. They decide to sell four limited partnerships in their enterprise for $15,000 each, with an agreed upon return of 14% per year for five years (after this, the limited partners' initial investment will be returned to them). Je'rod and Ira do this and have several very good years. The two partner-owners share in this prosperity equally, after they pay the limited partners under the terms of the limited partnership agreement.

Viewed from the other side of the window, limited partnerships allow investors a legal way to put money into a business, without incurring the responsibilities and risks inherent in full ownership. If the business succeeds, the limited partners receive a rate of return defined in the limited partnership agreement. This can be a set rate of return—for instance 10%, 12% or 15% per year. Or it can be a percentage of net business profits. Or even a percentage of gross income—though this is risky for the owner-partners because they are promising to pay their investors on what may be a substantial gross, even if there's no profit. In addition, the limited partners get their initial investment returned normally at the end of a preestablished number of years.

Limited partners do not face open-ended personal liability for the business's debts (unlike the general partners). Limited partners can only lose the amount they invest, no matter how great the debts of the business. Thus, limited partners are in much the same basic position as shareholders in a corporation. The maximum at risk for them is the amount they've invested.

As you may well recall, we briefly discussed limited partnerships in Chapter 1, Section E, as one way to organize your small business. You may want to reread that material before proceeding, if you're unsure how a limited partnership differs from a small business partnership or corporation. In this chapter, we'll further explore limited partnerships. We also present a sample limited partnership agreement that might prove useful for you if you decide to pursue the idea of using a limited partnership.

⚠ This chapter is not adequate to enable you to prepare a limited partnership yourselves. *In the absence of any excellent self-help book on this subject, you'll definitely need to see a lawyer before finalizing any limited partnership agreement. One reason for this is that each state's laws governing limited partnerships mandate technical legal requirements that must be met to establish a valid limited partnership.*

History Lesson # 7

Limited partnerships were first used in Italy in Pisa and Florence in the twelfth century as a method for owners of capital—mostly clergy and nobles—to invest their money without being known or named. Although anonymity didn't remain a feature of limited partnerships, the form itself proved useful. The limited partnership form spread to France and was then brought to America by French explorers and settlers in Louisiana and Florida.

Limited partnerships are fairly common in the small business world because they're such a good way to raise cash—either to open or to grow. New businesses usually have a hard time raising capital, except from the owners' pockets. Banks are quite reluctant, even in flush financial times, to loan money to a company with no, or little, track record (unless you provide the bank with adequate security, like a viable second mortgage on your home—but this is really taking the money from your own pocket). Similarly, it's not easy for a new business to obtain government loans, whether from the Small Business Administration (SBA) or other agencies. Even private investors in the business of providing start-up capital are often wary. And if they do provide money, they may demand a substantial share of ownership of the business in return.

Aside from borrowing money, the main alternative to a limited partnership is establishing a corporation. The corporation then sells stock to raise capital. While this approach can have considerable merit in some situations (see our discussion of incorporating in Chapter 1, Section D), raising money by selling stock, especially to people who are not closely linked to the corporation or its principal organizers, usually involves lots of red tape in the form of state, and sometimes federal, securities registration and disclosure paperwork.

For all these reasons, the best—indeed, often the only—way for many small business partnerships to raise additional capital is to sell interests to friends, friends of friends, and other investors they contact personally. Limited partnerships can be a practical way to structure these types of investments. We know a number of owners of small businesses (including owners of several restaurants, a house renovation company and a retail store), who have raised cash by selling limited partnership investments, mostly to friends and acquaintances who knew and trusted the general partners and their business.

⚠️ **Limited partnership interests are securities.** *Although most of us think of corporate stock as the main type of security regulated by the SEC, limited partnership interests also qualify as securities. This means that you'll need to comply with state and federal securities laws if you sell limited partnership interests, and you should get the help of an expert.*

A. How a Limited Partnership Works

A limited partnership must be attached to an ongoing business. That business must be managed and owned (except for the limited partners' interest) by a general partner, who has personal responsibility for all partnership debts. Although a limited partner requires the existence of at least one general partner, that general partner doesn't itself have to be a partnership. Sound odd? Not really, once you realize that a sole proprietor of a business can create a limited partnership with himself as the only general partner. This allows him to retain complete managerial control over the business at the same time that he raises money for expansion. Similarly, a corporation can be the general partner. Of course, a partnership, as an entity, can also be the general partner of a limited partnership.

The limited partners and the general partner define the limited partnership in a written agreement. (We present a sample limited partnership agreement in Section F of this chapter.) The partners must also file another document regarding the limited partnership, usually called a certificate of limited partnership, with an appropriate state agency. This certificate is a form of a registration statement, required by state law, which must list basic facts regarding the limited partnership. The partners usually file the certificate with the Secretary of State or whatever other bureaucracy handles corporate filing, such as the Commissioner of Corporations. You should be able to obtain the form for your state's certificate of limited partnership from this agency.

As we've said, it's legal and common to have a partnership that also has limited partners. In this situation, it's important to realize that there must be two agreements: one between the individual members of the partnership, who collectively are the general partner, and a separate agreement between this general partner and the limited partners.

Limited partnerships are generally governed by the Uniform Limited Partnership Act or the Revised Uniform Limited Partnership Act. Some form of one of these acts has been adopted, often with slight variations, in all states except Louisiana. For many purposes, especially for small business limited partnerships, the Revised Uniform Limited Partnership Act and the original Uniform Limited Partnership Act function similarly. In this text, when we refer simply and solely to the Uniform Limited Partnership Act (or ULPA), that means differences between the original Uniform Act and the Revised ULPA are not significant. Also, a state's partnership law can apply to limited partnerships, particularly if the general partner is a separate partnership.

The partners usually can't dispense with many of the provisions of a state's limited partnership law, even if they want to. For instance, legal duties, like filing the certificate of limited partnership (see Section D), cannot be ignored, even if the general partner and all limited partners want to. If the partnership doesn't comply with the limited partnership law, the entity won't be held to be a valid limited partnership, and the limited partners will lose their limited liability status.

Limited partners also risk losing their limited liability partnership status if they don't follow other rules. The most important rule is that limited partners must remain "passive" investors, meaning that they can't become actively involved in the day-to-day running of the business. The precise extent of business involvement a limited partner is allowed to engage in depends on state law. In most limited partnerships, this isn't a problem, because all the limited partner wants to be is a pure investor, receive a return on an investment and not bother with business management.

Sometimes, however, a limited partner wants to be involved in the business itself, perhaps as a way to impose controls that will protect his investment, or because the partnership is obviously in financial trouble.

⚠ **If you're a limited partner considering getting involved in management of the business, watch out!** *You'll need to review your state's laws (and maybe see a lawyer) regarding the extent a limited partner can become actively involved in a business and still retain limited liability status.*

When a business begins to fail, limited partners have been known to panic and try to intervene to save an investment that seems to be disappearing. This can be a bad mistake. If a limited partner gets too involved with the details of a floundering business, she may well be subjecting herself to unlimited liability for business debts if the business fails altogether, and is taking this risk precisely at the moment when the business is most in jeopardy. In a situation like this, proceeding without knowing your rights and responsibilities in depth is like trying to board a ship after it has hit an iceberg to try to protect the cargo.

Now it's time for the exceptions. What's a rule without exceptions? In the many states that have adopted the Revised ULPA, limited partners can engage in certain types of actions regarding ailing businesses. Authorized acts include assuming a management role or partnership position, and partnership salvage efforts generally. Also, under the Revised ULPA, limited partners can have certain rights, such as the right to vote on the election or removal of a general partner, without losing their passive investor status. Essentially, under the Revised ULPA, limited partners have rights similar to the minimum rights of voting shareholders in a corporation. (A few states—such as Nevada, Oregon and Washington—permit the limited partners to have the power to vote to remove the general partners in certain circumstances; most states generally don't allow this. Also, the Revised ULPA does permit the limited partners to participate in certain specified ways in management of the partnership business. As a practical matter, no small business owners we know of would become involved in limited partnerships if they thought they could wind up being expelled from their own businesses.)

To retain limited liability status for the limited partners, the limited partnership must be on the level: Attempts at manipulation, chicanery and other nefarious practices (often involving a "dummy" as a general partner, perhaps one person with no assets, while the limited partners have substantial wealth) can also cause a court to decide that so-called limited partners are legally general partners. However, as we've noted, almost all states permit a corporation—which itself creates limited liability for its owners—to be the general partner of a limited partnership. The corporate general partner of a limited partnership must be a bona fide corporation, which mostly means it must have sufficient cash (called adequate capitalization) to operate the business. If the corporation is a dummy—a shell, or a legal entity created without sufficient cash in order to protect the limited partners—these limited partners will lose the basic legal protection normally granted them, limited liability.

1. Contributions by Limited Partners

In many small business situations, the limited partners contribute a set amount of cash, all at once. This is what the owner, the general partner, generally needs. But this isn't the only way limited partners can make contributions. Sometimes, some limited partners contribute property. Or, the limited partners may make contributions over a set time period—so much down, and so much a month, or whatever time period the partners agree on. In this case, the limited partners generally each sign a promissory note, pledging to contribute a stated amount over a set time period. This note can then

often be used as collateral, by the general partner, to borrow money from a bank.

Our point here is simply to alert you that you can work out whatever contribution plan works best for all of you—the general partner and the limited partners. You're not stuck with one contribution method. One warning, though: Some limited partnership agreements authorize the general partner to require mandatory additional contributions from the limited partners, if at some future time the general partner decides the business needs more cash. Personally, we'd never agree to a deal where we might be stuck with putting up more money than we initially decided to. It could be that as the business got shaky, and you regretted putting any money into it, you'd be required to put in even more. A bad deal.

2. Transfer of Limited Partnership Interest

The ULPA provides that a limited partner may assign or transfer his or her interest in a limited partnership to third parties. (ULPA Section 9.) This is one legal provision that the partners can vary to some extent by agreement. And indeed, often the limited partnership agreement between the business (the general partner) and the limited partners does restrict transfer of the limited partners' interests. Because many owners of small businesses want to be sure they'll know who they'll be dealing with, they restrict the transfer of limited partnership interests to the extent possible. However, the ULPA doesn't permit a flat prohibition against any transfer of limited partnership interests. Instead, it provides that:

- The limited partnership interest is transferable if all the members of the partnership agree to this, or if the limited partnership agreement (or certificate) so provides. The person who receives the (former) limited partner's interest is called a substituted limited partner and acquires all the rights of any other limited partner.

• A third party can receive a former or substituted limited partner's interest, even if free transferability is not allowed under the limited partnership agreement. However, in this situation, the third party doesn't become a substituted limited partner. He only acquires a set financial interest in the partnership business, and he may only receive the return or profits the former limited partner was entitled to. He is not entitled to an accounting or any of the other inspection rights of full-fledged limited partners. (ULPA Section 9.)

3. Other Points About the Basic Nature of a Limited Partnership

As we've said, although we don't provide all the information you may need to prepare a valid limited partnership, we do want to give you enough so you'll at least have a sound overview of what is typically involved. This should be a big help if you talk to a lawyer about preparing one. Following are

a few more points about how a limited partnership works.

• As noted, it's vital that you understand that limited partnerships are legally regarded as investments, or securities, and are thus regulated by state and sometimes federal securities law, which attempts to curtail investment fraud. Check the materials on securities law in Section C of this chapter carefully. In garden-variety, small-business limited partnerships, you'll probably discover there's no serious risk you'll run afoul of the securities laws. However, if you have any doubt whether your deal does comply with the requirements of the securities laws, make sure you check with a knowledgeable lawyer. Mistakes here can be very costly. In this area, an ounce of prevention is worth many pounds of cure.

• The surname of a limited partner shouldn't be used in the partnership name, "unless it's also the name of a general partner, or unless the business had been carried on under a name in which the limited partner's surname ap-

peared, prior to the time when the limited partner become involved." (ULPA Section 5(b),(c).)

> **EXAMPLE:** If Herbert Crumb becomes a limited partner in the partnership of Cookie and Cake, it would be improper (as well as ridiculous) to change the partnership name to Cookie, Cake, and Crumb. However, if this was already the name of the partnership, because Herbert's uncle, Philip Crumb, was already a general partner, it would be proper for Herbert to join as a limited partner.

- Normally, limited partners don't become personally involved in lawsuits brought by, or against, the partnership (other than those suits brought by the limited partners themselves against the partnership).
- In any limited partnership, it's wise to provide for continuity of the business in case the one general partner dies, withdraws, etc. The partnership isn't dissolved if a limited partner withdraws, dies, goes bankrupt, etc., but unless the agreement provides otherwise, usually it is dissolved if a general partner withdraws, goes bankrupt or dies.
- Limited partnerships doing business in more than one state have to register in each state in which they do business.
- Limited partnerships can end by:
  - expiration of the terms set forth in the certificate of registration and limited partnership agreement. This method of ending a limited partnership is the wisest because everyone is clear as to what it involves from the start.
  - unanimous agreement of all the members of the limited partnership.
  - changing any of the matters set forth in the registration statement (that is, any change in the partnership requires a new registration statement).
  - judicial decree.

History Lesson # 8

The first American statute authorizing limited partnerships was adopted in New York in 1822. In those days, judges didn't like limited partnerships (we're not sure why), so the statutes were "strictly construed," and limited partnership status denied for trivial technical flaws, especially in registration statements. Eventually, this judicial hostility abated, especially after the promulgation of the Uniform Limited Partnership Act, which was first proposed in 1916. The ULPA was based on the traditional capitalistic notion that a willing investor should be able to put money in a limited partnership and depend upon others for "investment skills" without incurring personal liability in the process. In recent years, limited partnerships have become very widely used.

B. The Relationship Between the General Partner and the Limited Partners

Since limited partners are essentially passive investors, they must rely on the general partner to run a profitable and honest business. In theory, limited partners have the right to sell their limited partnership interest on the open market to whomever will buy it. In reality, however, there is often no available market, particularly if the business isn't making money or there have been conflicts with the general partner. The limited partners do have some legal rights with respect to the business and the general partner—they can file a lawsuit and demand a formal accounting or can bring allegations that the general partner violated his or her fiduciary duty (see Section B2). But a lawsuit is usually a disastrous business. A limited partner can easily eat up an amount equal to her investment in legal fees long before the matter comes to trial. Aside from that, lawsuits are emotionally draining. The truth is that the general partner controls the business and makes the decisions, and if a limited partner becomes disgruntled with that general partner, she has few effective remedies to protect herself. So, in any limited partnership, it's vital that the limited partners have a good working relationship with the general partner. If the limited partners' return is geared to the profits of the business, they'll want to know that the general partnership's books honestly reflect the operations of the business, particularly in the kinds of enterprises, such as bars or restaurants, in which skimming of cash has been known to occur.

1. Return to the Limited Partners

The return the general partner promises the limited partners on their investment is the key to the deal. As we've said, this return is defined in the limited partnership agreement. These terms can vary widely—from a flat percentage return on the investment, which is the equivalent of interest, to a percentage of gross income, to a percentage of the profits, or any combination. Likewise, the time span of the investment is determined by the agreement. Sometimes limited partners get their return for a set period of time, while in other situations their return continues until a certain dollar figure is reached. We know of some limited partnerships in which the limited partners get a share of the business in perpetuity, but we don't normally recommend this sort of arrangement. From the general partner's point of view (especially if the business is enormously successful), that's usually giving away too much.

From a limited partner's point of view, there can be problems with defining return based on the profits of the business. Since, by definition, the general partner has lots of authority to run the business, she is often in a position to make decisions that have the effect of substantially raising or lowering profits (for example, the decision to write down inventory can often be put off or moved up, with a major effect on profits). Also, if the general partner hires

friends or family members, or pays herself a generous management salary, it can wipe out profits. In short, many investors in a limited partnership would be wise to insist on a reasonable fixed return, in addition to a share of profits. Or, the rate of return can be geared to or based on gross income, which is less subject to manipulation (short of outright fraud) than are net profits.

We recommend two general principles regarding the return to limited partners to friends seeking to raise money by this method. First, be sure that the limited partners get a fair return on their investment. If in doubt, err a tad on the side of generosity. You don't want to lose your friends or suffer the headaches involved in dealing with frustrated limited partners who feel that they've been cheated. Second, be sure that once the limited partners have received a good return on their investment (however you define that), they're either automatically bought out, have their original investment returned or are somehow foreclosed from future participation in the business. This is particularly important if your business becomes very successful. In one real life situation we know of, four friends started a restaurant in San Francisco. They were all equal general partners. To raise some of the capital they needed at the beginning, they sold nine limited partnerships to friends of theirs. At that point, the limited partners worried only about the consequences of failure, so they demanded that the general partner (the four members of the restaurant partnership) be personally liable to them if their investments were lost. Everyone was so nervous about the new venture that nobody thought much about what would happen if the restaurant was a smashing success. The only provision about profits gave each limited partner a 10% yearly return on his or her investment, plus 1% of the restaurant's net profits. There was no buy-out clause or other provision limiting the term of the limited partners' investments.

Perhaps you can guess the rest of the story. The restaurant almost instantly became (and still is) one of the most popular and successful in San Francisco. People make reservations months in advance and delight in the wonderful food. Very quickly, the limited partners recovered their entire investment, made a good profit and had the prospect of a bonanza. The four members of the partnership realized that they had made a serious mistake. They had given away almost 10% of their total profits, forever, for an investment that, in hindsight, seemed very modest. Fortunately, this story has a happy ending. The limited partners—who were friends, after all—agreed it wasn't fair that they gain a lifetime interest in the business for their small investment. So the four members of the partnership (the general partners) were able to negotiate a fair buy-out, even though they had no legal basis to compel one.

General Partners Should Meet With Potential Investors

We think members of small partnerships seeking to raise money by selling limited partnership interests in their business should personally meet with all potential investors—who will likely be friends and family. Discuss possible options regarding limited partners' return and duration of the agreement, and try to arrive at mutually acceptable terms. If you can't, don't make the deal with those people. With a larger limited partnership, the terms are usually fixed at the start and the deal is offered, take-it-or-leave-it, to potential investors. However, in our experience, this sort of procedure doesn't work well for most small businesses.

EXAMPLE: When Roseanne and Claudette began to consider selling limited partnerships in their flower business, they knew that resolving what return their investors would receive was crucial. Rather than try to decide this by themselves, they came up with a couple of proposals, either of which was acceptable to them. The first consisted of 15% interest payments for two years, with the original investment returned

at the end of the term. The second was a flat 10% of the net profits for four years, and then the original investment returned. Then they had a meeting with several friends who liked them, loved flowers and thought the business looked promising. Most of the people with whom they discussed selling the limited partnerships said they preferred fixed payments, so they selected the fixed-interest method for payment of the limited partners.

2. Legal Rights of the Limited Partners

Most state's laws provide that a limited partner does have certain defined rights in the business, such as inspection of books and the right to an accounting. Also, a limited partner normally has the right to demand full return of his contribution, in cash, on the date specified in the certificate of limited partnership (see Section D), or, if none is specified, six months after giving written notice of this demand to the other members of the limited partnership. So, for the sake of certainty, it's almost always advisable for the general partner to specify a specific date for return of limited partners' contributions.

The general partner in a limited partnership has what are called fiduciary duties to the limited partners, similar to those a member of the board of directors of a corporation has to shareholders. This means that the law holds the general partner to a special duty of trust to the limited partners and requires the general partner to protect the limited partners' interests. But the sad truth is that if a general partner acts adversely to the limited partners interests, all they can do is protest, and then sue. As we've repeatedly warned you throughout this book, getting involved in a lawsuit means you're enmeshed in a financial and emotional nightmare.

Anyone contemplating an investment in a limited partnership should understand that they are, in terms of the real world of power, in a very weak position relative to the general partner. If you don't trust the general partner, don't do the deal. It's that simple.

3. Competition by a Limited Partner

Unless the limited partnership agreement or certificate prohibits it, a limited partner can legally engage in competition with the partnership business—and in fact, this frequently happens, especially in real estate. Also, a limited partner legally can do business with the partnership—loaning it money or purchasing its products or services. However, there are certain activities that limited partners can't engage in. Under the ULPA, a limited partner cannot:

- receive or hold as collateral or security any property of the partnership, or
- receive from a general partner, or the partnership, any money payment or release of liability, if at that time the partnership assets are insufficient to pay partnership debts (to outsiders other than general or limited partners) (ULPA Section 13).

4. Potential Conflicts of Interest When Preparing a Limited Partnership Agreement

Clearly, in any limited partnership, there is potential for serious conflict of interest between the general partner and the limited partners. Even if everyone starts as friends, tensions can surely develop if the business begins losing money. One tension can be—is it really losing money? The limited partners can wonder if the figures they are receiving from the general partner are truthful. Or, if the limited partners' return is geared to profit, the reverse can be a problem. The general partner and the books say there's no profit. But is this really true? How come the members of the general partnership buy new cars every year? What about those family members the general partner put on the payroll? Sadly, we could give quite a few examples of situations where the limited partners and the general partner were at odds. As we've warned you, the limited partners have very little real world power in conflicts with the general partner.

Does this mean that each group—the general partner and the limited partners—must hire its own lawyer when drafting the limited partnership agreement? We discuss lawyers in Chapter 10, Section A. Here we'll simply note that while a conventional lawyer would advise you that each group must always hire its own lawyer, we won't be so rigid. We urge you to recognize in advance that a possibility of conflict exists. Explore that possibility as thoroughly as possible. If you all feel you can trust each other, and the terms of the limited partnership agreement are clear and spelled out, it may be a waste of money to hire two lawyers. But if anyone feels at all uncomfortable with having only one lawyer—usually, the general partner's lawyer—hire another one. Better a second lawyer's fee now than a lawsuit later.

C. Securities Aspects of Limited Partnerships

A limited partnership is primarily a money-raising method, a way of investing in a business without forming a corporation and issuing stock. As such, a limited partnership interest is legally a "security." A security is conventionally defined as an investment in a business enterprise managed by others, in which the investor's expectation of return depends primarily on the effort of others. The most common form of a security is shares of stock issued by a corporation. However, there are numerous other types of securities. Most of these, including limited partnerships, are subject to federal and state laws that regulate the sale of any security.

1. Federal Regulation

The sale of securities has, historically, been an area fraught with fraud and chicanery. Swindlers and con men have sold securities in all sorts of worthless or nonexistent businesses to the gullible and greedy.

As a result, the sale of securities is governed by strict regulations. A series of federal laws, including the Securities Act of 1933, the Securities and Exchange Act of 1934, the Investment Advisors Act of 1940 and others, put the sale of many securities under supervision of the Securities and Exchange Commission (SEC) and other federal regulatory agencies. In addition, the states have passed their own securities laws, usually referred to as "blue-sky" laws, which also control the sale of securities in each state.

Complying with federal securities laws is a real hassle, not to mention very expensive. It often requires that immense amounts of paperwork be filed by those who are selling the securities. The drafting of SEC security prospectuses has become a major, and quite lucrative, lawyers' industry. Also, those businessmen involved in selling securities covered under federal law usually have to register with the SEC as broker-dealers. Any small business forming a limited partnership wants to avoid having to comply with these federal laws. Small partnerships surely don't need to deal with the paperwork meant to inhibit million-dollar frauds. Happily, you won't normally have to bother with these laws if you keep things small. The federal securities laws are designed to apply to big guys and big deals. These laws provide two exceptions from their coverage which apply to almost all small-business limited partnerships. As you read on, you'll probably conclude that any limited partnership you're considering will be exempt from the federal securities laws.

History Lesson #9

You might think that the term "blue sky" is a strange way to describe state securities laws. Popular wisdom attributes the name to a judge from the early 1900s who noted that people should be protected from putting their money into speculative investments that had "as much value as a patch of blue sky."

⚠️ **Don't assume you're exempt from complying with securities laws.** *If you believe there's any possibility that federal securities laws could apply to what you're planning, you'd better hire a securities lawyer. And get ready to spend a pile of money.*

2. Limited Partnership Exemptions From Federal Securities Regulations

You will not have to register your limited partnership interests under federal securities laws if you qualify under either of these exemptions (neither exception applies if there is any fraud involved):

1. **Intrastate offerings are not subject to the federal securities law.** Intrastate offerings are those that are offered and sold only in the state where the limited partnership was formed and the registration certificate filed. If you're relying on this exception, be sure you know the source of the funds used to buy each limited partnership. If Frank gets the money he used to buy a limited partnership from his Uncle Jason living in another state, this could be sufficient to make it an interstate (that is, more than one state) transaction—thus subject to federal securities laws.

2. **Private offerings are not subject to federal securities laws.** A private offering is more restricted than the sale of securities to the general public, which is called a public offering. There's no one simple test for determining what qualifies as a private offering. SEC Rule 146 supposedly makes the test more objective—but not a whole lot more. Several factors are involved (*SEC v. Ralston Purina Co.*, 346 U.S. 119 (1953)):

   • The people offered the security ("offerees" in legalese) must be kept to a minimum. State law, not federal law, defines the precise number of offerees or sales allowed in a private offering. You must be able to identify each offeree. If you're dealing with 35 or fewer buyers, you're usually safe regarding the number of people involved in most states. If you're dealing with ten or fewer, you're safe in all states. If you're raising money from more than ten investors, you should realize you're about to get involved in a fairly complicated transaction; be sure you want to do it.

State law may impose other requirements that must be met for a sale to qualify as a valid private offering. For example, in California a lawyer must sign a notice form stating that, in her opinion, the sale complies with all private sale requirements. These additional rules can vary widely. You'll need to review them in each state where you'll sell limited partnerships. (By definition, there will be at least two; if there was only one state involved, you'd be exempt from federal law under the all-in-one state exemption.)

The other factors involved in determining whether a sale of a security in more than one state is exempt from federal securities regulation are all subjective; their purpose is simple, though—to prevent sharp sellers from taking advantage of unsophisticated buyers. These other factors include:

- the relation of the investors (offerees) to each other and the seller (offeror)
- the number of units offered and the size of the offering
- the manner of the offering
- the sophistication of the investors, and
- the investors' access to financial and other information about the partnership and its business.

All of this may seem rather vague. What does it mean to you? First, if you're offering limited partnership interests only to buyers in one state, you don't have to worry about federal laws, period.

Second, if you intend to sell limited partnership interests to people living in more than one state, be sure that sale qualifies under federal law as a private offering. This means you must comply with each involved state's securities laws regarding private sales.

When it comes to the subjective elements required by federal law to qualify as a valid private offering, the only safe course is honesty. General partners should fully and completely disclose all significant facts about the business—including its risks—to all prospective purchasers of limited partnerships. In big-money private offerings, this often requires a bulky document, prepared by securities lawyers, full of disclaimers, figures and legalese. Frankly, if two partners are planning to raise money from their friends, we don't believe a formal disclosure full of technical language is necessary or helpful. (If you're engaged in a rather complicated and expensive transaction, you may need to prepare, or have prepared, a full disclosure memorandum, which usually isn't too different from what is required for full SEC registration.) Put your assessment of the basic risks you foresee into a simple written document that explains, in common sense terms, the ways "we could go belly up." Give that letter to all prospective buyers. But remember that you can't foresee every danger. Honesty isn't clairvoyance. If you think there's a chance that a limited partner might become quite angry no matter what goes wrong, and claim he was cheated and had no inkling such things were possible, don't sell to him.

EXAMPLE: Let's return to Je'rod and Ira and their limited partnership honey business that we discussed in the beginning of this chapter. They might write the four limited partners a letter such as the following before finalizing the deal:

_____ (Date)

Dear _____,

We're pleased that you're planning to invest $15,000 in Fatbee, our partnership honey business, in exchange for a limited partnership interest. In this connection, we thought that it would be appropriate to review the prospects for our business in writing. We've operated Fatbee as a general partnership for four years and have made a substantial profit on a relatively small investment. We believe that expansion and equipment modernization will produce greater profits.

However, we do want to emphasize that there is risk involved in the honey business. Bad weather and disease can affect our little flying workers, and our prices are dependent on national and international factors beyond our control. In addition, a new type of "killer bee" has entered the United States via Mexico. While it seems unlikely that it will penetrate as far as Oregon in the next generation, it's not impossible that this could occur. If it does, and the killer bees invade our hives, the yield of honey from our hives may decrease, since the killer bees are not only aggressive, they produce only about 25% of the honey produced by the variety we currently raise.

As attachments to this letter, we enclose the general partnership agreement between ourselves; the proposed limited partnership agreement (which will also function as our registration certificate and will be filed with the secretary of state's office); and our partnership tax returns for the last three years.

If you have any questions, please give either of us a call. We're looking forward to pleasant (and hopefully profitable) business relations.

Sincerely,

Je'rod Sweet

Ira Clover

3. State Regulations

A state's laws governing the sale of securities in that state are often almost as detailed and burdensome as federal laws. In other words, even if you have to comply only with state securities laws, you'll have to do considerable self-education or pay substantial lawyers' fees. Fortunately, state securities laws also exempt private offerings from their requirements. Generally, if you're offering limited partnership shares to 35 or fewer people in your state (ten in a few states), and don't do it often, you'll have little to worry about. Since we recommend you hire a lawyer in each state where you'll sell limited partnership interests, one of that lawyer's tasks is to be sure you've complied with that state's rules for private offerings.

As we've said, state securities, or blue sky laws, vary considerably with regard to exemptions for private limited partnership offerings. In many states the offer and sale to a limited number of persons during a specified period is exempt. In some states, the exemption is based on the number of offers made within a 12-month period. In other states, the limitation is based on the number of sales, not offerees. In some other states, the numerical test isn't applied to all offers, but only to offers to residents of that state and so on. Also, different requirements may apply to different types of securities. For example, in New York, a "syndication for interests" (through limited partnerships) is subject to special registration rules.

D. Certificate of Limited Partnership

As we've told you, a limited partnership must complete and file a certificate of limited partnership, in some states called a "Registration Statement," with a government agency, such as the Secretary of State or Corporations Commissioner, in the state where it does business. Whatever it is called, this document must contain required information about the composition of the limited partnership. In some states, the information is very detailed; in other states, only some basic facts must be listed. If a limited partnership does business in more than one state, it must

file a certificate in each state where it transacts business.

The primary purpose of the certificate is to protect creditors of the limited partnership by giving them information that allows them to better assess the risks involved in the partnership business. It also protects potential limited partners, because it reveals to them the composition of the business and allows state authorities to examine the situation to see if fraud seems likely.

Many states, such as California, have a specific certificate form you must use. (You can download California limited partnership forms directly from the Secretary of State website, www.ss.ca.gov/business/business.htm, or you can get them by writing California Secretary of State, Limited Partnership Unit, P.O. Box 944225, Sacramento, CA 94244-2250.) In other states, there's no set governmental form for the certificate. In a number of states, the certificate must be filed with the Secretary of State. However, that's not always true. Each state decides where the certificate must be filed. Also, in some states, a certificate must be filed in more than one place. For example, in Connecticut, it must be filed both with the corporate division of the Secretary of State and the local town clerk. In other states, the certificate must also be published in a local legal paper. To determine where you have to file in your state, you'll need to contact your Secretary of State, Corporations Commissioner or a knowledgeable lawyer. This agency will always have an office in your state capital and may have regional offices in major cities. Names for the appropriate government agency vary somewhat from state to state. If you have any trouble finding the correct one, find out where incorporation papers are filed. Limited partnership certificates are normally filed at the same location. If this is not the case, the staff will be able to direct you to the correct agency office.

The fees charged by the state agency for filing the certificate vary from state to state. In a number of states, they are substantial. For example, in California the fee is $70, plus an $800 franchise tax payment.

1. Basic Requirements of the Certificate

Some states, like California, require only a minimum of basic information to be provided in the certificate:

- name of the limited partnership (California requires that the name of the limited partnership end with "…a California Limited Partnership"; this requirement is fairly typical)
- names and addresses of all general partners
- number of general partners required to amend the certificate
- name and address of the agent for service of process (legal papers), and
- term or duration of the limited partnership.

Other states require a more detailed certificate. All of the above information must be listed, and also all or most of the following:

- brief description of the character or purpose of the business
- location of the principal place of business
- names and resident addresses of all limited partners
- amount of cash, and a summary description of and the agreed value of any other property, contributed by each limited partner
- additional contributions that must be made by limited partners, including the time of contribution and any conditions placed on it
- details of any agreements to return limited partners' investments
- arrangements for profit-sharing, compensation or other means of return to the limited partners
- how (and if) limited partners can substitute others in their place (that is, transfer provisions)
- rights, if any, of general partners to admit new limited partners
- how profits will be distributed, and who has priority
- right, if any, of a general partner to continue the partnership business upon the withdrawal, retirement or death of another general partner

- date of the expected dissolution of the general partnership (if planned) or expiration of any limited partnership interest, and
- right, if any, of any limited partner to demand and receive back, his initial contribution.

2. Complying With Certificate Requirements

If a state has a mandatory certificate form, as most do, you must use it. States that have no mandatory form still require certain information to be listed. In those states, you have two options:

1. You can create and file your own certificate form containing all the information required, or
2. You can have the limited partnership agreement also function as the certificate form. In that case, be sure that the agreement contains all of the information required by state law.

3. Amendments to the Certificate

You must keep your certificate up-to-date. You do this by amending the certificate when any information required by law has changed. Normally, any amendment must state where the original certificate was recorded and what changes have been made in that certificate, and it must be personally signed by all partners. However, the limited partners can authorize the general partners to sign for them by duly executing a legally valid power of attorney for this purpose.

In many states, amendments to the certificate are required if any of the following changes occur:

- partnership name is changed
- amount or character of any of the limited partners' contribution changes
- new limited partner is added or substituted

- general partner retires, dies, becomes insane or withdraws and the partnership business is continued
- character of the partnership business is changed
- time date for dissolution of the limited partnership, or return of a partnership contribution, is changed, or
- limited partners receive voting rights over management of the partnership business.

E. Tax Aspects of Limited Partnerships

Here we provide you with the most basic information about the tax aspects of limited partnerships. If you want more sophisticated information or maneuvers, you'll have to see a tax expert.

A limited partnership itself isn't subject to federal income tax. The overall entity must file an informational partnership tax return. If the general partner is a partnership, the partnership can file one single informational tax return for both the general and limited partnership.

1. Income Received by the Limited Partners

Income from a limited partnership received by general or limited partners must be reported on their individual return. Income or losses to the general partner(s) is generally active income. Income or losses received by limited partners is passive or investment income. As previously explained (see Chapter 7, Section I), passive or investment income received by the limited partners must, for IRS purposes, be treated separately from all active income.

2. Corporate Look-Alikes

As we've noted, limited partnerships are similar to corporations in the sense that investors gain limited liability status. However, if a limited partnership becomes too much like a corporation, there's a real danger that the IRS will determine that the entity really is a corporation, and tax it accordingly. This isn't desirable because it means that investors in the so-called limited partnership will find that the venture's corporate profits are taxed twice—both at the corporate and personal level—not passed through, as a partnership's would be. This isn't something you have to worry about if you're a typical small business—a relatively simple enterprise with just a few general partners raising operating money by selling limited partnership interests in the business. However, in a more complicated limited partnership transaction, the question of whether the business is really a corporation for tax purposes can become troublesome.

> **EXAMPLE:** Suppose several partners have created a successful business manufacturing leather purses. Now there are eight factories, a management committee and complicated partnership provisions designed to ensure that the business continues, no matter what happens to any individual partner or partners. To raise substantial amounts of money, limited partnership interests are sold to 25 wealthy investors. Is this, in reality, a corporate transaction? It might be held to be one. The IRS is likely to examine complex limited partnerships such as this one to see if the traditional attributes of a corporation are present.

The taxation of limited partnerships as corporations can become exceedingly complex. However, these complexities will apply to so few of our readers that it doesn't make sense to give you more detail here. The IRS will issue advance rulings on whether a limited partnership will be recognized as such for income tax purposes. If your limited partnership becomes a complicated business matter, it's wise to be sure, in advance, that there will be no trouble with the IRS. Discuss this matter with your accountant or lawyer in detail.

F. Limited Partnership Agreements

In this section we present a sample limited partnership agreement. This agreement assumes there's already a separate partnership agreement between members of the partnership which is the general partner. (This kind of agreement, of course, is the type covered in the bulk of this book.)

Finally, in Section 2, we provide additional clauses you can use, or adapt as you wish, in your draft legal partnership agreement.

1. Sample Limited Partnership Agreement

This is a sample agreement only. *It should not be relied on to prepare a final limited partnership agreement. The purpose of this sample agreement is to aid you to understand what you might want to cover in your limited partnership agreement, and to prepare a rough draft of that agreement. You must see a lawyer before preparing a final version of any limited partnership agreement.*

SAMPLE LIMITED PARTNERSHIP AGREEMENT

AGREEMENT OF LIMITED PARTNERSHIP OF

[partnership business name]

By this Agreement the signers form a limited partnership under the laws of the State of _____, as of _____ *[date]* _____, and agree to the following terms and conditions:

1. Members

The general partners are _____, _____,
_____, _____, *[etc.]*

The limited partners are _____, _____,
_____, _____, *[etc.]*

[You might want to list the limited partners in an attached Exhibit A, if they might change with some frequency.]

2. Place of Business

The partnership's principal place of business shall be at _____.

[If you want to be cautious, add "or such other place as the general partners determine in the future."]

3. Purpose

The purpose and character of the business of this limited partnership are _____
_____.

[Give a summary description.]

4. Term

[Be sure you coordinate this with Paragraph 7(b) on Return on Contribution.]

This partnership begins on the date of this Agreement and shall continue until _____, 20___, at which time it shall dissolve, as under the terms provided here, and the contributions of the limited partners shall be returned.

[As we discussed in Section B, usually it's wise to limit the duration of a limited partnership to a set time. If you do adopt another approach, you can substitute for the above "shall continue indefinitely," or "shall continue indefinitely, subject to the buy-out provisions of this Agreement," etc. If you do so, be sure to specify a date for the return of the limited partners' contributions.]

5. Formalities

    a. The general partners shall do what is needed to:
        1. Record a certificate of limited partnership.

2. Record a fictitious business name statement.

3. Deliver to each limited partner within _____ days of the close of the fiscal year the financial report of the partnership's activities for that year prepared under Section 6(C).

[You may add as many specific provisions here as you want. Our preference is to keep them to a minimum.]

b. Power of Attorney

Each limited partner grants each general partner a limited power of attorney, with the power to execute, acknowledge, and file any of the following documents in his or her name:

1. The original and any amendment to the certificate of limited partnership, and any other instruments that may need to be recorded or filed by the partnership.

2. All documents that may be required in the event that the partnership is terminated.

3. A fictitious business name statement.

6. Accounting and Records

a. The partnership shall use the _____*[cash, or accrual]*_____ method of accounting.

b. At all times during the duration of this limited partnership, the general partners shall keep books of accounts in which each partnership transaction shall be fully and accurately entered. These books of account shall be kept at the partnership's principal office and shall be available during reasonable business hours for inspection and examination by any limited partner or representative, who shall have the right to make copies of any of those books at his or her own expense.

c. At the close of each fiscal year, the general partners shall hire an accountant to prepare a financial statement, including net profit or loss, for that year, which shall be delivered to each limited partner.

7. Contributions and Return of Limited Partners' Capital

a. Contributions

Each limited partner shall initially contribute to the partnership, as capital, cash or property with an agreed-upon value as follows:

[Name] _____ : *[Cash/$]* _____

[also describe any other contribution with an agreed $ value]
[Total Contribution] _____

[Name] _____ : *[Cash/$]* _____

[also describe any other contribution with an agreed $ _____ value]
[Total Contribution] _____

[Name] _____ : *[Cash/$]* _____

[also describe any other contribution with an agreed $ _____ value]
[Total Contribution] _____

[Name] _____ : *[Cash/$]* _____

[also describe any other contribution with an agreed $ _____ value]
[Total Contribution] _____

  b. The capital contributed by each limited partner shall be returned to _*[him/her]*_ on _*[list a*_
      _specific date, or you can state "date of partnership dissolution"]* .

(As we've noted, in most states, if the limited partnership agreement and certificate don't specify a time for the return of a limited partner's contribution, he may demand its return six months after he gives written notice to all partners. This is normally undesirable, so you'll want to be specific. By using a specific date or the "date of partnership dissolution" (assuming that has a set date), you're in effect saying that the limited partner will receive the return of his capital after a set time.

If the limited partner doesn't get a fixed return, but a share of profits or losses, his initial contribution may have diminished by the return date, so you can substitute:

"The capital account of the limited partners shall be returned to them on _*[dissolution date]*_ ."

Further, in case property has been contributed, you may want to state that only the cash value of that property, or its current worth in the capital account, will be returned.)

  c. Capital Accounts

      An individual capital account shall be maintained for each partner. Each partner's capital account shall consist of his or her original capital contribution increased by any additional capital contributions, and decreased by distributions in reduction of partnership capital and his or her share of partnership losses, and other gains or losses attributed to the capital account.

8. Returns to Limited Partners

[The following is for a situation in which the limited partners' returns are geared to the profits— or losses—of the business.]

During the term of the partnership, the partnership's annual net profits and losses shall be determined by an accountant using the accounting procedures used on the partnership tax return filed. Each limited partner shall then receive the percentage of profits specified below, if the business has been profitable for that year:

Name   Return

_____ _____%

_____ _____ %

_____ _____ %

_____ _____ %

If the limited partners are due a return based on the yearly profits, that payment shall be made within
_____ days of the close of the fiscal year.

_[This is the crucial provision and, as you'd expect, can be arranged in innumerable ways. There
could be quarterly payments, for example. Or the return could be fixed at 15% yearly interest on
the capital contributions. Again, it's not really the drafting here that can be hard—it's working
out between all the general and limited partners a mutually acceptable method and rate of
return.]_

9. Management

   a. The partnership business shall be managed by the general partners. Limited partners shall have
no right to take part in the management of the partnership or to transact any business on its
behalf.

   b. The limited partners, either individually or collectively, may participate in other business
ventures of every kind, whether or not those other business ventures compete with the
partnership.

10. Assignments

_[As we discussed earlier, you can't totally prohibit transfer or assignment of a limited partner's
interest to another party. You can restrict that right, though, so that the person buying that interest doesn't have the full right of regular limited partners. We present sample clauses covering this
below.]_

Option A. _[If you want free transferability, this does it.]_

A limited partner's partnership interest is freely assignable, and the assignee [i.e, the buyer] shall become
a substituted limited partner, effective when the appropriate amendment to the certificate of limited
partnership is made.

Option B. _[Restricted transferability.]_

A limited partner's partnership interest shall not be assignable without the written consent of _[for example,
all general partners, all general and limited partners, etc.]_ .

If any limited partner shall assign his or her interest without receiving the consent of the general partners,
his or her assignee shall have no right to an accounting of partnership transactions or to inspect the
partnership books. On giving notice of the assignment to the general partners, the assignee [that is,
buyer] shall be entitled to receive only a return of the assignor's contribution to capital and the share of

profit to which the assignor would have been entitled, diminished by the assignor's share of losses, if any.

11. Withdrawals of Partners, Dissolution and Termination

Events Not Causing Dissolution:

Dissolution shall not be caused by the (a) death or disability of a limited partner, (b) withdrawal or expulsion of a limited partner, (c) admission of a new limited partner.

12. Arbitration Clause

[Include an arbitration clause.]
The parties of this limited partnership agreement have all executed it below, effective as of the day and year written there.

[Typed names go below signature lines.]

Signatures of General Partners   Residence Addresses of General Partners

_____   _____

_____   _____

_____   _____

Signatures of Limited Partners   Residence Addresses of Limited Partners

_____   _____

_____   _____

_____   _____

2. Additional Clauses for Limited Partnership Agreements

Limited partnership agreements can be every bit as complex, and indeed more so, as general partnership agreements. Clauses used for general partnership agreements can be used or adapted to limited partnership agreements. Also, below we've included some additional clauses specifically geared to limited partnership situations. However, they're not included on the forms disk; instead, you'll have to add them to your agreement yourself.

COMPOSITION OF THE PARTNERSHIP

General Partners

Departure Causes Dissolution

☐ On the death, insanity or withdrawal of the general partner, the partnership shall dissolve. It shall thereafter conduct only those actions necessary to wind up its affairs.

Departure Does Not Cause Dissolution

☐ On the death or insanity of a general partner, the partnership business shall be continued by the remaining general partners. The executive guardian, or other successor to the partnership interest of the general partner, shall be a limited partner.

Transfers by General Partners Prohibited

☐ The general partner shall not assign, pledge, encumber, sell or otherwise dispose of all or any part of his or her interest as a general partner in the partnership.

Transfers by Limited Partners

Written Transfer Required

☐ A limited partner may sell, assign or transfer only his or her entire partnership interest and only by a written document acceptable in form to the general partners; a copy of that document shall be delivered at the partnership's principal place of business before the transfer can become effective.

Right of First Refusal

☐ If a limited partner desires to sell or exchange his or her partnership interest, he or she shall give written notice to the partnership. The notice shall set forth the purchaser's name, the terms on which the interest is to be sold or exchanged and the price. For ___ days after the notice is given, the partnership shall have the right to purchase the partner's entire interest for the price and on the terms stated in the notice.

Substituted Limited Partners

☐ The purchaser of a limited partner's interest shall become a substituted limited partner. The substitution shall become effective when the appropriate amendment of the certificate of partnership is recorded. In the absence of such a designation, he or she shall be entitled to receive only the share of profits or other compensation by way of income and the return of capital contribution to which his or her assignor would have been entitled.

Contributions and Profits/Losses

Failure to Make Contributions: Partnership Can Purchase Limited Partners' Interest

☐ If, within the time provided, any limited partner fails to make a required contribution, the partnership may, within a period of ___ days after the contribution was due, purchase the defaulting partner's partnership interest at a price equal to the balance in the partner's capital account as of the end of the time the capital contribution was due.

If Partnership Elects Not to Purchase Interest

☐ If the defaulting limited partner's interest is not purchased by the partnership or other limited partners, the defaulting partner shall not withdraw, but shall retain his or her partnership interest. The interest of all the partners in the partnership's profits and losses shall be adjusted to reflect the changes in capital contributed by all partners.

Other Partners Can Make Up Contribution

☐ If, within the time provided, any partner or partners fail to make a required capital contribution, the interest of each partner in profits and losses shall be adjusted accordingly. The general partners shall notify each partner in writing of the total amount of contributions not made, and within ___ days, each other partner who wishes to do so may make a capital contribution in an amount determined by the general partners.

Loans

☐ If any limited partner shall, with the general partners' prior consent, make any loan to the partnership or advance money on its behalf, the loan or advance shall not increase the lending limited partner's capital account, nor entitle the lending partner to any greater share of partnership distributions, nor subject him or her to any greater proportion of partnership losses. The amount of the loan or advance shall be a debt owed by the partnership to the lending partner, repayable on the terms and conditions and bearing interest at the rate agreed on by the lending partner and the general partners.

Withdrawal of Capital

☐ The general partners may permit limited partners to withdraw capital at any time when, in their judgment, funds in excess of reasonable business needs are available. Any such withdrawal by limited partners shall be in the ratio of their respective capital accounts.

Return to Limited Partners

Varied Percentages, Based on Profits

☐ As return for their investment, the limited partners shall receive an aggregate of ___ percent of net partnership profits, up to total profits of $_____, then ___ percent of net profits, up to total profits of $_____, then ___ percent to net profits up to total profits of $_____. Beyond total net profits of $_____, the limited partners shall receive no further return.

Priority to Certain Limited Partners

☐ _[Names of limited partners]_ shall be entitled

to the first $_____ of net profits, if any, each year. Any net profit in excess of $_____ shall be distributed according to the limited partners' shares in partnership profits. _____*[Names]*_____ shall be credited with any amounts distributed to them under this priority.

Management Fees

Based on Net Profits

☐ If the net profits of the partnership total at least $_____ during any past fiscal year, the general partners shall be entitled to a management fee of ___ percent of those net profits, which shall be paid by of the following year.

Based on Partnership Capital

☐ Management fees shall be paid to each general partner on ___*[dates]*___ in an amount equal to ___ percent of the total partnership capital as of the close of the last fiscal year.

Many other types of compensation to general partners can be included in the agreement, including payments for:
- general management fee
- leasing commissions
- broker's commissions, and
- insurance commissions.

Liquidation

Priorities

☐ In the event of a voluntary dissolution, the partners shall continue to share profits and losses during the period of liquidation in the same proportion as before. Proceeds for the liquidation of partnership assets shall be applied according to the following priority:

1. Payment of partnership debts to creditors, other than general partners, in the priority provided by law.
2. Payments to limited partners for their share of profits.
3. Payments to limited partners for the credit balances of their capital accounts.
4. Payments to general partners for any amounts the partnership owes them other than for their share of profit or their capital accounts.
5. Payments to general partners for their share of profits.
6. Payments to general partners for the credit balances in their capital accounts.

Signature Provisions

These can eliminate burdensome signature requirements.

☐ An amendment to the certificate of limited partnership may be signed personally, or under a duly authorized power of attorney, by:

1. A general partner and the new partner if the amendment is caused by the addition of a new partner.
2. A general partner, the substituted limited partner and the assigning limited partner if the amendment is caused by the substitution of a limited partner.
3. A general partner if the amendment is caused by the retirement, death or insanity of a general partner and the partnership business is continued.

■

Lawyers and Other Professionals/ Doing Your Own Research

Will you have to deal with professionals or experts when you prepare your partnership agreement with the help of this book? How about when you run your business? As we've said before, for partnership business purposes, there are two different types of professionals who may become important to you: business lawyers and tax experts. Many people can prepare their own partnership agreement without recourse to a lawyer; others do need or want to see one. But when it comes to taxes, as we said in Chapter 7, all ongoing businesses need the services of a competent tax professional.

A. Lawyers

A lawyer—"one skilled in circumvention of the law."
—Ambrose Bierce

Can you really prepare your partnership agreement yourself? Won't you wind up having to see a lawyer? Our answer here is—it depends. Many readers will not need to see a lawyer to prepare their partnership agreement. The best proof we know of this is that in the two decades since the initial publication of this book, many thousands of people have actually used this book and created effective partnerships, without recourse to a lawyer. On the other hand, other readers who have had more complicated situations, or simply wanted to have their work checked, have consulted lawyers.

If your business arrangement is relatively straightforward, and you feel confident all partners trust each other and are confident that you've discussed and covered the basic problems in your partnership agreement, why pay lawyers' fees merely to get an authority figure's stamp of approval? But if your partnership involves more than normal complexities, whether financial, personal or both, seeing an attorney—or other expert, if appropriate—can be very sensible. Certainly, there are situations in which an experienced lawyer

Hiring a Lawyer to Review Your Draft Agreement

To partners, having a lawyer review your draft partnership agreement often sounds like a good idea. It shouldn't cost much, and seems to offer a comforting security. But there can be a serious catch to hiring a lawyer solely to review a partnership agreement you've prepared. Sadly, it may be difficult or even impossible to find a lawyer who is willing to accept the job. While this is unfortunate, we're not willing to excoriate lawyers who won't review a do-it-yourself partnership agreement. From their point of view, they are being asked to accept what can turn into a significant responsibility for what they regard as inadequate compensation, given their usual fees. Any prudent lawyer sees every client as a potential occasion for a malpractice claim or, at least, serious later hassles—the call four years later that begins, "We talked to you about our partnership agreement and now…" So, many—indeed most—experienced lawyers want to make sure they avoid this kind of exposure and risk, unless they are getting paid enough to make it worthwhile. Also, many lawyers feel that they simply don't get deeply enough into a situation if they're only reviewing someone else's work to be sure of their opinions. So where does this leave you if you want your work reviewed but not done over from scratch? Not in an easy place. Keep trying—there are some sympathetic lawyers who will help. But make an effort to see the issue from the lawyer's point of view and be willing to pay for enough of her time so she feels she can adequately study the partnership agreement you have drafted and possibly suggest changes. Also, point out to the lawyer that you are also looking for someone to work with in the future, on occasions when your business needs legal help.

or tax expert can be of great assistance, and others where their work supplies only an expensive redundancy.

For the intrepid, there is another option: doing your own legal research. Learning how to research partnership law can provide real benefits. Not only are you likely to save money on professional fees, you'll gain a sense of mastery over an area of law, generating a confidence that you've handled a difficult question about your partnership yourself. Also, this will give you a head start should you ever want to research other legal questions. (We discuss this option further in Section C.)

1. Using a Lawyer

There are a lot of lawyers out there these days; some are both ethical and competent. For any of a number of reasons, you may decide that it's sensible for your budding partnership to hire a lawyer to advise you.

What Kind of Expert Help Do You Need?

Before you run off to a lawyer, consider whether another type of expert, such as an accountant or financial planner, would serve you better. Questions about federal taxes, or how to calculate tax basis on the sale of appreciated property, can often be better answered by an experienced CPA than a lawyer. Similarly, for some financial decisions, such as what type of insurance to buy, you may be better off talking to a financial planner. We discuss this in more detail in Section B of this chapter.

Here are some common reasons people forming a partnership hire a lawyer:

Personality concerns or doubts: If one or more prospective members of the partnership feels uncomfortable or insecure about the relationship or potential relationship between the partners, it's usually wise to discuss these concerns with a lawyer. You'll want an experienced lawyer here, one who's got a good feel for the human dynamics that can be involved in a partnership. In a real sense, the lawyer is being asked to serve as therapist as much as technician. You want her to help spot problems you only vaguely sense, draw you out and see if resolution is possible. This can be particularly important if one (or more) potential partners feels another could be overbearing. In many cases, a lawyer will help you explore whether you and your partners can actually work together with the equality a partnership demands.

A potential problem with discussing potential personality conflicts with a lawyer is that many lawyers will respond that they cannot truly represent all the parties to the partnership. Perhaps the lawyer will be willing to give some advice and try to assist you to work matters out, but it's understandable why he might not want to represent the partnership itself, or more than one partner, when you've sought him out precisely because you feel there may be conflict. In this situation, each partner may end up having to see her own lawyer. Expensive as this can be, it will surely prove to be much less costly, and pain-filled, than entering a partnership and having grave personal conflicts erupt later.

Tax matters: If after you've read this book any partner has concerns or doubts regarding any tax matter, see a partnership tax expert. This will usually be a CPA, but it can be a tax lawyer, particularly when you're setting up a new partnership. Suppose, for example, that you're setting up a partnership to run a restaurant and you're contributing a building you already own. Do you transfer it outright to the partnership? Lease it? Rent it? How is depreciation on the building to be apportioned? If one partner has a much higher income than the others, can all the depreciation be allotted to him? These types of problems, as we explained in Chapter 7, Section E, can become complicated in a hurry. It's necessary not only to understand applicable tax rules, but to be sure this understanding is reflected in the drafting of your partnership agreement.

Creation of a limited partnership: Creating a legal limited partnership (see Chapter 9), necessarily requires knowledge of your state's securities laws and rules for the Certificate of Limited Partnership. Unless you're comfortable researching these matters yourself, you'll need to see a lawyer about them.

Complicated buy-out provisions: Some partnerships desire sophisticated, complex buy-out provisions. We discuss this issue in some detail in Chapter 5, Sections A and B, but we don't get into nearly as much complexity as is possible. If you want to explore this area further, prudence dictates that you have custom-tailored buy-out clauses drafted, or at least reviewed, by a knowledgeable lawyer.

How Many Lawyers Will You Need?

What's this? A trick question? A light bulb joke? Sadly, no. Where one partner is dominant, it can be best for that partner to use a separate lawyer from the other partners. The purpose is to prevent any later claim that the agreement was unfair, that the dominant partner (and his lawyer) took advantage of the other less sophisticated ones. In extreme cases, each member of a partnership has chosen to be represented by a different lawyer. Or perhaps a lawyer representing all partners will require them to sign a waiver agreeing that there was no conflict of interest.

Happily, few partnerships need or benefit from this costly caution. If all the prospective partners feel basically equal, at most you'll need one lawyer, and quite likely none, as we've stressed throughout this book.

2. What Kind of Lawyer Do You Need?

For sure, you want a lawyer with plenty of experience working with small businesses, and at least some experience advising partnerships. (This does raise the question of how an inexperienced lawyer can get experience. But that's not your concern. The usual method for a young lawyer to learn the ropes is to work with an experienced one.) Effective, meaningful legal advice about a partnership is difficult, if not impossible, to acquire simply by studying law books. Partnership legal work is an art, and real-life experience is a necessary component of that art.

If you want to consult a lawyer, what else do you look for aside from one having experience advising business partnerships? That depends largely on what your problems are. If you want a general review of your agreement (and to make sure you haven't overlooked something basic), any good business partnership lawyer who'll accept the job should do. If your needs are more special, you may well need a lawyer with more specific expertise. For example, if partners will make complex property contributions, you'll surely be better off with a lawyer well versed in partnership taxation. Or, if you're creating a limited partnership, you'll want a lawyer knowledgeable about your state's limited partnership rules.

It's important that all partners feel a personal rapport with their lawyer. You want one who treats you as an equal. When talking with a lawyer on the phone or at a first conference, ask specific questions that concern you. If the lawyer answers them clearly and concisely—explaining but not talking down to you—fine. If he acts wise, but says little except to ask that the problem be placed in his hands (with the appropriate fee, of course), watch out. You are either talking with someone who doesn't know the answer and won't admit it (common), or someone who finds it impossible to let go of the "me expert, you peasant" way of looking at the world (even more common).

It's no secret that lawyers are expensive. They normally charge fees ranging from $150 to $400 or more per hour. While fancy office trappings, three-piece suits and solemn faces are no guarantee (or even a good indication) that a particular lawyer will provide top-notch service in a style with which you will feel comfortable, this conventional style will almost always ensure that you will be charged at the upper end of the fee range. At Nolo, our experience tells us that high fees and quality service don't necessarily go hand in hand. Indeed, the attorneys we think most highly of tend to charge moderate fees (for lawyers, that is), and seem to get along very nicely without luxurious law office trappings.

3. Working With a Lawyer Over the Long Term

Many partners in small businesses apply the same logic to their business's legal affairs that they do to their own: Avoid lawyers and hope that common sense will carry the day.

This approach may have worked a generation or two ago, but it's almost sure to fail today. Small businesses are affected by a growing mountain of legal rules, some of which didn't exist the day before yesterday. And even if you scrupulously comply with all of them, outsiders may still cause legal problems: a wrongful termination lawsuit by an angry former employee; a major customer's failure to pay; the rip-off of a copyright, patent or trademark by a competitor; or a subcontractor's breach of contract.

So sooner or later—probably sooner—you will have to cope with legal problems. And unless you are a very fortunate small business owner, you can't afford to buy all the legal information you need from a lawyer at $150 or more per hour. Because the survival of your business may depend on mastering this information, you need to get it some other way.

a. Build a Legal Information Library

Fortunately, there are many affordable sources of good legal information.

Business magazines: You may get some good legal and practical tips from general business magazines.

Newsletters: In many fields, monthly or bimonthly newsletters from trade associations or consultants specialize in keeping business owners up-to-date on practical—and occasionally legal—information specific to their field. Newsletters are often pricey, but the best are worth it. Free sample copies are often available at trade shows. Ask others in your field what they rely on.

Books: Every small business should build a library of legal and management books. The most valuable legal books will offer specific information about your field. For example, a landlord needs an up-to-date set of state laws, a commonsense property management book such as *Every Landlord's Legal Guide*, by Marcia Stewart, Ralph Warner and Janet Portman (Nolo).

Software: Should your business need a contract, lease or other legal agreement, you may find guidance in an unexpected place: your computer. With an excellent computer program, it's not too difficult to draft legal documents on your own. Before finalizing your work, you may want it checked by an experienced lawyer, but this should cost far less than asking a lawyer to draft documents from scratch. You can also obtain much valuable business information, as well as many handy business forms, from *Quicken Lawyer 2002 Business Deluxe* (Nolo).

b. Line Up a Lawyer

Sometimes, after your business is underway, you may need a lawyer's advice. For example:

- A trusted employee may quit and take your confidential customer list.
- An employee may dump toxic fluids out the back door just as a city health inspector shows up.
- Your landlord may refuse to make repairs to try to force you to accept a big rent increase.
- A disgruntled customer may sue you.

If you don't have a relationship with a lawyer before trouble hits, you may pay too much and receive lousy service when you do seek out a lawyer.

The unprepared business owner suddenly faced with a serious legal problem typically gets mad, gets scared, calls a lawyer and demands an immediate appointment. If he gets bad advice, he may make a quick decision fueled by the angst of the moment—a decision that may even put the business at risk.

You're simply not likely to find a good lawyer in a hurry. The 80-20 Rule sums up the situation: in any field, only the top 20% (at most) of the people are excellent. Finding a lawyer in that category is not easy when you are under time pressure. Excellent lawyers seldom need to solicit business through advertising or referral services.

Even if you are lucky enough to find good legal help, you will be charged a premium, because the lawyer must drop other projects and spring to your side.

4. Finding a Lawyer

Sounds fine, you may be thinking, but how do we find a good lawyer? Here are a few tips to help you find a lawyer suited to your taste and needs, if you should need one.

- Look for a lawyer who represents other small business owners, preferably in the same or a similar field as yours. For example, if you intend to run a bar, check out lawyers who have other bars as clients. You can get the benefit of a lawyer's experience with everything from obtaining a liquor license, to dealing with city inspectors, to setting up an employee benefits policy.
- Look for a lawyer who is interested in your business. It may make sense to have an experienced lawyer personally check out your business and make practical suggestions about how to reduce legal risks.
- Look for a lawyer who is willing to help you learn about the laws that affect your business. Again, you know you can't afford to pay for information you find on our own. The trick is to find a lawyer savvy enough to understand this.
- Avoid lawyers who are desperately looking for you. In many communities, mediocre general practitioners anxiously prospect for small business clients; if you have been to lunch at a local service club, you have probably met half-a-dozen.
- Avoid lawyers who pepper you with slick, image-enhancing brochures. You want a lawyer smart enough to see this sort of silliness for what it is.
- Be cautious when dealing with bar associations' referral panels and those run as private businesses. There's often a charge for referral. While lawyers are supposed to be screened

as to their specialty, in some areas this is perfunctory. Don't assume a bar association referral is some sort of seal of approval. Question the lawyer and make your own judgment, just as you would if you got the referral in any other way.

Agree in advance on the fee for any initial consultation. *Then, at your first meeting, talk your problems over with the lawyer and see how open and knowledgeable she is. If the first meeting goes well, you may want to talk about establishing a continuing relationship. If you have any doubts, go home and think about them. Even if you have to pay several consulting fees before finding the right person, it will be vastly better than ending up with someone you don't like.*

5. Paying a Lawyer

Lawyers sell their time. You can save money by using self-help legal resources so you don't need to pay for lots of lawyer time, not by using a cheap lawyer. A lawyer who has expertise with your type of business and who will sincerely help you educate yourself may be a bargain even at a relatively high hourly rate. For example, if you have a copyright problem, it will cost far more to pay a novice to learn about copyright law at $100 an hour than it will to pay a pro $300 to deal with the same problem. And because the novice won't have the experience to supplement the textbook knowledge, the advice you receive is unlikely to be as good.

Paying by the hour is usually best. The alternative of paying a lawyer a fixed sum each month or year as a retainer can also make sense after you've been in business for a while, and only then if you have predictable needs. For example, you might want the lawyer to attend several partnership meetings each year, look over occasional contracts and be available once a month to discuss miscellaneous problems. In this situation, paying a retainer may turn out to cost less than paying by the hour;

the lawyer may be willing to charge less in exchange for a guaranteed monthly income. But don't expect heroic amounts of work for a modest monthly retainer. If you need substantial legal help, be ready to pay for it.

Finally, be aware that at any time your economic interests and the lawyer's may diverge. A lawyer who wants to run a profitable business needs to sell a lot of his time. Litigation is often the best way to accomplish this; America's court system is so constipated, complicated and convoluted it runs up lawyers' bills faster than the Pentagon wants new weapons. But as we've stressed, litigation is seldom in the best interests of your psyche or wallet. If a lawyer recommends going to court, ask these questions:

- How much will it cost? Ask for a written estimate of the total cost. Then ask if it's a worst-case estimate. It's likely to be a lot higher—and a lot more realistic.
- What do other lawyers think? Get a second and maybe a third opinion from knowledgeable lawyers with no financial stake in the potential lawsuit. This takes time and money, but it's cheap compared to a lawsuit.
- What happens if I do nothing? Sometimes, the best course is to let the passage of time and cooling of emotions settle the situation. For example, if a former employee opens a competing business using your trade secrets, and you know it is bound to fail for a variety of reasons, you might be better off to relax and let it happen.

B. Partnership Tax Experts

If your business gets off the ground, you'll need a partnership tax expert no matter how uncomplicated your tax situation was at the start. You will also need someone to do routine bookkeeping and file routine paperwork for workers' compensation, unemployment insurance, sales tax and the like. (We discuss these issues in Chapter 8.) A two-tier system of experts for your financial recordkeeping is generally the best system. Here's how it works.

1. Hire a competent bookkeeper to actually set up your books, make necessary entries each week (or day), and prepare your routine tax forms. You don't need a professional accountant, let alone a CPA, to do these types of chores, and you shouldn't have to pay accountant's fees. Most small businesses can start with part-time bookkeeping help; if you ask around, you'll find a lot of small bookkeeping services that will provide you with the hours you need at a reasonable cost.

2. Coordinate your bookkeeping arrangements with those of a certified public accountant or other tax expert who specializes in small businesses and has extensive experience with partnerships. Make sure your tax expert reviews and approves the work of your bookkeeper. In this area, we've found that good accountants are typically more knowledgeable, and cheaper, than tax lawyers.

To find your tax expert, follow routes similar to those we suggested for finding a lawyer. Talk to friends with business needs similar to yours. Choose your tax expert carefully; you'll want to avoid both slipshod operators and large expensive firms that specialize in big business. Your accountant's role is primarily one of a tax advisor. A good advisor will almost always be able to make tax savings suggestions that will more than pay for her services. Many small business people we know only need to sit down with their expert a couple of times a year, thus minimizing this expense.

C. Doing Your Own Research

As far as tax law goes, our advice about doing your own research is clear—don't do it. Tax statutes and regulations are astoundingly unclear, laden with cross-references, such as "Except as provided by Section 3(A)b-2(iii) (c)," with that section itself being totally obtuse. Understanding the broad outlines of tax rules and how they affect your business is a sensible

use of your time and energies. In our opinion, investing the time and energy to understand them in great detail is not. And even if you managed to understand them formally, you still wouldn't know how the rules are applied in the real world, which is an art gained through experience by tax experts.

General partnership law, by contrast, is more amenable to a self-help approach. Learning how to do your own research into partnership law can provide real benefits. Lawyers, after all, are experts at recycling information and charging large amounts for the service. When doing this, the lawyer (more often her secretary or paralegal assistant) is doing no more than opening a book of legal forms or information and copying out the answers. Armed with the information in this book, why can't you do this if you need a specific clause we don't provide? Often you can, if you know where to look.

In Appendix 1 at the back of this book, you'll find a list of research materials on small-business operation and organization in general and on partnership law in particular. These materials are a good place to start.

Some hardy spirits may wish to go beyond the list of resources we provide, and dig into law books. Why not? There's nothing particularly hard about reading law books (boring, yes—hard, no). In many states, county law libraries (and sometimes specialized business libraries) that are free and open to the public have good collections of business law materials. Also, the law libraries of most publicly-funded law schools can be used for research by members of the public, particularly if you courteously explain your needs to a librarian. In both circumstances, we've found law librarians to be very helpful and considerate.

Unfortunately, in using any law library, you'll quickly see that legal resources are arranged following a different code than the Dewey Decimal or Library of Congress system followed in public libraries. Until you master how various legal resources are organized, meaningful legal research will be impossible. For an excellent explanation of how to conduct your own legal research, see *Legal*

Research: How to Find and Understand the Law by Stephen Elias and Susan Levenkind (Nolo).

Another way to approach your research is to use a computer. You can conduct significant amounts of legal research by using the World Wide Web.

 *You can use Nolo's website for access to state partnership laws and other partnership matters. You can find us at www.nolo.com.*

A related approach is to call your local law library to see if they have a phone service. Perhaps you can have someone in the library assist you with your computer research, if not by phone at least by assisting you when you visit that library.

Here are a couple of general hints for the adventurous legal researcher. Each state has its own partnership laws and partnership cases. All the states except Louisiana have adopted the Uniform Partnership Act, or Revised Uniform Partnership Act, but most states have made at least some changes. You can start your research by reading your state's version of the Uniform Act. It's unlikely that your state will have a separately-bound volume labeled "Uniform Partnership Law," or any name referring to partnerships. Often your state's partnership statutes will be included in a general volume of business laws, or commerce codes, or corporation law. So to find your state's Uniform Partnership Law, you'll need to know how to do rudimentary legal research, as it's unlikely to be in a separate volume.

Once you locate the volume with your state's Uniform Partnership Code, the annotated version will provide you with excerpts and citations (references) to relevant judicial decisions. There are also useful legal encyclopedias arranged by topic, and form books (collections of sample legal forms, including partnership forms). Your law librarian should be able to direct you to many of these.

Finally, don't be intimidated by the hush of law libraries, or the legal jargon you'll find in the books. This isn't quark physics, or neurosurgery, just words about people and their rights. ■

Drafting Your Own Partnership Agreement

Okay, now you get to do it yourselves. It's time to prepare your own partnership agreement. This chapter takes you step-by-step through each basic topic we believe you should or may want to cover in your agreement. In Appendix 3, you'll find a tear-out Partnership Agreement, which includes every clause we've previously introduced in Chapters 3 through 6. Perhaps you're a bit surprised at how much material you had to cover before you reached the pencil-to-paper or computer stage, but we hope you also understand why a standardized form partnership agreement is dangerous. At any rate, this is where your hard work pays off, since you should now have enough information to carefully draft a document that expresses your specific desires and needs.

The clauses in this chapter are not accompanied by explanatory materials. If you have any doubts whether you want, or need, to include a specific clause in your agreement, turn back to the discussion of that clause in the appropriate section of Chapters 3 through 6. In these chapters we asked you to mark the clauses you thought you'd want to include in your agreement and write in your initial decisions about what you wanted in your clauses.

Now it's time to assemble the clauses you selected into a coherent agreement. (Of course, we mean a general partnership agreement. Limited partnerships are discussed in Chapter 9.) Putting your agreement together will give you a chance to review, once again, your thoughts and any problems you can foresee arising in your partnership. If there are any problem areas that you haven't yet resolved, this is your final chance to do so.

A. How to Prepare Your Agreement

Read through this entire chapter first, so you thoroughly understand how to put your agreement together. Then follow the steps described below to assemble your partnership agreement.

Step 1: Detach the Partnership Agreement

This agreement is printed on perforated paper. Detach it and, with a large paper clip, fasten together all pages so they don't get separated or lost. But before you do, make a backup photocopy or two, so if you do lose a page or muck one up too much working on your draft, you'll have clean replacement pages on hand.

If you have a computer with a word processor, use the forms disk that comes with this book to draft your agreement.

Computer users should first work through the clauses on paper. *Even if you intend to use the forms disk and your word processor to create your document, follow these steps and work through all the sample clauses* on paper, *checking the clauses you want to include and filling them in as appropriate.*

Using the CD-ROM to Create a Partnership Agreement

You can create a custom Partnership Agreement using the word processing files on the CD-ROM at the back of this book. (These files have the same sample clauses as the tear-out Partnership Agreement in Appendix 3.)

To create your agreement, follow Steps 1 through 8 in this section. For instructions on how to install and copy the form files from the CD-ROM onto your computer, please refer to Appendix 2.

Note to Mac users: This CD-ROM and its files should work on Macintosh computers. Please note, however, that Nolo cannot provide technical support for non-Windows users.

Work through the forms on paper first. Before you use these files and your word processor to create your agreement, we suggest you work through all the sample clauses on paper first. Place a check mark next to the clauses you want to include in your Partnership Agreement and fill in the appropriate blanks.

Finding the Clauses You Want

Windows users

- Each clause is installed to the appropriate \Clause subfolder within the \Partnership Forms subfolder in the \Program Files folder of your computer.

- Open a clause by selecting its "shortcut" as follows: (1) click the Windows "Start" button; (2) open the "Programs" folder; (3) open the "Partnership Forms" subfolder; (4) open the appropriate "Clause" subfolder; and (5) click on the shortcut to the clause you want to work with.

Mac users

- Each clause is located in the appropriate "Clause" subfolder in the "Partnership Forms" folder.

- Open a file as follows: (1) use the Finder to go to the appropriate "Clause" folder; (2) open it; and (3) double-click on the specific file you want to open.

As each sample clause is introduced and explained in Chapters 3-6, its corresponding file name and directory are given.

Drafting Your Partnership Agreement

When selecting and completing clauses and assembling your agreement, follow these rules:

- Read and understand Chapters 3-6, where each clause is explained in detail and information on how to complete them is provided.

- Work through all the sample clauses on paper, checking the clauses you want to include and filling them in as appropriate.

- Follow the step-by-step instructions in this section on how to complete your agreement. Although these instructions are not specifically for computer users, they should be followed nevertheless. It is only in Steps 6 and 7, when you actually draft your agreement, that you begin to work with the clause files.

- When you open a clause file, you'll see that it contains blank lines, which show you where you need to type in information. In some cases, the blanks are followed by bracketed instructions about what information is required. *Be sure to delete the blank underlines and the bracketed instructional text from your final document.*

- After filling in a clause, use your word processor's "Save As" command to save and rename the file. Because all the files are "read-only", you will not be able to use the "Save" command. This is for your protection. *If you save the file without renaming it, the underlines that indicate where you need to enter your information will be lost and you will not be able to create a new document with this file without recopying the original file from the CD-ROM.* If you do not know how to use your word processor to save a document, you will need to look through the manual for your word processing program—Nolo's technical support department will *not* be able to help you with the use of your word processing program.

- The clauses in the clause files are not numbered, and some captions included in the sample clauses in the book are not included in the clause files. Follow Step 6 and use the OUTLINE file, adding the numbers and captions as required.

Step 2: Select the Clauses You Want for Your Agreement

You've already read through Chapters 3-6 and should have identified the clauses you want in your agreement by putting a check in the box to the left of each one you want to include. Now, carefully transfer these check marks to the clauses set out in the agreement. Almost all the clauses follow the order of the earlier chapters, so this should be easy. However, there are three exceptions we want to caution you about.

1. Clauses governing amendments to the tear-out partnership agreement, including the addition of a new partner, are found in a different sequence in our agreement than they originally appear in Chapter 4. The reason for this change in sequence is simple. In the earlier text we wanted to cover problems involving amendments when the issue first arose, in the context of the growth of your business. But since an amendment clause naturally can apply to any clause in the agreement, we place that amendment clause near the end of the tear-out agreement, so you can include it near the end of your partnership agreement.

2. In the tear-out agreement, the clauses concerning the expulsion of a partner are included with those that deal with the continuity of partnership business should a partner leave or die. This is a slightly different approach than the one we took in Chapter 5, Section D, where we have a separate heading for expulsion clauses. We do not provide a separate heading for expulsion clauses here, since it's been our experience that few partners actually choose to include such a clause in their agreement.

3. In the tear-out agreement, Clause 12, General Provisions, includes some standard legal provisions that lawyers call boilerplate. These clauses are aptly called boilerplate because

they are routinely attached to most partnership agreements. These boilerplate clauses were not presented in the earlier text because they cover obvious matters you normally don't need to discuss.

For example, one of our boilerplate clauses states that your written agreement contains the entire understanding of the partners regarding their rights and duties in the partnership, and no alleged oral modification is valid. Perhaps this seems obvious, but if one partner subsequently tries to claim that an oral agreement between you has altered the written terms of this agreement, it will prove handy to have this boilerplate clause in your agreement.

If you have any question about what a clause means, or whether it makes sense for you to include it in your agreement, reread the discussion pertaining to that clause in the appropriate earlier chapter.

Step 3: Finish the Clauses You've Selected

Now comes the vital task of completing all clauses you've selected. We want to remind you once again that this may involve more than simply filling in the blank lines of our sample clauses. Many partnership agreements require some modification and adaptation of our sample clauses to fit partners' specific situations.

EXAMPLE: In the sample agreement at the end of this chapter, their Clause 4, CONTRIBUTIONS, contains some subclauses which adapt the clauses in the tear-out agreement to their individual needs. Subclause 4.B, CASH CREDIT, adapts cash contribution provisions to an uncommon situation where one partner gets contribution credit for below-market rent of a building. And subclause 4.C, CONTRIBUTION

OUT OF PROFIT, adapts our subclause covering this issue to an individual situation. Our subclause provides that a partner shall not make any cash contribution, but shall make her entire contribution out of her future profits. However, in the sample agreement, one partner is making some cash contributions at the beginning, so only part, but not all, of her total contribution will be paid out of her future profits. Accordingly, these partners had to adapt our clauses to reflect what they were actually doing.

Hopefully, you've made notes for the clauses you want, and sketched in any modifications or changes you need, when you originally read through Chapters 3 through 6. If you did that, now pin down precisely how you want all of your clauses and subclauses to read. Smooth out any rough spots from your earlier work. Fill in all blank lines from our sample clauses that you use. If you didn't make notes on a clause the first time through, you can still complete or adapt that clause here, if you're sure you understand how that clause works, what your needs are and what you want your clause to contain. And of course, you simply turn back to the text where a particular clause was first discussed if you have questions.

Here's an example of how you actually complete a clause. This is the initial clause in your agreement. You simply fill in the date you plan to sign your final, typed agreement, along with the names of the partners, as shown below.

 The following clause is in the file **OUTLINE**.

☐ This Partnership Agreement is entered into and
effective as of _____ June 19 _____ , 20 ___
by the partners ___ Eli Manstein ___ ,
Alon Talmi ___ ,
Kathleen O'Brien ___ ,
_____ .

Completing the general provisions.
In the boilerplate clauses under 12, GENERAL PROVISIONS (these clauses are included on the forms disk in directory Clause12), you'll complete one clause you haven't seen before, where you list the name of the state whose laws will govern your partnership. This is usually the state where you live and will do business. If you plan to operate in more than one state, or the partners live in more than one state, you should normally select the state where you have your principal place of business.

Drafting Two-Person Partnership Agreements

In preparing the partnership clauses set out in this chapter, we assumed there will be three or more partners. This means that if you're preparing an agreement for a two-person partnership, you have to make some minor changes to some of our printed clauses. For example, some buy-out clauses refer to a "partnership," or "partners," that remains after one partner leaves. But if there were only two partners originally, and one departs, there's only one person left, so there can't be "remaining partners," or a "partnership." This means that when drafting an agreement for a two-person partnership, you will need to change these clauses to refer to the "remaining owner," as shown below.

☐ If any partner leaves the partnership, for whatever reason, whether he quits, withdraws, retires, or dies, his estate shall be obligated to sell his interest in the partnership to the remaining owner, who may buy that interest under the terms and conditions set forth in this Agreement.

So, if you are in a two-person partnership, read through each clause of your agreement with care to check that it is phrased correctly for you.

Step 4: Complete Any New Clauses You've Prepared

If you've decided to create new clauses yourselves, different from any presented in this book, now is the time to pin down the precise wording of these clauses. If you have trouble doing this, or have any doubt as to a provision's legal effect, see a lawyer.

Step 5: Delete All Unnecessary Information

Now that you've prepared all the clauses for your agreement, including filling in the blanks for all the clauses from this book, you need to delete all extraneous material from that document in order to produce a document ready for typing. In other words, on the pages in the tear-out agreement, you need to indicate what material you want to include in your agreement and what you want to exclude. To do this, draw a heavy pencil line through all material that you don't want in your final agreement, and include whatever other marks you need so that whoever prepares a typed draft will know what's in and what's out.

Material that should be deleted includes:

- all clauses that you decide not to use
- any headings or subheadings you decide not to use
- all those little margin boxes, along with your check marks (good-bye, little boxes)
- in clauses you complete, the blank lines (those you filled in or left blank).

EXAMPLE:

This Partnership Agreement is entered into and effective as of July 10, 2002, by the partners:

(⌖ is a standard mark meaning "delete.")

⚠ Important!
Do not delete the number and general caption for a basic clause, such as:
"1. Names"
"2. Terms"
"3. Purpose"
"4. Contributions"
The reason you leave these in is because they identify the basic units of your agreement. You use them as the base for outlining your agreement as explained in Step 6, below.

Step 6: Outline Your Agreement

As noted, we've provided the basics for the structure of your agreement. As you'll see, at the beginning of the document it says "Partnership Agreement." Next, you list the names of the partners and the date of the agreement, as shown in the previous example. This first clause is not given an identifying number, but after that, we have divided your agreement into basic units, each with a number and identifying caption:

"1. Names"
"2. Term of the Partnership"
"3. Purpose"
"4. Contributions"
"5. Profits and Losses"
"6. Management Powers and Responsibilities"
and so on.

In some of these basic units, you'll use more than one clause. We call this using "subclauses." For example, in basic Clause 4, CONTRIBUTIONS, you may have selected two subclauses, one for contributions of cash and another for contributions of property. Your concern now is how you should identify those two subclauses.

Your job is to provide sufficient names and identifying symbols (such as capital letters, small letters, or numbers) for subclauses, so that your agreement is structured coherently. Doing this may seem a little daunting at first, but all you're really doing is preparing an outline, as most of you have surely done many times in high school. For those others of you who may have difficulty with this (we confess we never found outlining a snap, no matter how often we did it in the 10th grade), we offer some further suggestions.

When you wish to include two or more subclauses, place an "A" in front of one. Following this approach, your contributions clause would look like this:

4. CONTRIBUTIONS

A. [Specific Cash Clause]

B. [Specific Property Clause]

A related concern is whether you want to give identifying names to each subclause. There is no legal requirement that you do so, but we've provided a caption for every subclause in the text, should you prefer this extra element of structure. Also, we provide more general headings for groups of subclauses related to one subject. It's up to you to decide if you want to structure your agreement with names for subclauses. If you do, your contributions clause could be structured as:

4. CONTRIBUTIONS

A. Cash

[Specific Cash Clause]

B. Property

[Specific Property Clause]

You may well have sub-subclauses. For example, you may have in your agreement:

4. CONTRIBUTIONS

A. Cash

(i) cash contribution
[specific cash contributions clause]

(ii) initial work contribution
[specific initial work contribution clause]

(iii) extra cash loaned by a partner
[specific cash loan clause]

Tip for forms disk users.
If you prepare your partnership agreement using the computer disk, you'll find the basic, first-level headings in the file OUTLINE. Each clause is in its own separate file, and you cut and paste text from the clause files you've chosen and filled in into the OUTLINE file to create your agreement. In each clause file, you'll find the appropriate second-level, subclause heading and the third-level or sub-sub-clause heading, if any. You can select which, if any, of these headings you want to use and add them to your draft agreement (in other words, transfer the headings you want to the OUTLINE file).

You have considerable discretion as to how you outline and structure the subclauses (and sub-subclauses, etc.) of your agreement. As long as you come up with an order that is clear and works for all of you, you're fine.

Now, one final editing note. If you decide not to use any of our captions or headings for subclauses you include in your agreement, be sure to cross those captions and headings out, so the typist won't include them.

Step 7: Prepare a Draft of Your Agreement

Once you've fully prepared a coherent draft of your agreement and double-checked to be sure you haven't omitted anything and have deleted all unnecessary material, it is time to put together a final version of your agreement typed. Computer word processors are ideal here, as you'll save much time and expense if revisions prove necessary, as they usually do.

Step 8: Review Your Draft

Have the draft reviewed by all the partners. Most likely there will be some changes, hopefully minor. But don't get discouraged if more work and changes are needed before all feel comfortable that a fully acceptable final draft has been achieved. We rewrote the current edition of this book 11 times, and we do this for a living.

Step 9: Prepare Your Final Agreement

Finally, prepare a final draft of your agreement. Plain bond paper is fine. Have each partner sign and date the agreement at the end.

A partnership agreement doesn't have to be notarized unless it entails the ownership of real property and you want to record it at your local land title recording office. Notarization has nothing to do with making a contract binding, but does serve to establish that the signatures are legitimate.

Each partner should be given a photocopy of the signed agreement. Keep the original in a safe place.

B. After You've Drafted Your Agreement

Now, that wasn't so terribly complicated, was it? (Well, maybe it was. If so, double congratulations!) Many partnership agreements contain only five or six pages. Still, it's extremely important that all of your clauses fit together to make an orderly whole. So check and double-check if you need to, to be sure you have an agreement that you all understand and that reads coherently.

The Story of a Partnership

Now that you've gone through the entire book and argued, bickered, discussed, wheedled, cajoled and finally drafted your partnership agreement (or maybe you haven't quite gotten to drafting it yet, but now you have a much better idea of what will be in your agreement), we'd like to relate the story of how two friends came up with a great idea and set up a partnership. We hope you will like them and find them interesting, as we do. (It's best to confess that these two people are fictional, although drawn using bits and pieces from a number of real friends.) Perhaps they are much like yourselves—excited about setting up their own business, optimistic about success and a little scared about embarking on a journey into uncharted waters. Also like you, they are unique, distinct individuals. We've chosen them for their value in illustrating a process of establishing a good partnership and a sound partnership agreement, not because we expect your business or partnership agreement to mirror theirs. So now, let's meet our future partners, Pete and Laurie.

Two years ago, Pete and Laurie had little in common but their habit of walking their dogs in the same park at roughly the same time each evening. But, as most dog owners can tell you, where dogs lead, owners often follow.

When Pete Johnston, 33, meets Laurie, he is working as a sales manager for Karlsbraat Engineering, a wholly-owned subsidiary of Jameson Constructors, whose worldwide offices had recently been acquired by Grede International. Pete is one of those rare individuals who enjoys, not merely tolerates, selling. He makes friends anywhere, never forgets a name or face and even likes getting on the telephone and contacting prospective customers. He can do this not only because he is gregarious, but because he believes that Karlsbraat offers the finest engineering products and services on the market.

Pete likes his job but delights in the view from his office windows—a spectacular panoramic vista of the Rocky Mountains. This is where Pete's heart truly lies. When he isn't at work, he can usually be found in the mountains, skiing or rock climbing, depending on the season. He loves to buy the latest outdoor equipment, and his generous salary at Karlsbraat provides for all the expensive toys in his garage—the cross-country and downhill skis, climbing ropes, ice axes, ice boots, a plethora of camping equipment and three different kinds of climbing shoes for three different kinds of rock. His salary has also enabled him to recently buy a new Ford Explorer, with special quarters for his dog and several new business suits.

Now let's meet Laurie Mendez. Laurie is 38, only five years older than Pete, but what a world of difference between them. Laurie was born in Venezuela, and immigrated to the United States 17 years ago with her husband, Santiago, a remodeling contractor. She is the mother of three children, including twin daughters. For the past four years, Laurie has worked as a nutritionist in a local hospital for 15 hours a week, but her primary commitment has always been to family—her husband and children, and her parents, whom she brought here from Venezuela.

One evening, as Laurie strolls past the baseball diamond at the edge of the park, her dog, Paco, catches sight of a golden retriever and takes off after him. When Laurie finally catches up to Paco, she sits down to catch her breath and makes polite conversation with the golden retriever's owner, whose name is Pete. After the obligatory dog-talk, Pete begins to talk about his passion, rock climbing.

"My children are climbers," Laurie says. "They are absolutely insane about the rocks. Maybe someday you'll see my two twin girls hanging from a cliff face. When it comes to climbing, they are totally defiant of their father, their mother and the laws of gravity."

Pete suspects that he already knows Laurie's daughters. There's only one set of twins who climb in Mountain Valley, and they're already local leg-

ends. He hopes the woman doesn't know the kinds of risky rock climbing her daughters engage in.

Thus begins one of those innocuous but pleasant associations between casual acquaintances. Pete and Laurie see each other frequently in the park over the coming months and engage in easy, gradually more personal conversation.

Then one night, high above Mountain Valley, Pete finds himself tying into the same belay ledge as Laurie's twins, who are also on a two-day climb. Accidentally, Pete's climbing partner drops the haulbag containing their food, and the twins offer to share theirs. Pete is treated to one of Laurie's special recipes—a toasted, baked, energy bar which, the twins explain, "contains lipoproteins for a quick start, semi-carbs for the long haul, macrosugars for essential surges and chamomile for peace of mind." Maybe so, but Pete wonders what else she put in them—Chiles? Mole? Cayenne pepper? Corn? Garlic? The taste is unbelievable; far superior to most of those bland, if wholesome, "power bars" on the market. Pete is impressed.

Some weeks later Grede Industries, which had so recently taken over Jameson, and therefore Karlsbraat, is itself taken over by RR&K. In a spinoff, RR&K sells Karlsbraat Engineering to the much bigger Rochester Engineering, which decides to merge Karlsbraat into its own operations. Rochester lays off most of Karlsbraat's entire marketing division. Karlsbraat's number one salesman, Pete, is offered a chance to transfer to Trenton, N.J. Faced with leaving his beloved Rocky Mountains or becoming unemployed, Pete chooses unemployment.

Feeling rather low, despite the generous check for his severance and uncollected vacation pay in his pocket, Pete walks Nugget toward the park and mulls over his situation. With no other good-sized engineering firms in town, he will clearly have to adapt his marketing skills to another industry or move. Relocating means working with an engineering firm in a big city, leaving his beloved Rockies behind. A third choice, he realizes, is to consider an entirely new career. As long as he works with people, and makes a decent enough salary to support his skiing and mountaineering, Pete believes he would probably be content, no matter what company he worked for. But also, he thinks to himself, the product must be good.

Laurie is sitting on a bench, watching Paco chase after squirrels across the grass. He disappears behind the trees. She, too, is deep in thought, pondering something which, unbeknownst to her, will lead to her upcoming partnership with Pete.

"Hi," Pete greets Laurie, putting aside his concerns momentarily. "Paco's got a new collar, I see." He immediately senses that Laurie is preoccupied and asks her if everything is all right. After a pause, Laurie responds, somewhat shakily, "I just found out that my daughters have been accepted at Cornell."

"Those kids are certainly upwardly mobile," quips Pete.

"Such a great honor," she says wryly. "They go to an elite school and the family goes broke."

Laurie is obviously distressed. He remembers that private colleges can cost over $30,000 a year; times two—who could afford that?

"Even though they may qualify for partial scholarships and student loans, I will have to work full-time if we're going to swing this," says Laurie. "But business around here is very slow, and that new hospital is on hold; not good prospects for nutritionists. And since I've only been working part-time, I may even be let go."

They commiserate for a time, Pete telling Laurie about his own recent layoff. Then, without thinking, Pete blurts out, "You know what we should do? We should go into business marketing your power bars—the ones you make for your daughters. I tasted a few of them one night on the Crow's Nest, and they were incredible."

Laurie turns toward him, her eyes wide. "The twins climbed the Crow's Nest?" She was clearly horrified. "Well, if that's what they've been up to, I guess I should be grateful that they're going off to Cornell. If nothing else, it will keep them off the Crow's Nest."

"Laurie, I'm serious. What do you think about going into business together?"

"Where did you get such an idea, Pete? I've never even considered going into business for myself, let alone selling power bars," Laurie retorts. But then, as an afterthought, she adds, "Of course, it does make a lot of sense for a nutritionist to produce wholesome food. And it would probably sell well, since most outdoors people know the difference between good stuff and junk." She looks at him. "Pete, are you really serious about this?"

"Well, the idea came to me out of the blue, but I think I am at least serious about exploring it," Pete answers, half-laughing. "It could certainly solve both our problems. And I think this is an ideal town for trying this kind of business. Want to think about it?"

"Let's mull it over for a few days. I'll see what my husband thinks," Laurie responds. But it's not her husband she's concerned with, it's herself. She likes Pete, but she doesn't know him well, and they don't seem to have much in common except a love of animals—she's married and has a family, he's single with no kids. She's quiet and introverted, he's outgoing and gregarious. Laurie is concerned that if they go into business together, their differences will make it more difficult to come to agreement over problems that will inevitably come up.

After a couple of days of serious thinking, Laurie decides their differences don't have to be a barrier to working well together. After all, she and her husband have many differences, yet their marriage has worked out very well. Perhaps, she concludes optimistically, her differences with Pete will make their partnership more dynamic. And since Pete doesn't have a family, that means he can operate as more of a free agent, which will allow them more flexibility.

Several days later, Pete and Laurie realize they are growing more and more excited about going into business together. One afternoon, they load Nugget and Paco into the back seat of Pete's car and drive to a nearby outdoor equipment store, which they knew stocked various trail mixes and foods. They check out the ingredients of the store's energy bars, buy a few of each (Paco and Nugget will have to share), and ask the salespeople for their opinions on the quality of the bars. Then they return to the park, unwrap and sample the competition.

"You're right. They could taste better," announces Laurie, as they bite into one bar after another. Both become more and more enthusiastic, sensing they may be onto something.

"I told you," Pete says. "I've never tasted anything like your bars. They're light years better than the rest of this stuff."

They agree that over the next week, Laurie will make up a batch of energy bars, listing her ingredients and costs. She will then talk to a friend who works at a small local food company to help with estimating the costs of mass production. Both Laurie and Pete know that many small food companies start by contracting out actual manufacture, because that is less costly than making the product themselves. Both wonder about doing this. Is it possible to really assure top quality if you don't handle production yourself? Pete will look into distribution and marketing costs, focusing on how hard and expensive it is likely to be to get a power bar widely distributed. Both prospective partners will read as many technical books and trade magazines about small food companies they can get their hands on.

"Oh, and I'll also check out the legalities," Pete adds.

"What legalities?" Laurie asks, arching an eyebrow.

"The legalities of setting up a business," Pete answers. "We're talking about a partnership, right? Well, what does that mean, exactly? What paperwork does it involve, and will we have to file formal papers?"

"Of course," Laurie says. "In all of our excitement, I guess we neglected one or two small details."

"There's a lot to consider," Pete continues. "We don't even know if a partnership is the best way to go. My uncle Jim, who's an architect in Atlanta, told me it's sometimes better to organize a business as a corporation because it qualifies you for limited liability. That might be quite an advantage if our business fizzles. Also, we have to figure out a tax structure that isn't going to bury us. And there are

lots of other questions that need answering about licenses, permits and so on. The food business is more heavily regulated than most."

"Hum," Laurie frowns. "Maybe we should get a lawyer and let her figure out this stuff."

Pete appears horrified. "At $250 an hour?! No way. I'm sure there's a way to get good information without going into debt before we even get started. Once we know what's involved, then we can decide if we need a lawyer or not—and if we do, how we can keep the costs down."

"That's fine with me, Pete," Laurie says. "You worry about the business end, and all the paperwork, and I'll get started on the product end of it. Let's compare notes in a week."

One week later, Pete is stunned at all that Laurie has accomplished. She presents him with sixteen samples—four recipes for four different bars—which she wants him to take into the mountains and pass out to his buddies. In addition, she's priced ingredients, wrapping machines and industrial-sized mixers. She has also talked to two local food processing companies that already have the necessary equipment and permits about how much they would charge to do contract manufacturing.

Though he doesn't express his concerns aloud, Pete is a little taken aback by the prospect of going into business with someone so organized and focused. He hopes her expectations of him will not far exceed what he is willing or able to give to the business. He knows he's a hard worker, but he does not intend to work 70 hours a week or give up his hobbies. After all, one of his reasons for working for himself is so he can remain close to his beloved Rocky Mountains and indulge his outdoor passions.

"Well…I did do some research," Pete tells her. "I've talked to a health inspector about the kind of facilities we'll need if we do our own production and got some information about federal food labeling rules. I've also given some preliminary thought to how much we can charge and what sort of a wholesale discount structure we'll have to offer."

Pete continues. "Remember my Uncle Jim in Atlanta? Well, I called him and he said we can create a partnership agreement ourselves with a good legal self-help reference book. He recommended a book called *The Partnership Book,* by Denis Clifford and Ralph Warner. [You didn't think we'd let them get their partnership information anywhere else, did you?] He said it would help us figure out whether to set up as a partnership or corporation. I picked up a copy and studied it the last couple of nights—from what I've read, I can't see any advantage to us incorporating. Plus, it would involve lots of paperwork and cost a few hundred dollars."

"Do most partners go through this process before going into business together?" Laurie asks Pete. The fact that Pete was insistent about formalizing their relationship seemed sensible and professional from a business point of view, but it also caused her to question if he trusted her (and by inference, whether she should trust him). To her, it seemed a little like being asked to sign a prenuptial wedding agreement instead of focusing on the romance.

Pete tries to reassure her. "I don't know if everyone goes through this process, but I've heard some real horror stories about people who just winged it. I'm convinced that it's worth taking the time to figure this stuff out now. I want to make sure that we're absolutely clear with each other about how we want to run this business, what we want to get out of it and where we want it to go."

"But can't we just talk things out?" Laurie asks. "We pretty much agree on everything so far."

"Maybe so," Pete responds, "But going through this process will force us to pay attention to lots of issues we might never have thought of if we relied just on talking." He adds, "I bought a copy of *The Partnership Book* for you as well. I think we should both read up on the different business forms before we decide on anything else."

Several days later, Laurie invites Pete over for coffee at her house. She explains that it's important to include her husband in what they are planning and make sure that he and Pete are comfortable with each other.

When Pete arrives, Laurie gets right down to business. "Well, I've read *The Partnership Book*—at least the part on partnerships and corporations. I asked Santiago to read it, too. We both agree with you. It makes sense for us to start out as legal partners. If we buy enough insurance, the fact that corporations give their owners limited liability doesn't really help us." Then she adds, "And by the way, I now understand why you insisted that we formalize our agreement. I don't want our business to risk being a casualty because we didn't pin down what we wanted at the start."

At that moment, the phone rings, and a voice from another room calls, "Mom, it's your sister. I told her you were busy, but she says she needs to talk to you for just a minute."

"Excuse me a minute," Laurie says. "I'll be right back."

Waiting for Laurie to return, Pete begins to feel uneasy. His own home life is so solitary, and Laurie's so traditional; he wonders if this will have an effect on their business relationship. Laurie enters the room and suggests that Santiago, and the twins if they are interested, join her and Pete in the living room.

Once seated around the coffee table, Pete begins to share his view of the partnership business and why he feels it will prosper.

"Have you come up with a name for the bars yet?" asks one of the twins.

"Twin Bars?" jokes Pete.

"No way," the twins say, almost in unison. Then one of them launches into an explanation of the burden of being seen as a double. Naming the bars Twin Bars would cause both of them psychological damage, she insists.

The second twin says, "I have an idea. Pete, do you remember where the three of us met, the night we gave you one of mom's energy bars?"

"Sure," Pete responds. "It was in the Crow's Nest."

"Well, how about Crowbars?" the twin says.

Everybody seems to like that idea, except Laurie, who shudders every time she thinks of the twins up in that Crow's Nest.

"Let's all think about it some more, but I like that," Pete says. "It's simple, it resonates and it's got several meanings, all of which work. But still, it doesn't pay to fall in love with a marketing idea without lots of thought. Also, we'll need to do a federal trademark search to be sure someone else hasn't already reserved that name, or something too similar."

"Great," the twins say, excusing themselves from the room. At this point, only Laurie, Santiago and Pete remain.

"I've worked out some of the start-up figures. Can we go over them now?" Pete says to Laurie, wondering if Santiago is going to remain for the entire discussion.

"Sure," Laurie says. "Do you mind if Santiago stays? For better or for worse, we're a family, which means, frankly, I need his agreement and support to really commit to this."

"That's fine," Pete replies, not entirely certain that it is, but not willing to say no at this point. He makes a mental note to clarify with Laurie how she sees Santiago's role in their business. "The way I see it, we'll need a considerable amount of start-up cash to buy equipment, supplies, ingredients, and get the word out. Of course, if we contract out manufacturing and concentrate on marketing until we see how sales go, we can save some. At any rate, I think I can come up with about $35,000. How about you?" he asks Laurie.

"I have about $9,000 I can throw in. But I don't think I can come up with much more than that," Laurie says, looking at Pete for his reaction.

"But remember, Papa Juan will give you $4,000," Santiago says to Laurie, "so that would bring your contribution up to $13,000."

"Pete, if we contribute unequal sums, how does that affect our partnership? We want to be equal partners then, don't we?" Laurie asks.

"Definitely," Pete answers. "So we'll have to work on what we put in and come up with something fair. And there's a lot more we have to hash out. For instance, what if after a couple of years one or the other of us wants out? What happens to that person's share of the business?"

"Right," Laurie says. "Or what happens if the business really takes off and we want to bring

someone into the partnership midstream? We have to have an agreement about that, no?"

"Exactly," says Pete. "Or, God forbid, suppose something happens to one of us? What then? What happens to that person's share of the partnership's profits or debts?"

"Can we back up a minute?" Santiago asks. "Pete, why do you think this business will work? Obviously, the food business is dominated by huge companies, which means you need to gear up for a national or even international market. How can you compete with them?"

"I've worked in sales for ten years, so I know what you're asking, and believe me, I think a bit of skepticism that a start-up can succeed in the food business makes sense," Pete responds. "But despite the obstacles, we have a chance if we really have a product that's better. Remember, we're after a niche market—mountaineers, climbers and other serious outdoors people. These folks are serious about what they do—people don't climb with third best rope or just pretty good pitons. They want the best and will pay for it."

"The other advantage we have," Pete goes on, "is that most mountaineering shops are willing to try new products, especially if we can get our product favorably reviewed in the climbing magazines. At least at the beginning, we should avoid mass merchants. Of course, if the customers don't like Crowbars, we won't last long. But if we really do have the best product, and I think we do, the business side can work. For example, I have a number of ideas as to how we can get samples into the hands of hardcore climbers and let them spread the word for us. It's unbelievable how fast positive word-of-mouth can get the word out on a new product that's really better."

"I guess we have a lot more work to do in coming up with a written partnership agreement," Laurie says.

"Definitely," Pete agrees. "I have a suggestion. Why don't we each study the sample clauses in *The Partnership Book* and see how they would apply to our situation. Then, if we don't agree with something in them, or we find they don't cover our business exactly, we can add some more, or alter what's there. In addition, I think we should invest a few of our dollars in getting the help of a small business consultant. Before we get too deep into this, we need a business and marketing plan, a proposed profit and loss forecast and a cash flow analysis. I know this sounds tedious, but we can't start flying blind. If the bars do well, we need to know that we have the financial ability to increase production while we wait for the money to come in."

"Pete, that's an excellent idea," Laurie says. Santiago agrees. "How about getting together again next week and trying to draft a preliminary agreement. That ought to give us time to study the book more."

"Perfect," Pete says.

After meeting with Laurie and her family, Pete is a bit overwhelmed. He's not sure if he's ready to commit to the business, and, in the process, to Laurie and Laurie's family.

Three days later, Laurie calls Pete to tell him she's found a wonderful building that is presently being renovated by her Uncle Carlos, who will rent space to them cheap. She also says that the equipment they will need to make the bars can be purchased used at a very reasonable cost. She adds that, if possible, she favors doing their own production because that way quality will be assured. Finally, she tells Pete that she sees a potentially big expense for them in packaging equipment and is working on that.

Once again, Pete is impressed by Laurie's energy and now sees both her high-spiritedness and her big family as a real business asset rather than a burden. Working with her is turning into an exciting venture, albeit a scary one. Everything is happening pretty fast. Losing his job at Karlsbraat is something he'd never anticipated happening, and he's been fighting his sense of insecurity about the future. This business venture is clearly a gamble, and he takes it very seriously. At the same time, he doesn't want the job to eat him alive. For him, it's a means to an end—to allow him plenty of time for skiing

and rock climbing. He knows that he and Laurie have to talk about this just to be sure there is no misunderstanding. But he senses that Laurie's love of family and her desire to have time to spend with them is as strong as his passion for the out-of-doors and hopes they will be in rough agreement. In the meantime, Pete decides to hop on a jet and go to a big climbing gear trade show in Los Angeles. This will give him a chance to talk to prospective sales reps and wholesalers and get a better feel for the business. He is confident that he knows mountaineering and he knows selling, but he doesn't know enough about selling to mountaineering stores and direct-mail catalog marketers.

When he returns later that week, he and Laurie meet at an old brick mill, now empty, which Uncle Carlos intends to subdivide into several work spaces. The building is at the bottom of a gravel driveway, surrounded by a grassy expanse. Pete finds the setting comforting. It's not quite the panoramic view of the Rockies he had at Karlsbraat, but it has a good feeling, and he senses he would be happy coming to work here. He learns that an indoor gym is under construction a couple of blocks away, and notices that a couple of coffee houses have already sprouted up to serve the artists and artisans who have gravitated to the area. Best of all, Laurie's uncle is offering to lease them space in the building for a year, with an option to renew for several more, at what Pete knows to be a very favorable rate.

Carlos invites them to follow him inside. They find themselves in a large bare room, with a concrete floor, brick walls, and skylights. Laurie walks around it energetically, enumerating all the things they'll need: shelves for bulk ingredients, a king-sized refrigerator, work tables, industrial mixers, ovens, a cooling space and a conveyor belt that attaches to a packaging machine, which will, theoretically, wrap their product.

Once they are outside the building, Pete extends his hand to Carlos. "We really like the space, Carlos," he says, "and appreciate your generosity, but before we accept, we need about two weeks to work on our profit-and-loss statement and to be sure we can handle doing our own manufacturing. We need to at least look at bids to contract it out and then do a comparison, and so on."

"That's fair," Carlos tells him. "I'll hold the space that long at no charge and then we'll talk business. But I don't promise to hold it a day longer." He speaks with solemnity. "I'm as serious about my business as you are." Carlos adds, "And one more thing. I'm proposing a low rent because I want to help Laurie, and because I like your business idea, but if you do well, I want the option to renew to bring your lease up to market rate."

"Agreed, Carlos!" Pete replies, laughing. "By the way, do you mind if we set up a camp table and a couple of stools on the lawn? Laurie and I have some paperwork to do, and I can't think of anyplace better to do it."

"Help yourselves," Carlos says.

The next day, Pete loads a table and chairs into his Explorer and drives over to their new space. By the time Laurie pulls up, she finds Pete hard at work, with his copy of *The Partnership Book,* quite dog-eared by now, on the table in front of him. He is making notes on a long legal pad.

Laurie reaches into her pack and pulls out her own copy of the book. It is tagged with lots of little yellow Post-It notes.

"Well, are we ready?" Laurie asks Pete. "Did you study the clauses in the book? Can we use any of them?"

"Well, there were many clauses I think we can use, but first we have to work out the problem of how we can be equal partners when we don't put in the same amount of money," Pete answers.

"I agree," says Laurie. "I mean, I like you, Pete, or I wouldn't be considering going into business with you, but that doesn't mean I want you as my boss. This has got to be an equal partnership."

"You know I agree. So how do we balance out that I'll be putting in more money? Are you willing to put in more hours until you catch up?" Pete asks.

"I don't know. To make this work, we'll both have to be working very hard, and I can't imagine putting in extra hours on top of that. I don't think my family would be very happy with that arrangement either, since they're used to me working a 15-hour week."

So they talk some more, broach new ideas, shoot them down, and come up with more new ones. Finally, Laurie suggests that perhaps she should get some contribution credit for the low rent that Carlos has offered them on the building. Pete agrees that this is fair. They work out that her contribution will include the difference between their rent and conventional rents in the area for the first year of the lease period. In addition, he suggests that Laurie's recipes should be given a value. Laurie is delighted that he is being so fair, but indicates she is still worried that the shares aren't 50/50.

"We can figure out the details later," Pete says, "but how about your leaving half of your profits in the partnership until your total contribution equals mine?"

"You mean, we split the profits 50/50, but I don't get paid half of my half?" Laurie asks.

"Right, but only until your contribution, including a fair amount for the rent and a couple thousand dollars for the recipes, equals my $35,000 contribution," Pete replies.

"That's certainly a possibility," Laurie says. "I hadn't thought of that."

They talk about it some more. Laurie remembers that she needs money to help pay the twins' tuition at Cornell and proposes that 25% of her profits be retained by the business until her total contributions equal Pete's.

Pete agrees and then asks, "How about decision-making? Do we confer on every aspect of the business?"

"I don't think so. Doesn't it make sense for me to make the production decisions—you know, what ingredients to order, and when, and whether to add a pinch more sugar, or a few grains less salt—while you make the marketing decisions? I don't know anything about hiring sales reps or collecting accounts. Maybe we can set it up so that we both can write checks, but if it involves over $1,000, we both have to sign."

"That's good. I like that," Pete agrees.

"What about dividing the work responsibilities?" Laurie continues. "It's clear that I'll do the cooking and supervise packaging, and you'll take care of marketing and distribution, but what about the bookkeeping? Do we hire someone? And what happens when we have an equipment failure? Who takes care of repairs?"

"I think I can handle most of the repairs myself, but if I can't, I'll take care of finding someone who can," Pete says. Then he adds, "But we need to hire a combination bookkeeper/order taker right from the beginning, even if it's only part time. It's essential that we set up a good invoice and billing system—as well as good books—from the start. It will make it so much easier down the road, don't you agree?"

"I do. And I certainly don't want to keep the books myself!" Laurie says emphatically. She goes on, "Also, I feel pretty strongly that I don't want to work more than an eight- or nine-hour day. Even with my mother taking care of the kitchen, and the twins away at school, I've got to be home for dinner. Dinner has always been a ritual in our house— and Santiago and I are committed to maintaining that at all costs."

"Fine by me," Pete concurs. "What about vacations? I'm willing to commit to six months a year of nonstop work. After that, if I can't get some skiing and mountain climbing in, I won't be a very happy camper, I can tell you that!"

"Same here. Every year we go back to Venezuela so my mother and father can visit with my sister and brother. They can't travel alone, and these trips have become another family ritual," Laurie explains. "And I want to take a few days off at Christmas, because the girls will be home from college, and I want to spend as much time with them as I can. Also, if possible, I'd love to take Thanksgiving weekend."

"I'm not so concerned about holidays, because the ski slopes and trails are too busy at those times. But once we get up and running, I do need to be able to take some three- and four-day weekends now and then. And every couple of years, I'd like to take a month or two to go on bigger adventures," Pete says.

"A month or two?" Laurie asks, a little concerned.

"I'm saying it now, so it won't surprise you later," Pete says. "That's one of the reasons I'm willing to work so hard now. Money has never been my main objective—freedom is. If I thought I'd be permanently tied down to the business, I'd scrap it before it got started."

"Hopefully by then we'll be doing well enough to be able to hire competent people, maybe even a manager," says Laurie. "Realistically, if we don't sell enough to bring in others by that time, we'll probably give up anyway. In the meantime, I think it will work out just great. You can spell me over the holidays, and I'll cover for you on your long weekends. It sounds perfect."

They agree to meet again in a week and to redraft a partnership agreement, incorporating the decisions they'd arrived at that day.

Laurie and Pete are surprised at how much discussion has gone into working out the details of their partnership agreement. Still, they haven't hit any major stumbling blocks so far, nor have they had many tense moments.

"We'd better wait before we pat ourselves on the back," Laurie says, laughing. "*The Partnership Book* says we're just reaching the hardest part."

"You're right," Pete says, getting down to business. "Next subject. Buy-outs. What happens if we do pretty well, but one of us wants to quit?"

"You're quitting already?" Laurie says, teasing him.

Pete doesn't bite. He wants to get this thing tacked down. "Say, five years from now, you and Santiago decide to move to Tampa, Florida. What happens then?"

"We move, of course," Laurie answers.

"Right, and what happens to the business? I'm not exactly a whiz in the kitchen, you know. And I wouldn't want to run the business alone," Pete adds.

"Or what if you're skiing in the Alps one year and I get a telegraph saying you've married some ruddy-cheeked Heidi person and you're not coming back? I'm not sure I'd want to give up the business, but I wouldn't want to have to come up with an outrageous sum of money to buy you out, either," Laurie says.

Peter smiles. "Exactly. This stuff can get complex. We've got to work it out now. Neither of us wants to be stuck holding the bag sometime down the road."

Laurie agrees. "First we have to determine what the business is worth, right? How do we do that? Do we just estimate the worth of the inventory? No, that can't be right," she corrects herself. "Because what happens if we're making a lot of money? The business will be worth more than just the inventory."

"Correct," Pete says. "Let's hope the business is worth a lot more four years from now than our stock-on-hand and the value of our equipment."

"Should we just agree on an arbitrary amount now? Like maybe $50,000?" Laurie suggests.

"I don't think it's realistic. We don't have any track record yet," Pete says. "Anyway, neither one of us is likely to be able to come up with that much money in one lump sum. Especially if the remaining partner wants to continue the business. Having to pay out a large sum of money would almost certainly break the business, even if it was successful."

Laurie agrees. Then she says, "I'm confused. Where do we go from here?"

Pete opens his copy of *The Partnership Book.* "I've gone over the different ways to value a business. I think we ought to use what they call the asset-valuation method now—for a while—until we really get off the ground. Basically, this means the business is worth the market price of all our specific assets—the ingredients, the machinery, even the lease. What it won't cover is if Crowbars becomes a valuable brand name—like you could sell just the name for a lot of money."

"That hasn't quite happened yet," Laurie notes.

"True," Pete concedes.

"And if you leave in a year, I don't want to pay you for a name that probably won't have much value by then," Laurie adds.

"But in five years, it might," Pete responds.

"It certainly will!" Laurie states emphatically.

"Let's agree to meet every year and consider if a different valuing method works better," Pete suggests. "If it does, we'll amend our agreement."

"Every year? We'll be seeing each other almost every day, unless you know something I don't know," Laurie quips.

"I mean a formal meeting, specifically to discuss valuation," Pete says.

"Okay," Laurie agrees. "That makes sense."

"I have another question for you," Pete continues. "What happens if I do move to Switzerland, but I have a friend who's willing to buy me out for $50,000, or whatever we've decided to be the worth of the business at that time? Do I have the right to sell my share to him and introduce him to you as your new partner?" Pete asks.

"Well, what's he like," Laurie replies, going along with the story.

"Let's say he's a great businessman, but he poisons dogs."

"No way," Laurie says, laughing. "Hmmmm. I guess we need a clause giving each other the right to buy the other out before either of us gets snagged with someone we hate. I don't believe in arranged marriage, so why would I go along with an arranged partnership?" Laurie adds.

"Exactly. Now, what happens if, God forbid, I'm killed in a ski accident and my will leaves everything to my brother?" Pete continues.

"I didn't even know you had a brother," Laurie says, with curiosity.

"I do. He lives in New York, on Staten Island. He's an actor." Pete says. "And believe me, as much as I love him, I have to say that you don't want to do business with him."

"So, I have to pay him for your half of the business, right?" Laurie asks.

"Yup."

"Hmmm, wait a minute. There's something else I read that we should think about. Suppose you quit because you want to ski all the time. It seems to me I shouldn't have to pay as much as if you died, or had to move," Laurie says.

"Okay," Pete muses. "Yeah, I know I'd feel more generous toward you if you had to leave out of some kind of family necessity than if you just wanted to go off to the Bahamas or Tampa to live in the sun."

"Well, we need to cover this," Laurie states. "Let's come up with something reasonable."

After considerable discussion and review of *The Partnership Book,* Pete and Laurie realize there isn't anywhere they can go to find out what is "reasonable." Once again, they have to work it out themselves. Eventually they decide that what they are really concerned about is one partner simply deciding to bail out, leaving the other one stuck with the business. By contrast, if a partner dies or becomes disabled, or must leave, they are inclined to say that that partner should get full price.

"Do we define 'must leave'?" Pete asks.

"I don't think so," Laurie replies. "After all, we could write a novel about all the possible scenarios that could happen."

"At least a soap opera," Pete notes.

They finally decide that if a partner leaves for reasons other than personal or family necessity (or disability or death), the buy-out price would be reduced. They want the reduction to be substantial, and settle on 35% of the regular price as a fair figure.

Laurie's and Pete's partnership officially begins. They sign a lease, find a company that will lease them a used packaging machine cheap because they want future business and set up a deal with a local graphics designer, who agrees to design package and original promo art dirt cheap with the idea of getting lots of follow-up business if all goes well. They buy stoves, mixers, trays—all the production equipment they need. Laurie orders the ingredients to make 5,000 Crowbars. Pete contacts stores about sending samples.

But before all this actually got underway, they hammered out and signed their actual partnership agreement, using *The Partnership Book.* Here is their final agreement.

For Laurie and Pete, preparing many of the clauses in their agreement required no more than filling in the blanks of a sample clause of *The Partnership Book.* For some of their clauses, though, they had to make some adjustments of the book's clauses to fit their specific needs. For example, there is no sample clause covering contributions out of profits when that partner has already made a cash contribution, as Laurie did. However, there is a sample clause for contribution from profits. So Pete and Laurie adapted that clause to their situation. They needed to make phrasing changes in other clauses, especially in the buy-out clauses, because there are only two partners.

PARTNERSHIP AGREEMENT

This Partnership Agreement is entered into and effective as of June 6, 2004, by Laurie Mendez and Peter ("Pete") Johnston, the partners.

1. NAME

   The name of the partnership shall be: Mendez and Johnston.

   The name of the partnership business shall be: Crowbars.

2. TERM OF THE PARTNERSHIP

   The partnership shall last until it is dissolved by all the partners, or a partner leaves, for any reason, including death.

3. PURPOSES OF THE PARTNERSHIP

   The purposes of the partnership are: to produce and sell Crowbars, high quality climbers' food, and other high quality food products.

   The specific purposes of the partnership are set out above. In addition, the goals and dreams of each partner are set out below. The partners understand that this statement is not legally binding, but include it in the Partnership Agreement as a record of their hopes and intentions. Both partners hope to create a prosperous business that sells a quality product, and which allows them to live the lives they want. Laurie wants to help provide for her family, including her children's college educations, and pay for travel. Pete wants to continue his mountain climbing, skiing and travel.

4. CONTRIBUTIONS

   The initial capital of the partnership shall consist of the following:

   A. Cash Contributions

Name	Amount
Laurie Mendez	$13,000
Peter Johnston	$35,000

   Each partner's contribution shall be paid in full by July 10, 2004.

   B. Cash Credit

   Laurie Mendez shall receive a credit of $5,000 towards her contribution because of the below-market rent provided by her uncle for the first year of the lease of the premises at 56 Holloway Street (etc.) and $2,000 credit for use of her recipes.

C. Contribution Out of Profit

Laurie shall subsequently contribute to the partnership capital twenty-five percent (25%) of her share of the partnership profits for each fiscal year, beginning June 6, 2004, until her total contribution, including cash and cash credit, equals Peter's.

D. Ownership of Partnership Business

Each partner's ownership share of the business shall be:

Name	Share
Laurie Mendez	50%
Peter Johnston	50%

5. PROFITS AND LOSSES

The partners will share all profits equally, and they will be distributed at least monthly. All losses of the partnership shall also be shared equally.

6. MANAGEMENT POWERS AND DUTIES

A. Skills Contributed

All partners shall be actively involved and materially participate in the management and operation of the partnership business.

Each partner named below shall participate in the business by working in the manner described: Laurie shall be in charge of the production of Crowbars. Peter shall be in charge of the marketing of Crowbars.

B. Partnership Decisions

All major decisions of the partnership business must be made by a unanimous decision of both partners. Minor business decisions may be made by an individual partner. Major decisions are defined as the expenditure of $1,000 or more.

C. Hours Worked

Except for vacations, holidays, and times of illness, each partner shall work at least thirty (30) hours per week on partnership business.

D. Leaves of Absence

Any partner can take a leave of absence from the partnership upon agreement by the other partner.

E. Accountings

1. Accounting on Request by a Partner:

Accountings of any aspect of partnership business shall be made upon written request by any partner.

2. Accountant to Determine Profits and Losses:

The partnership's net profit or net loss for each fiscal year shall be determined as soon as practicable after the close of that fiscal year. This should be done by a certified public accountant in accordance with the accounting principles employed in the preparation of the federal income tax return filed by the partnership for that year, but without a special provision for tax-exempt or partially tax-exempt income.

F. Outside Business Activities: Permitted, Except for Direct Competition

Any partner may be engaged in one or more other businesses as well as the business of the partnership, but only to the extent that this activity does not directly and materially interfere with the business of the partnership and does not conflict with the time commitments and other obligations of that partner to the partnership under this Agreement. Neither the partnership nor any other partner shall have any right to any income or profit derived by a partner from any business activity permitted under this section.

G. Ownership of Business Assets

1. Trade Secrets:

All trade secrets used or developed by the partnership, including customer lists and sources of supplies, will be owned and controlled by the partnership.

2. Business Name:

The partnership name of Crowbars shall be partnership property. In the event of the departure of a partner, and/or dissolution of the partnership, control and ownership of the partnership name shall be determined pursuant to this Agreement.

7. TRANSFER OF A PARTNER'S INTEREST

A. Sale to Partnership at Its Option

If any partner leaves the partnership, for whatever reason, whether he or she quits, withdraws, is expelled, retires or dies, he or she or his or her estate shall be obligated to sell his or her interest in the partnership to the remaining owner, who may buy that interest, under the terms and conditions set forth in this Agreement.

B. The Partnership's Right to First Refusal Upon Offer From Outsiders

If any partner receives a bona fide legitimate offer, whether or not solicited by him or her, from a person not a partner, to purchase all of his or her interest in the partnership, and if the partner receiving the offer is willing to accept it, he or she shall give written notice of the amount and terms of the offer, the identity of the proposed buyer, and his or her willingness to accept the offer to the other partner. The other partner shall have the option, within thirty (30) days after the notice is given, to purchase that partner's interest on the same terms as those contained in the offer.

C. Refusal of the Remaining Partners to Buy

If the remaining partner does not purchase the departing partner's share of the business, under the terms provided in this Agreement, within thirty (30) days, the entire business of the partnership shall be put up for sale, and listed with the appropriate sales agencies, agents or brokers.

D. Requiring Advance Notice of Withdrawal

Unless physically prevented from giving notice, a partner shall give sixty (60) days written advance notice of his or her intention to leave the partnership. If he or she fails to do so, the buy-out price shall be reduced by twenty percent (20%).

E. Conflicts Regarding Right to Buy: The Coin Flip

If the partners cannot agree on who has the right to purchase the other partners' interest in the business, that right shall be determined by the flip of a coin.

8. BUY-OUTS

   A. The Asset-Valuation Method

   Except as otherwise provided in this Agreement, the value of the partnership shall be made by determining the net worth of the partnership as of the date a partner leaves, for any reason. Net worth is defined as the market value, as of that date, of the following assets:

   1. All tangible property, real or personal, owned by the business;
   2. All the liquid assets owned by the business, including cash on hand, bank deposits, and CDs or other monies;
   3. All accounts receivable;
   4. All earned but unbilled fees;
   5. All money presently earned for work in progress;
   6. Less the total amount of all debts owed by the business.

   B. Revision of Valuation Method

   The partners understand and agree that the preceding business-valuation clause may not fully and adequately reflect the worth of the business after it has been successfully established, if the business has earned goodwill. Therefore, the partners agree that two years after the commencement of the business they will amend this business-valuation clause to include a method that will reflect any goodwill earned by the business.

   C. Variation of the Buy-Out Price

   The preceding method for calculating the value of the business shall be varied as stated below, for the reasons stated below:

   If a partner leaves not for reasons of death, disability or personal or family necessity, but to pursue other opportunities or plans, the buy-out price shall be reduced thirty-five percent (35%).

   D. Payment by Equal Monthly Payment

   Whenever the partnership (or the remaining owner) is obligated or chooses to purchase a partner's interest, it shall pay for that interest by promissory note of the partnership. Any promissory note shall be dated as of the effective date of the purchase, shall mature in not more than five (5) years, shall be payable in equal installments that come due monthly, and shall bear interest at the rate of ten percent (10%) per annum. The first payment shall be made sixty (60) days after the date of the promissory note.

9. CONTINUITY OF PARTNERSHIP BUSINESS

   A. Control of Partnership Name

   The partnership business name of Crowbars is owned by the partnership. Should any partner leave the business and desire to use the name Crowbars, and the remaining partner desires to continue the business and use the name Crowbars, ownership and control of the partnership business name shall be decided by mediation/arbitration.

10. MEDIATION AND ARBITRATION

A. Mediation

1. The partners agree that, except as otherwise provided in this Agreement, any dispute arising out of this Agreement or the partnership business shall first be resolved by mediation, if possible. The partners are aware that mediation is a voluntary process, and pledge to cooperate fully and fairly with the mediator in any attempt to reach a mutually satisfactory compromise to a dispute.

2. The mediator shall be as agreed on by the partners. If they cannot agree, the mediator shall be chosen by Catherine Howard, friend of both partners.

3. If any partner to a dispute feels it cannot be resolved by the partners themselves, he or she shall so notify the other partners, and the mediator, in writing.

4. Mediation shall commence within five (5) days of this notice of request for mediation.

5. Any decision reached by mediation shall be reduced to writing, signed by all partners and be binding on them.

6. The costs of mediation shall be shared equally by all partners to the dispute.

B. Arbitration with One Arbitrator

1. The partners agree that, except as otherwise provided in this Agreement, or the partnership business, shall be arbitrated under the terms of this clause. The arbitration shall be carried out by a single arbitrator who shall be agreed upon by the partners to the dispute. If the partners cannot agree on the arbitrator, the arbitrator shall be selected by Catherine Howard.

Any arbitration shall be held as follows:

2. The partner initiating the arbitration procedure shall inform the other partner in writing of the nature of the dispute at the same time that he or she notifies the arbitrator.

3. Within seven (7) days from receipt of this notice, the other partner shall reply in writing, stating his or her views of the nature of the dispute.

4. The arbitrator shall hold a hearing on the dispute within seven (7) days after the reply of the other partner. Each partner shall be entitled to present whatever oral or written statements he or she wishes and may present witnesses. No person may be represented by a lawyer or any third party.

5. The arbitrator shall make his or her decision in writing.

6. If the partner to whom the demand for arbitration is directed fails to respond within the proper time limit, the partner initiating the arbitration must give the other an additional five days' written notice of "intention to proceed to arbitration." If there is still no response, the partner initiating the arbitration may proceed with the arbitration before the arbitrator, and his or her award shall be binding.

7. The cost of arbitration shall be borne by the partners as the arbitrator shall direct.

8. The arbitration award shall be conclusive and binding on the partners and shall be set forth in such a

way that a formal judgment can be entered in the court having jurisdiction over the dispute if either partner so desires.

C. Combining Mediation with Arbitration

If the partners cannot resolve the dispute by mediation, the dispute shall be arbitrated as provided in the arbitration clause of this Agreement.

D. Time for Mediation

If the partners have not resolved their dispute within thirty (30) days of the commencement of mediation, the partners shall have failed to have resolved their dispute by mediation under this Agreement, and the dispute shall be arbitrated.

11. AMENDMENTS

Amendment by Unanimous Agreement

This Agreement may be amended only by written consent of all partners.

12. GENERAL PROVISIONS

A. State Law

The partners have formed this general partnership under the laws of the State of Colorado, intending to be legally bound thereby.

B. Attached Papers Incorporated

Any attached sheet or document shall be regarded as fully contained in this Partnership Agreement.

C. Agreement is All Inclusive

This Agreement contains the entire understanding of the partners regarding their rights and duties in the partnership. Any alleged oral representations of modifications concerning this Agreement shall be of no force or effect unless contained in a subsequent written modification signed by all partners.

D. Binding on All Successors and Inheritors

This Agreement shall be binding on and for the benefit of the respective successors, inheritors, assigns and personal representatives of the partners, except to the extent of any contrary provision in the Agreement.

E. Severability

If any term, provision, or condition of this Agreement is held by a court of competent jurisdiction to be invalid, void or unenforceable, the rest of the Agreement shall remain in full force and effect and shall in no way be affected, impaired or invalidated.

Signature: _Laurie Mendez_   Dated: _6/6/04_
Laurie Mendez

Signature: _Peter Johnston_   Dated: _6/6/04_
Peter Johnston

Epilogue

Five years later, after loads of hard work and periods of real anxiety, Crowbars has prospered to the point where sales are now well over $2 million annually and growing nicely. Laurie and Pete have had some arguments and a couple of serious fights, but have been able to work things out, and are now considering adding two new products. Paco and Nugget, the best of dog-friends, continue to crave Crowbars and pine to be allowed inside the manufacturing plant, particularly the kitchen. The twins are finishing up at Cornell, with one planning to go on to architecture school and the other wanting to take some time out to climb before starting law school. ("More tuition," moans Laurie, unsuccessfully masking her pride.) Paul is now a sophomore at the University of Colorado. Laurie and Santiago are personally, if not financially, freer than they have been since they were kids.

Pete's life has changed dramatically. Let's accompany Laurie as she stops by Pete's house for a short meeting one Friday afternoon before taking off for a weekend ski trip with Santiago.

"Hang out in the front room for a minute, will you Laurie?" Pete says as he lets her in, "I'm just finishing with Kevin's diapers, and he should conk out for an hour."

"Let's just hope Kevin doesn't bleed to death," Laurie laughs.

"You're showing your age, partner. Even cloth diapers come with Velcro fasteners these days," Pete calls out to her from the nursery.

Much to everyone's surprise, including his own, Pete has accepted, and sometimes enjoys, being a part-time house dad. His wife, Teresa, a veterinarian, has just opened a new pet hospital and has a more demanding work schedule than Pete these days. "I enjoy being with Kevin most of the time," he tells Laurie, "but don't think I'm not counting the days until I can take him out on the slopes. Do you think two years old is too young to get him started?" Then he grins, "I can't wait to see him in his little blue ski suit and toddler skis."

Amidst the chaos in Pete's living room, the two partners set to work. The subject for today is how to manage the steady growth of their business. Laurie has proposed that Patricia, who has managed Crowbars' production for the past two years, including responsibility for its 11 employees, be given a stake in the business. Pete, at first reluctant to give up any ownership ("After all, I've got my own kid's tuition to worry about in 17 years"), starts the meeting by saying, "Laurie, I've reconsidered. You're right about Patricia being invaluable to us. If she leaves, we'll be back to those ten-hour days."

"That's why I've been lobbying so hard to give her a share in the business. But I want to be sure that you and I maintain more than 50% ownership at all times. I think we should also allow for the possibility we will want to give others an ownership share, so I think cutting Patricia in for 5% is fair."

"I don't think Patricia will have a problem with that," Pete replies. "Let's talk it over with her and see if she has some ideas on how to do it."

"And, Pete, we need to talk with her about relocating to a bigger plant. We can't possibly expand Crowbars production in that kitchen."

"Move? No way! I love that place, Laurie."

"You're the one who's got to worry about college tuition now, remember?" Laurie retorts.

"You managed to put the both twins through Cornell in that kitchen, so I'm sure I'll manage to get Kevin through," Pete volleys back. He's silent for a minute and then knits his brow. "Hey, I just had an uncomfortable thought. If we take Patricia in as a part-owner, the two of you could outvote me on this."

"Or you me," Laurie answers.

"Hmmm, we're taking quite a risk here."

"I thought you mountain climbers loved risk," Laurie answers.

"Yeah, but not when it comes to business."

"Pete, we've got to go ahead with this, risk or no risk. We'll just have to expand the pie so there's plenty for you, me and Patricia, and perhaps even for other good people who come aboard later. We'll get nowhere trying to hold onto every possible morsel and all the control."

"I guess so," Pete concedes, reluctantly. "When do you want to meet with Patricia?"

Laurie consults her pocket calendar. "How about next Monday? Santiago and I will be back by then, I'm sure."

"Monday's fine," Pete says, standing up. "Now, if you'll excuse me, I'm going to do some sit-ups while Kevin's still asleep." He pats his stomach. "Middle age," he sighs.

May you approach your partnership business with a sense of excitement and take from it not only material success, but some personal fulfillment. Or, as some say in California, may you be blessed with the centeredness that comes with having lived your dream. And keep your sense of humor. You'll need it! ■

Resources

Resources for Further Research

Here is a list of some of the materials we found useful in writing this book. It isn't an exhaustive index of a legal materials on partnerships or small businesses, but it does contain books that we believe are useful to the reader who wishes to do further research.

The best book on doing your own legal research (something that's very helpful for small business people to know how to do) is *Legal Research: How to Find and Understand the Law,* by Stephen Elias and Susan Levinkind (Nolo).

1. General Resources for Drafting Partnership Agreements

Unfortunately, aside from this book, you're unlikely to find much in a library, whether a law or public library, that will assist you if you want more help drafting your agreement. Usually, the best you can do is locate books designed to assist lawyers to draft agreements, such as (in California) *Advising California Partnerships* (CEB) and subsequent annual supplements. But not only are these books often difficult to understand, even for lawyers, they are usually not very sophisticated about actual problems. Realistically, it's generally wiser to see an experienced lawyer about a partnership agreement drafting problem than to try to solve it through further research.

2. Partnership Taxation

There are some excellent resources here if you're the type who can comprehend tax jargon. Here are two of the best and most thorough:

- *Federal Taxation of Partnerships and Partners,* by William S. McKee, William F. Nelson and Robert L. Whitmire (Warren, Gorham & Lamont).

Also useful for business tax matters:

- IRS Publication 334, *Tax Guide for Small Business*, and, if you're just getting started, IRS Publication 583, *Starting a Business and Keeping Records.*
- U.S. Master Tax Guide (CCH, Inc.). Updated annually, it features in-depth explanations of many tax complexities.

Citations to State Uniform Laws

The Uniform Partnership Act and
*The 1994 Revised Uniform Partnership Act

State	Statutory Citation
*Alabama	Code 1975, §§ 10-8A-101 to 10-8A-1109
Alaska	AS 32.05.010 to 32.05.430 and 32.06.201 to 32.06-997
*Arizona	A.R.S. §§ 29-1001 to 29-1111
*Arkansas	A.C.A. §§ 4-42-101 to 4-42-702 and 4-46-101 to 4-46-1207
California	West's Ann. Cal. Corp. Code §§ 15001 to 15045
*Colorado	C.R.S. 7-60-101 to 7-60-143 and 7-64-101 to 7-64-1206
*Connecticut	C.G.S.A. §§ 34-300 to 34-499
*Delaware	6 Del.C. §§ 15-101 to 15-1210
*District of Columbia	D.C. Code 1981, §§ 41-151.1 to 41-162.3
*Florida	West's F.S.A. §§ 620.81001 to 620.9902
Georgia	O.C.G.A. §§ 14-8-1 to 14-8-43
Guam	Guam Code Ann, §§ 25101 to 25702
*Hawaii	HRS §§ 425-101 to 425-145
*Idaho	I.C. §§ 53-301 to 53-343 and 53-3-301 to 53-3-1205
Illinois	106 Ill. Comp. Stat. Ann. 2051/1 to 205/43
Indiana	Ind. Code Ann. §§ 23-4-1-1 to 23-4-1-43
*Iowa	I.C.A. §§ 486.1 to 486.47 and §§ 486A.101 to 486A.1302
*Kansas	K.S.A. 56A-101 to 56A-1305
Kentucky	KRS 362.150 to 362.360
Maine	31 M.R.S.A. §§ 281 to 323
*Maryland	Code, Corporations and Associations, §§ 9-101 to 9-1001 and §§ 9A-101 to 9A-1205
Massachusetts	M.G.L.A. c. 108A, §§ 1 to 44
Michigan	M.C.L.A. §§ 449.1 to 449.43
*Minnesota	M.S.A. §§ 323.01 to 323.43 and 323A.1-01 to 323A.12-03
Mississippi	Code 1972, §§ 79-12-1 to 79-12-85

State	Statutory Citation
Missouri	V.A.M.S. §§ 358.010 to 358.430
*Montana	MCA 35-10-101 to 35-10-644
*Nebraska	R.R.S. 1943, §§ 67-301 to 67-343 and 67-401 to 67-467
Nevada	N.R.S. 87.010 to 87.430
New Hampshire	RSA 304-A:1 to 304-A:62
New Jersey	N.J.S.A. 42:1-1 to 42:1-43
*New Mexico	NMSA 1978, §§ 54-1A-101 to 54-1A-1206
New York	McKinney's Partnership Law, §§ 1 to 75
North Carolina	G.S. §§ 59-31 to 59-73
*North Dakota	NDCC 45-13-01 to 45-21-08
Ohio	R.C. §§ 1775.01 to 1775.42
*Oklahoma	54 Okl. St. Ann. §§ 1-100 to 1-1207
*Oregon	ORS 67.005 to 67.810 and 68.010 to 68.650
Pennsylvania	15 Pa. C.S.A. §§ 8301 to 8365
Rhode Island	Gen. Laws 1956, §§ 7-12-12 to 7-12-55
South Carolina	Code 1976, §§ 33-41-10 to 33-41-1090
South Dakota	SDCL 48-1-1 to 48-5-56
Tennessee	T.C.A. §§ 61-1-101 to 61-1-142
*Texas	Vernon's Ann. Texas Civ. St. art. 6132b §§ 1.01-10.04
Utah	U.C.A. 1953, 48-1-1 to 48-1-40
*Vermont	11 V.S.A. §§ 3201 to 3313
*Virgin Islands	26 V.I.C. §§ 1 to 274
*Virginia	Code 1950, §§ 50-73.79 to 50-73.149
*Washington	West's RCWA 25.04.010 to 25.04.430
*West Virginia	Code, 47B-1-1 to 47B-10-5
Wisconsin	W.S.A. 178.01 to 178.39
*Wyoming	W.S. 1977, §§ 17-21-101 to 17-21-1003

Uniform Limited Partnership Act (1976) With the 1985 Amendments

State	Statutory Citation	State	Statutory Citation
Alabama	Code 1975, §§ 10-9B-101 to 10-9B-1206	Montana	MCA 35-12-501 to 35-12-1404
Alaska	AS 32.11.010 to 32.11.990	Nebraska	R.R.S. 1943, §§ 67-233 to 67-297
Arizona	A.R.S. §§ 29-301 to 29-366	Nevada	N.R.S. 88.315 to 88.645
Arkansas	A.C.A. §§ 4-43-101 to 4-43-1109	New Hampshire	RSA 304-B:1 to 304-B:64
California	West's Ann. Cal. Corp. Code §§ 15611 to 15723	New Jersey	N.J.S.A. 42:2A-1 to 42:2A-72
Colorado	C.R.S. 7-62-101 to 7-62-1201	New Mexico	NMSA 1978, §§ 54-2-1 to 54-2-63
Connecticut	C.G.S.A. §§ 39-4 to 34-38q	New York	McKinney's Partnership Law, §§ 121-101 to 121-1300
Delaware	6 Del. C. §§ 17-101 to 17-1107	North Carolina	G.S. §§ 59-101 to 59-1106
District of Columbia	D.C. Code 1981, §§ 41-401 to 41-499.25	North Dakota	NDCC 45-10.1-01 to 45-10.1-62, 45-12-01
Florida	West's F.S.A. §§ 620.101 to 620.186	Ohio	R.C. §§ 1782.01 to 1782.62
Georgia	O.C.G.A. §§ 14-9-100 to 14-9-1204	Oklahoma	54 Okl. St. Ann. §§ 301 to 365
Hawaii	HRS §§ 425D-101 to 425D-1113	Oregon	ORS 70.005 to 70.490
Idaho	I.C. §§ 53-201 to 53-267	Pennsylvania	15 Pa. C.S.A. §§ 8501 to 8594
Illinois	106 Ill. Comp. Stat. Ann. 210/100 to 210/2005	Rhode Island	Gen. Laws 1956, §§ 7-13-1 to 7-13-65
Indiana	West's A.I.C. 23-16-1-1 to 23-16-12-6	South Carolina	Code 1976, §§ 33-42-10 to 33-42-2040
Iowa	I.C.A. §§ 487.101 to 487.1105	South Dakota	SDCL 48-7-101 to 48-7-1105
Kansas	K.S.A. 56-1a101 to 56-1a609	Tennessee	T.C.A. §§ 61-2-101 to 61-2-1208
Kentucky	KRS 362.401 to 362.527	Texas	Vernon's Ann. Texas Civ. St. art. 6132a-1
Maine	31 M.R.S.A. §§ 401-530	Utah	U.C.A. 1953, 48-2a-101 to 48-2a-1107
Maryland	Code, Corporations and Associations, §§ 10-101 to 10-1105	Vermont	11 V.S.A. §§ 3401 to 3503
Massachusetts	M.G.L.A. c. 109, §§ 1 to 62	Virgin Islands	26 V.I.C. §§ 321 to 575
Michigan	M.C.L.A. §§ 449.1101 to 449.2108	Virginia	Code 1950, §§ 50-73-1 to 50-73-77
Minnesota	M.S.A. §§ 322A.01 to 322A.87	Washington	West's RCWA 25.10.010 to 25.10.690
Mississippi	Code 1972, §§ 79-14-101 to 79-14-1107	West Virginia	Code, 47-9-1 to 47-9-63
Missouri	V.A.M.S. §§ 359.011 to 359.691	Wisconsin	W.S.A. 179.01 to 179.94
		Wyoming	Wyo. Stat. Ann. §§ 17-14-201 to 17-14-1104

2

How to Use the CD-ROM

The tear-out forms in Appendix 3 are included on a CD-ROM in the back of the book. This CD-ROM, which can be used with Windows computers, installs files that can be opened, printed and edited using a word processor or other software. It is *not* a stand-alone software program. Please read this Appendix and the README.TXT file included on the CD-ROM for instructions on using the Forms CD.

Note to Mac users: This CD-ROM and its files should also work on Macintosh computers. Please note, however, that Nolo cannot provide technical support for non-Windows users.

How to View the README File

If you do not know how to view the file README.TXT, insert the Forms CD-ROM into your computer's CD-ROM drive and follow these instructions:

- Windows 9x, 2000, ME and XP: (1) On your PC's desktop, double-click the My Computer icon; (2) double-click the icon for the CD-ROM drive into which the Forms CD-ROM was inserted; (3) double-click the file README.TXT.
- Macintosh: (1) On your Mac desktop, double-click the icon for the CD-ROM that you inserted; (2) double-click on the file README.TXT.

While the README file is open, print it out by using the Print command in the File menu.

A. Installing the Form Files Onto Your Computer

Word processing forms that you can open, complete, print and save with your word processing program (see Section B, below) are contained on the CD-ROM. Before you can do anything with the files on the CD-ROM, you need to install them onto your hard disk. In accordance with U.S. copyright laws, remember that copies of the CD-ROM and its files are for your personal use only.

Insert the Forms CD and do the following:

1. Windows 9x, 2000, ME and XP Users

Follow the instructions that appear on the screen. (If nothing happens when you insert the Forms CD-ROM, then (1) double-click the My Computer icon; (2) double-click the icon for the CD-ROM drive into which the Forms CD-ROM was inserted; and (3) double-click the file SETUP.HLP.)

By default, all the files are installed to the \Partnership Forms folder in the \Program Files folder of your computer. A folder called "Partnership Forms" is added to the "Programs" folder of the Start menu.

2. Macintosh Users

Step 1: If the "Partnership Forms CD" window is not open, open it by double-clicking the "Partnership Forms CD" icon.

Step 2: Select the "Partnership Forms" folder icon.

Step 3: Drag and drop the folder icon onto the icon of your hard disk.

B. Using the Word Processing Files to Create Documents

This section concerns the files for forms that can be opened and edited with your word processing program.

All word processing forms come in rich text format. These files have the extension ".RTF." For example, the clause where you state the name of your partnership is on the file NAME.RTF. As each sample clause is introduced and explained in Chapters 3–6, its corresponding file name and directory are given.

RTF files can be read by most recent word processing programs, including all versions of MS Word for Windows and Macintosh, WordPad for Windows, and recent versions of WordPerfect for Windows and Macintosh.

To use a form from the CD to create your documents you must: (1) open a file in your word processor or text editor; (2) edit the form by filling in the required information; (3) print it out; (4) rename and save your revised file.

The following are general instructions on how to do this. However, each word processor uses different commands to open, format, save and print documents. Please read your word processor's manual for specific instructions on performing these tasks.

For specific instructions on how to use the CD-ROM forms to create a Partnership Agreement, please refer to the instructions in Chapter 11.

Do not call Nolo's technical support if you have questions on how to use your word processor.

Step 1: Opening a File

There are three ways to open the word processing files included on the CD-ROM after you have installed them onto your computer.

- Windows users can open a file by selecting its "shortcut" as follows: (1) Click the Windows "Start" button; (2) open the "Programs" folder; (3) open the "Partnership Forms" subfolder;

(4) open the appropriate "Clause" subfolder, if applicable; and (5) click on the shortcut to the form you want to work with.

- Both Windows and Macintosh users can open a file directly by double-clicking on it. Use My Computer or Windows Explorer (Windows 9x, 2000 or ME) or the Finder (Macintosh) to go to the folder you installed or copied the CD-ROM's files to. Then, double-click on the specific file you want to open.

- You can also open a file from within your word processor. To do this, you must first start your word processor. Then, go to the File menu and choose the Open command. This opens a dialog box where you will tell the program (1) the type of file you want to open (*.RTF); and (2) the location and name of the file (you will need to navigate through the directory tree to get to the folder on your hard disk where the CD's files have been installed). If these directions are unclear you will need to look through the manual for your word processing program—Nolo's technical support department will *not* be able to help you with the use of your word processing program.

Where Are the Files Installed?

- Windows Users: Files are installed by default to a folder named \Partnership Forms in the \Program Files folder of your computer.
- Macintosh Users: Files are located in the "Partnership Forms" folder.

Step 2: Editing Your Document

Fill in the appropriate information according to the instructions and sample agreements in the book. Underlines are used to indicate where you need to enter your information, frequently followed by instructions in brackets. *Be sure to delete the underlines and instructions from your edited document.* If you do not know how to use your word processor to edit a document, you will need to look through the manual for your word processing program—Nolo's technical support department will *not* be able to help you with the use of your word processing program.

Editing Clauses That Have Optional or Alternative Text

Some of the clauses have optional or alternative text:
- With optional text, you choose whether to include or exclude the given text.
- With alternative text, you select one alternative to include and exclude the other alternatives.

When editing these forms, we suggest you do the following:

Optional text

If you **don't want** to include optional text, just delete it from your document.

If you **do** want to include optional text, just leave it in your document.

In either case, delete the italicized instructions.

Alternative text

First delete all the alternatives that you do not want to include, then delete the italicized instructions.

Step 3: Printing Out the Document

Use your word processor's or text editor's "Print" command to print out your document. If you do not know how to use your word processor to print a document, you will need to look through the manual for your word processing program—Nolo's technical support department will *not* be able to help you with the use of your word processing program.

Step 4: Saving Your Document

After filling in the form, use the "Save As" command to save and rename the file. Because all the files are "read-only," you will not be able to use the "Save" command. This is for your protection. *If you save the file without renaming it, the underlines that indicate where you need to enter your information will be lost and you will not be able to create a new document with this file without recopying the original file from the CD-ROM.*

If you do not know how to use your word processor to save a document, you will need to look through the manual for your word processing program—Nolo's technical support department will *not* be able to help you with the use of your word processing program. ■

3

Partnership Agreements

Sample Partnership Termination Agreement

Tear-Out Short-Form Partnership Agreement

Tear-Out Partnership Agreement

Sample Partnership Termination Agreement

_____ ("AT") _____ and _____ ("KC") _____ agree as follows:

I. RECITALS

1. PARTNERSHIP. AT and KC have been and are now partners doing business under the name of AT & KC ASSOCIATES, with its principal place of business in Oakland, California.

2. PARTNERSHIP AGREEMENT. The partners entered into said partnership and have continued in partnership under the provisions of an agreement in writing, dated _____, 20__.

3. DESIRE TO DISSOLVE. The partners now desire to adopt a plan for a sale of part of the partnership and of dissolution for their partnership and liquidation of its affairs, in two steps.

4. VALUATION. The partners agree that each partnership asset disclosed in the partnership balance sheet has a present fair market value equal to its book value to the partnership and that consideration in excess of book value reflected in this Agreement is attributable to goodwill not shown on the balance sheet.

II. DISSOLUTION

1. PURCHASE BY AT. AT hereby purchases forty-nine percent (49%) of the partnership interest of KC, and KC hereby sells and irrevocably assigns to AT the said forty-nine percent interest in consideration of: (A) AT's $5,500 negotiable promissory note in the form of Exhibit A hereto and (B) AT's agreement to hold KC free and harmless from all partnership debts and liabilities.

2. GUARANTEED PAYMENTS. KC has received since January 1, 20__ and shall continue to receive through calendar year 20__, guaranteed payments from the partnership, by way of remuneration for services rendered, at the rate of $1,000 per month. Except for such guaranteed payments, KC shall receive no another amounts from the partnership.

3. AMENDMENT OF PARTNERSHIP AGREEMENT. The Agreement of Partnership is hereby amended to provide that from and after _____, 20__, AT alone shall exercise management and control over partnership decisions, and that from and after that date, the profits and losses of the partnership with corresponding items of taxable income or deductible loss will be shared ninety-nine percent (99%) for AT and one percent (1%) for KC.

4. COMPETITION PERMITTED. From and after _____, 20___ each partner shall be free to conduct consulting activities apart from the partnership, even to the extent of competing with the partnership.

5. INSURANCE. KC shall continue to receive health and automobile liability insurance coverage under the partnership's policies through December 31, 20___.

   Upon execution of this Agreement, KC shall be entitled to assume the life insurance policy on her life presently carried by the partnership.

6. LEASE. AT and KC both shall continue to be named a lessee under the existing lease for the partnership's present principal office. However, AT shall pay all rent accruing from and after _____, 20___.

7. ACCESS. KC shall, for the present term of the existing lease on the partnership's principal place of business, have full access to and use of an office in the partnership premises and access to its files.

8. NAME. AT shall not use the partnership's name or any name confusingly similar thereto in any new business conducted by him following liquidation of the partnership.

   a. During the period from _____,20___ through _____,20___ either partner shall be entitled to refer to the partnership name solely for purposes of indicating transition from the partnership to his or her new business.

   b. After _____,20___ either partner's use of the partnership name shall be only to the extent necessary to identify prior projects that either has completed.

9. TERMINATION AND LIQUIDATION. On December 31, 20___, the partnership shall purchase KC's remaining one percent (1%) interest for a price of $_____ and the partnership shall be dissolved, liquidated and terminated. Upon such termination and liquidation, AT shall own all of the assets of the partnership and shall satisfy all its debts and liabilities, subject to the restrictions on use of the partnership name as specified in Paragraph 8 of this Agreement. From December 31, 20___ on, except for the purposes of carrying out the liquidation of the partnership, neither of the partners shall do any further business nor incur any further obligations on behalf of the partnership.

III. LIQUIDATION

1. ACCOUNTING. As of December 31, 20___, the partners shall cause an accounting to be made by the then partnership accountants of all of the assets of the partnership and of the respective equities of the creditors and the partners in the assets as of the effective date of the dissolution.

2. DISCLOSURE. Except as appears by the books of the partnership, each of the partners represents that he or she has not heretofore contracted any liability that can or may charge the partnership or the other partner, nor has he or she received or discharged any of the credits, monies or effects of the partnership.

3. SETTLING ACCOUNTS. Upon completion of the accounting, the partners shall pay all of the liabilities of the partnership including those owing to the partners other than for capital in accordance with *[the applicable state law]*. Payment of liabilities owing to the partners shall include payment of profits for the current accounting period computed on the basis of actual cash receipts to completion of the accounting. All amounts received after completion of the accounting shall be the sole property of AT.

IV. EXECUTION AND ENFORCEMENT

1. SURVIVAL OF REPRESENTATIONS. The representations and agreements set forth herein shall be continuous and shall survive the taking of any accounting.

2. SUCCESSORS AND ASSIGNS. This Agreement shall inure to the benefit of and bind the successors, assigns, heirs, executors and administrators of the partners.

Executed on _____,20___ at Oakland California.

_____

AT

_____

KC

Short-Form Partnership Agreement

_____, _____,

_____, _____, and

_____, agree as follows:

1. That as of _____, 20_____, they are partners in a business known as

_____

_____.

2. That the general purpose of the business is _____

_____

_____

_____

_____

_____.

3. That the partners now agree that _____

_____

_____

_____

_____

_____

_____

_____

_____.

4. That the partners further agree that they will prepare, by _____, 20_____
   a final and complete partnership agreement governing the partnership, and that the agreement
   will cover at least:

   * Contributions of each partner to the partnership

   * Distribution of profits and losses

   * Management powers and responsibilities

   * Admission of new partners

   * The departure of a partner for any reason

   * Arbitration.

To formalize this short-form partnership agreement, each partner has signed his or her name on the date below:

Signature: _____ Dated: _____

Signature: _____ Dated: _____

Signature: _____ Dated: _____

Signature: _____ Dated: _____

Signature: _____ Dated: _____

Signature: _____ Dated: _____

Partnership Agreement

☐ This Partnership Agreement is entered into and effective as of _____ 20_____ , by:

_____

_____ , the partners.

1. NAME

☐ The name of the partnership shall be _____

_____ .

☐ The name of the partnership business shall be _____

_____ .

2. TERM OF THE PARTNERSHIP

Lasts Until Dissolved on Death of Partner

☐ The partnership shall last until it is dissolved by all the partners, or a partner leaves, for any reason, including death.

Lasts Until Dissolved or Partner Withdraws

☐ The partnership shall last until it is dissolved by all the partners or until a partner withdraws, retires, dies or otherwise leaves the partnership, under Sections _____ and _____ of this Agreement.

Lasts for Set Term of Years

☐ The partnership shall commence as of the date of this Agreement and shall continue for a period of _____ years, at which time it shall be dissolved and its affairs wound up.

Lasts Until Set Date

☐ The partnership shall continue until _____

_____ at which time it shall be dissolved and its affairs wound up.

3. PURPOSES OF THE PARTNERSHIP

☐ The purpose of the partnership is: _____

_____

_____

_____

_____

_____ .

Statement of the Partners' Goals

☐ The specific purposes of the partnership are set out above. In addition, the goals and dreams of each partner are set out below. The partners understand that this clause is not legally binding, but include it in the Partnership Agreement as a record of their hopes and intentions:

_____

_____

_____

_____

_____

_____

_____

_____

_____

_____

_____ .

4. CONTRIBUTIONS

Contributions of Cash

Equal Cash Contribution

☐ The initial capital of the partnership shall be a total of $_____ . Each partner shall contribute an equal share amounting to $_____ , no later than _____, 20___. Each partner shall own an equal share of the business.

Unequal Cash Contribution

☐ The initial capital of the partnership shall consist of cash to be contributed by the partners in the following amounts:

Name	Amount
_____	$_____
_____	$_____
_____	$_____

Each partner's contribution shall be paid in full by _____, 20___.

Each partner's ownership share of the business shall be:

Name	Amount
_____	_____
_____	_____
_____	_____

Equal Cash Contributions, With a Partner Loaning Additional Cash

☐ The initial capital of the partnership shall be a total of $_____. Each partner shall contribute an equal share amounting to $_____, no later than _____, 20____. In addition, _____ shall loan the partnership $_____ by _____, 20____. The partnership shall pay _____ percent interest on the loan.

Unequal Cash Contributions, to Be Equalized By One Partner's Extra Work in the Business

☐ The initial capital of the partnership shall consist of cash to be contributed by the partners in the following amounts:

Name	Amount
_____	$_____
_____	$_____
_____	$_____
_____	$_____

Each partner's contribution shall be paid in full by _____, 20____. In addition, to equalize the contributions, _____ shall contribute an extra _____ hours of work valued at $_____ until the amount contributed by all partners is equal.

Deferred Contributions

Monthly Installments

☐ _____ shall be a partner, but shall not make any contribution of cash or property to the initial capital of the partnership. _____ shall subsequently contribute to the partnership capital, and _____ capital account shall be credited, in the amount of $_____ per month, beginning _____, 20____, until _____ has contributed the sum of $_____.

Contribution Out of Profit

☐ _____ shall be a partner, but shall not make any contribution of cash or property to the initial capital of the partnership. _____ shall subsequently contribute to the partnership capital, and _____ capital account shall be credited _____ percent of _____ share of the partnership profits for each fiscal year, beginning _____, 20____, until _____ has contributed the amount of $_____.

Payment of Interest on Contributed Capital

No Interest Paid

☐ No partner shall be entitled to receive any interest on any capital contribution.

Interest to be Paid

☐ _____ shall be entitled to interest on his or her capital contribution accruing at the rate of _____ percent per year from the date the contribution is paid. This interest shall be treated as an expense to be charged against income on the partnership books and shall be paid to the partner entitled to it _____

_____.

Contributions of Property

Specific Property Contributed

☐ _____

shall contribute property valued at $_____, consisting of _____

_____ by _____, 20___.

Loans of Property to the Partnership

☐ In addition to the capital contributions defined in this Agreement, some partners have or will loan to the partnership additional items of property, as specified below:

_____ shall loan

_____.

_____ shall loan

_____.

Each item of property lent to the partnership shall remain the separate property of the lending partner and shall be returned to that partner _____.

Intellectual Property—Ownership Transferred to the Partnership

☐ _____, the owner of

_____ hereby agrees to transfer all _____ interest in this _____ to the partnership with the understanding that all _____ interest in the _____, including the sole right to license derivative works, shall vest in, and be owned by, the partnership and shall not be _____ separate property. In exchange for this transfer, it is agreed that _____

_____ shall be credited with a contribution of $_____ to the partnership. No sale or assignment of, or grant of license under the _____ shall be made without the consent of all the partners. Any monies resulting from any such sale, assignment or grant of license shall be divided _____.

Intellectual Property—Only Use Transferred to the Partnership

☐ _____, the owner of

_____ hereby contributes

to the partnership the nonexclusive use of that _____, to the partnership, with

the understanding that _____ shall retain sole ownership of the _____,

along with the sole right to license its use to third parties, and it shall not become a partnership

asset. _____ further agrees that until the termination

of the partnership, or until _____ death or retirement from it, _____ will not, without the

consent of all other partners, sell, assign or grant licenses under this _____.

Any money accruing from a sale or assignment of, or the grant of licenses under such

_____, which are so authorized, shall be the sole property

of _____. For the purpose of profit-sharing

only, and not for participation in the distribution upon the termination and winding up of the

partnership, the partnership will credit _____

_____ with a contribution in the amount of $_____.

Contributions of Service

Contribution of Services

☐ _____ shall make

no cash or property contribution at the commencement of the partnership. _____

_____ shall donate _____

and energies to the partnership for a period of _____ and for those

services _____ shall be entitled to _____ percent ownership of the business.

Contribution of Profits from Service Partner

☐ Should _____ share of the profits, as defined

in this Agreement, exceed _____, _____ shall contribute the excess

to _____ capital account in the business until the total amount of _____ capital account

shall _____.

Failure to Make Initial Contribution

Partnership Dissolves

☐ If any partner fails to pay his or her initial contribution to the partnership as required by this
Agreement, the partnership shall immediately dissolve and each partner who has paid all or
any portion of his or her initial contribution to the partnership's capital shall be entitled to a
return of the funds and properties he or she contributed.

Partnership Continues for Partners Who Have Made Contributions, and No Additional Contribution Required

☐ If any partner fails to pay his or her contribution to the partnership's capital as required by this Agreement, the partnership shall not dissolve or terminate, but it shall continue as a partnership of only the partners who have made their initial capital contributions as required and without any partner who has failed to do so. In that case, the share in the partnership's profits and losses allocated under this Agreement to any partner who has failed to make his or her initial contribution shall be reallocated to the remaining partners in proportion to their respective shares of partnership profits and losses as specified in this Agreement.

Partnership Continues—Additional Contributions Are Required

☐ If any partner fails to pay his or her initial contributions to the partnership's capital as required by this Agreement, the partnership shall not dissolve or terminate, but shall continue as a partnership of the partners who have made their initial capital contributions and without any partner who shall have failed to do so, but only if the remaining partners pay the initial capital contribution that was to have been made by the noncontributing partner or partners. The partnership shall promptly give written notice of this failure to all partners who have made their initial capital contributions. The notice shall specify the amount not paid. Within _____ days after the notice is given, the remaining partners shall pay the amount of the defaulted contribution in proportion to the respective amount they are required to pay to the partnership's capital under this Agreement. That share of the profits of the partnership belonging to noncontributing partners shall then be reallocated to the remaining partner in proportion to their respective shares of partnership profits and losses under this Agreement.

Failure of Service Partner to Actually Perform Service

☐ If _____ fails to contribute the services promised, the partnership shall proceed as follows:

_____

_____

_____ .

Additional Future Contributions

If Future Contributions Needed

☐ If, at any future time, more money is required to carry on the partnership business, and all partners vote to increase the capital contributions required by partners, the additional capital shall be paid in by the partners _____

_____ .

Requirement of Annual Contributions by Partners

☐ Each partner shall contribute annually _____ percent of his or her share of each year's profits
[or $_____] to the partnership's capital for a period of _____ years.
If any partner fails to make such contribution, _____.

No Voluntary Contributions Without Consent

☐ No partner may make any voluntary contribution to the partnership without the written content
of all the other partners.

5. PROFITS AND LOSSES

Distribution of Profits and Losses

Equal Shares

☐ The partners will share all profits equally, and they will be distributed _____
_____.

All losses of the partnership shall also be shared equally.

Unequal Shares: Set Percentages

☐ The partnership profits and losses shall be shared among the partners as follows:

Name	Percentage
_____	_____ %
_____	_____ %
_____	_____ %
_____	_____ %

Unequal Shares: Different Percentages for Profits and Losses

☐ The partnership profits and losses shall be shared among the partners as follows:

Name	Percentage of Profits	Percentage of Losses
_____	_____ %	_____ %
_____	_____ %	_____ %
_____	_____ %	_____ %
_____	_____ %	_____ %

Unequal Shares: Profits and Losses Keyed to Capital Contributions

☐ The partnership's profits and losses shall be shared by the partners in the same proportions as
their initial contributions of capital bear to each other.

Draws to Partners

Draws Authorized

☐ Partners _____ and

_____ are entitled to

draws from expected partnership profits. The amount of each draw will be determined by a vote

of the partners. The draws shall be paid _____

_____ .

Draws Prohibited

☐ No partner shall be entitled to any draw against partnership profits. Distributions shall be made

only as provided in this Agreement, or upon subsequent unanimous written agreement of the

partners.

Draws Exceeding Partners' Actual Shares of Profits To Become Loans to Partners

☐ Notwithstanding the provisions of this Agreement governing drawing permitted by partners, to

the extent any partner's withdrawals for draws under those provisions during any fiscal year of

the partnership exceed his or her share in the partnership's profits, the excess shall be regarded

as a loan from the partnership to him or her that he or she is obligated to repay within _____

days after the end of that fiscal year.

Retention of Profits for Business Needs

General Limitation on Distribution to Retain Cash Business Needs

☐ In determining the amount of profits available for distribution, allowance will be made for the

fact that some money must remain undistributed and available as working capital as determined

by _____ .

Specific Limitation on Distribution to Retain Cash Business Needs

☐ The aggregate amounts distributed to the partners from the partnership profits shall not exceed

_____ percent of any net income above $_____ .

Salaries

Salaries to Partners

☐ Partners can be paid reasonable salaries for work they perform in the partnership business.

No Salaries to Partners

☐ No partner will be paid any salary, except those that may in the future be decided on by

unanimous written consent of all partners.

6. MANAGEMENT POWERS AND DUTIES

Skills Contributed

☐ Each partner named below shall participate in the business by working in the manner described:

Partner   Type of Work

_____   _____

_____   _____

_____   _____

_____   _____

Hours Worked

☐ Except for vacations, holidays and times of illness, each partner shall work _____ hours per week on partnership business.

Leaves of Absence

☐ Any partner can take a leave of absence from the partnership under the following terms and conditions:_____

_____

_____.

All Partners Work in Business

☐ All partners shall be actively involved and materially participate in the management and operation of the partnership business.

Decisions

All Decisions Unanimous

☐ All partnership decisions must be made by the unanimous agreement of all partners.

Major/Minor Decisions

☐ All major decisions of the partnership business must be made by a unanimous decision of all partners. Minor business decisions may be made by an individual partner. Major decisions are defined as:_____

_____.

Unequal Management Powers

In Accordance With Contributed Capital

☐ Each partner shall participate in the management of the business. In exercising the powers of management, each partner's vote shall be in proportion to his or her interest in the partnership's capital.

By Fixed Percentage as Agreed on by Partners

☐ In the management, control, and direction of the business, the partners shall have the following percentages of voting power:

Name   Percentage

_____ _____ %

_____ _____ %

_____ _____ %

Financial Matters

Periodic Accountings

☐ Accountings of _____ shall

be made every _____.

Accounting on Request by a Partner

☐ Accountings of any aspect of partnership business shall be made upon written request by any partner.

Accountant To Determine Profits and Losses

☐ The partnership's net profit or net loss for each fiscal year shall be determined as soon as practicable after the close of that fiscal year. This should be done by a certified public accountant, _____ in accordance with the accounting principles employed in the preparation of the federal income tax return filed by the partnership for that year, but without a special provision for tax-exempt or partially tax-exempt income.

Power To Borrow Money

☐ A partner can borrow money on behalf of the partnership in excess of $_____ only with prior consent of all partners.

Expense Accounts Authorized

☐ An expense account, not to exceed $_____ per month, shall be set up for each partner for his or her actual, reasonable, and necessary expenses during the course of the business. Each partner shall keep an itemized record of these expenses and be paid once monthly for them on submission of the record.

Expense Accounts Not Authorized

☐ The partners individually and personally shall assume and pay:

- All expenses for the entertainment of persons having relations with firm.
- Expenses associated with usual business activities.

Signature Required on Partnership Checks

☐ All partnership funds shall be deposited in the name of the partnership and shall be subject to withdrawal only on the signatures of at least _____ partners.

Prohibition Against Commingling

☐ All partnership funds shall be deposited only in bank accounts bearing the partnership name.

For Businesses Receiving Funds To Be Held in a Trust Account

☐ All trust and other similar funds shall be deposited in a trust account established in the partnership's name at _____ bank, and shall be kept separate and not mingled with any other funds of the partnership.

Meetings

☐ For the purpose of discussing matters of general interest to the partnership, together with the conduct of its business, partners shall meet _____ or at such other times agreed upon by the majority of the partners.

Maintenance of Records

☐ Proper and complete books of account of the partnership business shall be kept at the partnership's principal place of business and shall be open to inspection by any of the partners or their accredited representative at any reasonable time during business hours.

Vacation

☐ Each partner shall be entitled to _____ weeks paid [or unpaid] vacation per year.

Sick leave

☐ The partnership's sick leave policy for partners is:

_____

_____

_____.

Outside Business Activities

Permitted, Except for Direct Competition

☐ Any partner may be engaged in one or more other businesses as well as the business of the partnership, but only to the extent that this activity does not directly and materially interfere with the business of the partnership and does not conflict with the time commitments and other obligations of that partner to the partnership under this Agreement. Neither the partnership nor any other partner shall have any right to any income or profit derived by a partner from any business activity permitted under this section.

Permitted

☐ It is understood and agreed that each partner may engage in other businesses, including enterprises in competition with the partnership. The partners need not offer any business opportunities to the partnership, but may take advantage of those opportunities for their own accounts or for the accounts of other partnerships or enterprises with which they are associated. Neither the partnership nor any other partner shall have any right to any income or profit derived by a partner from any enterprise or opportunity permitted by this section.

Specific Activities Permitted

☐ The list below specifies business activities that each partner plans or may do outside of the partnership business. Each partner is expressly authorized to engage in these activities if he or she so desires: _____

_____

_____

_____.

Restricted

☐ As long as any partner is a member of the partnership, he or she shall devote his or her full work time and energies to the conduct of partnership business, and shall not be actively engaged in the conduct of any other business for compensation or a share in profits as an employee, officer, agent, proprietor, partner, or stockholder. This prohibition shall not prevent him or her from being a passive investor in any enterprise, however, if he or she is not actively engaged in its business and does not exercise control over it. Neither the partnership nor any other partner shall have any right to any income or profit derived from any such passive investment.

Ownership of Business Assets

Trade Secrets

☐ All trade secrets used or developed by the partnership, including customer lists and sources of supplies, will be owned and controlled by the partnership.

Patents

☐ Any ideas developed by one or another of partners pertaining to partnership business that are the subject of an application for a patent shall be partnership property.

Copyrights

☐ All copyrighted materials in the partnership name are, and shall remain, partnership property.

Business Name

☐ The partnership business name of _____
_____ shall be partnership property. In the event
of the departure of a partner and/or dissolution of the partnership, control and ownership of the
partnership business name shall be determined pursuant to this Agreement.

Provision for a Managing Partner

Authority of Managing Partner

☐ The managing partner shall be _____. The
managing partner shall have control over the business of the partnership and assume direction
of its business operations. The managing partner shall consult and confer as far as practicable
with the non-managing partners, but the power of decision shall be vested in the managing
partner. The managing partner's power and duties shall include control over the partnership's
books and records and hiring any independent certified public accountant the managing
partner deems necessary for this purpose. On the managing partner's death, resignation or
other disability, a new managing partner shall be selected by a majority of the partners.

Limited Authority for Managing Partner

☐ The managing partner shall be _____.
The managing partner shall have control over routine business transactions and day-to-day
operating decisions. The managing partner shall not make any major or basic decisions without
consent of a majority of the partners. A major or basic decision is defined as: _____
_____
_____.

Salary of Managing Partner

☐ The managing partner shall be paid a monthly salary of $_____ or such other amount
that may be determined by the unanimous written agreement of the partners. This salary shall
be treated as a partnership expense in determining its profits or losses.

Managing Partner Handles All Money of the Partnership

☐ All partnership funds shall be deposited in the partnership's name and shall be subject to
withdrawal only on the signature of the managing partner.

Managing Partner Handles Operating Fund Only

☐ All partnership funds shall be deposited in the partnership's name and shall be subject to
withdrawal only on the signatures of at least _____ partners, except that a separate
account may be maintained with a balance never to exceed $_____. The amounts in
that separate account shall be subject to withdrawal on the signature of the managing partner.

7. TRANSFER OF A PARTNER'S INTEREST

Sale to Partnership at Its Option

☐ If any partner leaves the partnership, for whatever reason, whether he or she quits, withdraws, is expelled, retires, becomes mentally or physically incapacitated or unable to function as a partner or dies, or if the partner attempts to or is ordered to transfer his or her interest, whether voluntarily or involuntarily, he or she or his or her estate shall be obligated to sell his or her interest in the partnership to the remaining partner or partners, who have the option, but not the obligation, to buy that interest. However, if the departing partner receives a bona fide offer from a prospective outside buyer, the Right of First Refusal Clause of this Agreement shall apply.

The Right of First Refusal Upon Offer from Outside

☐ If any partner receives a bona fide, legitimate offer, whether or not solicited by him or her, from a person not a partner, to purchase all of his or her interest in the partnership, and if the partner receiving the offer is willing to accept it, he or she shall give written notice of the amount and terms of the offer, the identity of the proposed buyer, and his or her willingness to accept the offer to each of the other partners. The other partner or partners shall have the option, within _____ days after the notice is given, to purchase that partner's interest on the same terms as those contained in the offer.

Refusal of the Remaining Partners To Buy

☐ If the remaining partner or partners do not purchase the departing partner's share of the business, under the terms provided in this Agreement, within _____ the entire business of the partnership shall be put up for sale, and listed with the appropriate sales agencies, agents or brokers.

Requiring Advance Notice of Withdrawal

☐ Unless physically prevented from giving notice, a partner shall give _____ written advance notice of his or her intention to leave the partnership. If he or she fails to do so _____.

Conflicts Regarding Right to Buy

The Coin Flip

☐ If the partners cannot agree on who has the right to purchase the other partners' interest in the business, that right shall be determined by the flip of a coin (to be flipped by _____ _____).

Auction Bidding

☐ If the partners cannot agree who has the right to purchase the other partners' interest in the business, that right shall be determined by an auction, where each group of partners shall bid

on the business. The group eventually offering the highest bid shall have the right to buy the lower bidder's shares of the business. The buying group shall pay for the purchased share of the business under the terms provided in this Agreement.

8. BUY-SELL AGREEMENT

Specific Buy-Out Methods

Asset-Valuation Method

☐ Except as otherwise provided in this Agreement, the value of the partnership shall be made by determining the net worth of the partnership as of the date a partner leaves, for any reason. Net worth is defined as the market value, as of that date, of the following assets:

1. All tangible property, real or personal, owned by the business;

2. All the liquid assets owned by the business, including cash on hand, bank deposits and CDs or other monies;

3. All accounts receivable;

4. All earned but unbilled fees;

5. All money presently earned for work in progress;

6. Less the total amount of all debts owed by the business.

Set-Dollar Method

☐ Except as otherwise provided in this Agreement, the value of a partner's interest in the partnership shall be determined as follows:

1. Within _____ days after the end of each fiscal year of the partnership, the partners shall determine the partnership's value by unanimous written agreement, and that value shall remain in effect from the date of that written determination until the next such written determination.

2. Should the partners be unable to agree on a value or otherwise fail to make any such determination, the partnership's value shall be the greater of (a) the value last established under this section, or (b) _____

   _____

   _____.

3. _____

   _____

   _____

   _____.

Revision of Valuation Method to include Goodwill

☐ The partners understand and agree that the preceding business-valuation clause may not fully and adequately reflect the worth of the business after it has been successfully established, if the business has earned goodwill or has other valuable intangible assets. Therefore, the partners agree that _____ after the commencement of the business they will meet to consider amending this business-valuation clause to include a method that will reflect any goodwill earned by the business.

Post-Departure Appraisal

☐ Except as otherwise provided in this Agreement, the value of the partnership shall be determined by an independent appraisal conducted, if possible, by _____ _____. If all partners cannot agree on appraiser, the departing partner and the remaining partners shall each select an independent appraiser. If the two selected appraisers are unable to agree on the fair market value of the partnership business, then the two appraisers shall mutually select a third appraiser to determine the fair market value.

The appraisal shall be commenced within _____ days of the partner's departure from the partnership. The partnership and the departing partner shall share the cost of the appraisal equally.

The Capitalization of Earnings Method

☐ Except as otherwise provided in this Agreement, the value of the partnership shall be determined as follows:

1. The average yearly earnings of the business shall be calculated for the preceding _____ _____.

2. "Earnings," as used in this clause, is defined as: _____.

3. The average yearly earnings shall then be multiplied by a multiple of _____ to give the value of the business, except as provided for in Section 4, below;

4. Additional factors: _____ _____ _____ _____.

Varying the Buy-Out Price

☐ The preceding method for calculating the value of the business shall be varied as stated below, for the reasons stated below:

_____
_____
_____
_____

Insurance Proceeds: Disability or Death of a Partner

☐ If a partner becomes disabled or dies, the value of his or her interest in the partnership, including for estate purposes, shall be the proceeds paid by the disability or death insurance policy maintained by the partnership [or other partners] for that partner.

Consent of Spouse

☐ I, _____, the _____ of _____, have read and understand this Partnership Agreement and hereby consent to all clauses and terms in it. I specifically agree that the business valuation method contained in the Agreement shall be used in any legal proceeding to determine the value of any interest I may have in the business.

Dated: _____   _____

Payments

Equal Monthly Payments

☐ Whenever the partnership is obligated or chooses to purchase a partner's interest in the partnership, it shall pay for that interest by promissory note of the partnership. Any promissory note shall be dated as of the effective date of the purchase, shall mature in not more than _____ years, shall be payable in equal installments that come due monthly [and shall bear interest at the rate of _____ percent per annum] [and may, at the partnership's option, be subordinated to existing and future debts to banks and other institutional lenders for money borrowed]. The first payment shall be made _____ days after the date of the promissory note.

Lump Sum, Then Equal Monthly Payments

☐ Whenever the partnership is obligated to, or chooses to, purchase a partner's interest in the partnership, it shall pay for that interest as follows:

First: It shall pay the departing partner _____ within _____.

Second: After that initial payment, it shall pay the balance owed by promissory note of the partnership. Any promissory note shall be dated as of the effective date of the purchase, shall mature in not more than _____ years, shall be payable in equal installments that come due monthly [shall bear interest at the rate of _____ percent per annum] [and may, at the partnership's option, be subordinated to existing and future debts to banks and other institutional lenders for money borrowed]. The first payment shall be made _____ days after the date of the promissory note.

Cash Payment

☐ Whenever the partnership is obligated or chooses to purchase a partner's interest in the partnership, it shall pay for that interest in cash within _____.

Assumption of Departing Partner's Liabilities

☐ The continuing partnership shall pay, as they come due, all partnership debts and obligations that exist on the date a partner leaves the partnership, and shall hold the departing partner harmless from any claim arising from these debts and obligations.

9. CONTINUITY OF PARTNERSHIP BUSINESS

Partnership Continues

☐ In the case of a partner's death, permanent disability, retirement, voluntary withdrawal, expulsion from the partnership or death, the partnership shall not dissolve or terminate, but its business shall continue without interruption and without any break in continuity. On the disability, retirement, withdrawal, expulsion or death of any partner, the others shall not liquidate or wind up the affairs of the partnership, but shall continue to conduct a partnership under the terms of this Agreement.

Noncompetition Clause

☐ On the voluntary withdrawal, permanent disability, retirement, death or expulsion of any partner, that partner shall not carry on a business the same as or similar to the business of the partnership within the _____ for a period of _____.

Control of the Business Name

Partnership Continues To Own Name

☐ The partnership business name of _____ is owned by the partnership. Should any partner cease to be a member of the partnership, the partnership shall continue to retain exclusive ownership and right to use the partnership business name.

One Partner Owns Name

☐ The partnership business name of _____ _____ shall be solely owned by _____ _____, if _____ ceases to be a partner.

Control of Name To Be Decided at Later Date

☐ The partnership business name of _____ is owned by the partnership. Should any person cease to be a partner and desire to use the partnership business name, and the remaining partners desire to continue the partnership and continue use of the partnership business name, ownership and control of the partnership business name shall be decided by _____.

Dissolution: Majority Owns Name

☐ In the event of dissolution, the partnership business name of _____ _____ shall be owned by a majority of the former partners. Any other former partner is not entitled to ownership or use of the partnership business name.

Expulsion of a Partner

☐ A partner may be expelled from the partnership by a vote of _____

_____

_____

_____

_____.

Expulsion shall become effective when written notice of expulsion is served on the expelled partner. When the expulsion becomes effective, the expelled partner's right to participate in the partnership's profits and his or her other rights, powers and authority as a partner of the partnership shall terminate. An expelled partner shall be entitled to receive the value of his or her interest in the partnership, as that value is defined in this Agreement.

A Partner's Bankruptcy and Expulsion

☐ Notwithstanding any other provision of this Agreement, a partner shall cease to be a partner and shall have no interest in common with the remaining partners or in partnership property when the partner does any of the following:

1. Obtains or becomes subject to an order of relief under the Bankruptcy Code.
2. Obtains or becomes subject to an order or decree of insolvency under state law.
3. Makes an assignment for the benefit of creditors.
4. Consents to or accepts the appointment of a receiver or trustee to any substantial part of his or her assets that is not vacated within _____ days.
5. Consents to or accepts an attachment or execution of any substantial part of his or her assets that's not released within _____ days.

From the date of any of the preceding events, he or she shall be considered as a seller to the partnership of his or her interest in the partnership as set forth in this Agreement.

If a partner is expelled for one of the above reasons, the partnership shall not be dissolved, but shall continue to function without interruption.

Expulsion and Arbitration

☐ Any decision of expulsion made by the partners pursuant to this Agreement shall be final and shall not be subject to arbitration or other review, including review by any court.

Insurance and Partner's Estate Planning

Cross-Purchase of Life Insurance

☐ Each partner shall purchase and maintain life insurance [and disability insurance] on the life of each other partner in the face value of $_____.

Partnership Insurance Policies

☐ The life insurance policies owned by the partnership on the lives of each partner are assets of the partnership only in so far as they have cash surrender value preceding the death of a partner.

Insurance Polices and Partner's Departure

☐ On the withdrawal or termination of any partner for any reason other than his or her death [add "or disability" if the partners purchase disability insurance on each other], any insurance policies on his or her life ["or health"], for which the partnership paid the premiums, shall be delivered to that partner and become his or her separate property. If the policy has a cash surrender value, that amount shall be paid to the partnership by the withdrawing partner, or offset against the partnership's obligations to him or her.

10. MEDIATION AND ARBITRATION

Mediation

☐ 1. The partners agree that, except as otherwise provided in this Agreement, any dispute arising out of this Agreement or the partnership business shall first be resolved by mediation, if possible. The partners are aware that mediation is a voluntary process, and pledge to cooperate fully and fairly with the mediator in any attempt to reach a mutually satisfactory compromise to a dispute.

2. The mediator shall be _____.

3. If any partner to a dispute feels it cannot be resolved by the partners themselves, after mediation has been attempted, he or she shall so notify the other partners, and the mediator, in writing.

4. Mediation shall commence within _____ days of this notice of request for mediation.

_____

_____.

5. Any decision reached by mediation shall be reduced to writing, signed by all partners, and be binding on them.

6. The costs of mediation shall be shared equally by all partners to the dispute.

Arbitration

Arbitration With One Arbitrator

☐ 1. The partners agree that, except as otherwise provided in this Agreement, any dispute arising out of this Agreement, or the partnership business, shall be arbitrated under the terms of this clause. The arbitration shall be carried out by a single arbitrator _____

_____.

Any arbitration shall be held as follows:

2. The partner(s) initiating the arbitration procedure shall inform the other partner(s) in writing of the nature of the dispute at the same time that he or she notifies the arbitrator.

3. Within _____ days from receipt of this notice, the other partners shall reply in writing, stating their views of the nature of the dispute.

4. The arbitrator shall hold a hearing on the dispute within seven days after the reply of the other partner(s). Each partner shall be entitled to present whatever oral or written statements he or she wishes and may present witnesses. No partner may be represented by a lawyer or any third party.

5. The arbitrator shall make his or her decision in writing.

6. If the partner(s) to whom the demand for arbitration is directed fails to respond within the proper time limit, the partner(s) initiating the arbitration must give the other an additional five days' written notice of "intention to proceed to arbitration." If there is still no response, the partner(s) initiating the arbitration may proceed with the arbitration before the arbitrator, and his or her award shall be binding.

7. The cost of arbitration shall be borne by the partners as the arbitrator shall direct.

8. The arbitration award shall be conclusive and binding on the partners and shall be set forth in such a way that a formal judgment can be entered in the court having jurisdiction over the dispute if either party so desires.

Arbitration With Three Arbitrators

☐ The partners agree that, except as otherwise provided in this Agreement, any dispute arising out of this Agreement or the partnership business shall be arbitrated under the terms of this clause. The arbitration shall be carried out by three arbitrators. Each partner or side to the dispute shall appoint one arbitrator. The two designated arbitrators shall appoint the third arbitrator.

The arbitration shall be carried out as follows:

1. The partner(s) initiating the arbitration procedure shall inform the other partner(s) in writing of the nature of the dispute at the same time that they designate one arbitrator.

2. Within _____ days from receipt of this notice, the other partners shall reply in writing naming the second arbitrator, and stating their view of the nature of the dispute.

3. The two designated arbitrators shall name a third arbitrator within ten days from the date the second arbitrator is named. If they cannot agree _____

_____ .

4. An arbitration meeting shall be held within _____ days after the third arbitrator is named.

5. Each partner shall be entitled to present whatever oral or written statements he or she wishes and may present witnesses. No partner may be represented by a lawyer or any third party.

6. The arbitrators shall make their decision, in writing.

7. If the partner(s) to whom the demand for arbitration is directed fails to respond within the proper time limit, the partner(s) initiating the arbitration must give the other an additional five days' written notice of "intention to proceed to arbitration." If there is still no response, the partner(s) initiating the arbitration may proceed with the arbitration before the arbitrators, and their award shall be binding.

8. The cost of arbitration shall be borne by the partners as the arbitrators shall direct.

9. The arbitration award shall be conclusive and binding on the partners and shall be set forth in such a way that a formal judgment can be entered in the court having jurisdiction over the dispute if either party so desires.

Combining Mediation with Arbitration

☐ If the partners cannot resolve the dispute by mediation, the dispute shall be arbitrated as provided in the arbitration clause of this Agreement.

Time for Mediation

☐ If the partners have not resolved their dispute within _____ of the commencement of mediation, the partners shall have failed to have resolved their dispute by mediation under this Agreement, and the dispute shall be arbitrated.

11. AMENDMENTS

Amendment

By Unanimous Agreement

☐ This Agreement may be amended only by written consent of all partners.

As Specified

☐ This Agreement may be amended by _____

_____ .

Admission of New Partner(s)

Addition by Unanimous Written Agreement of All Partners

☐ A new partner or partners may be added to the partnership only by unanimous written consent of all existing partners.

Addition by Less Than All Partners

☐ A new partner may be admitted to the partnership with the written approval of _____
_____ .

Admitting a New Partner When You've Failed To Plan Ahead

☐ _____
_____ have been engaged in business at
_____
_____ as a partnership under the firm name of _____
_____ . They now intend to admit
_____ to their
partnership, and all the members of the expanded partnership desire to amend and clarify the
terms and conditions of their Partnership Agreement and to reduce their agreement to writing.

No Dissolution of the Partnership When a New Partner Joins

☐ Admission of a new partner shall not cause dissolution of the underlying partnership business,
which will be continued by the new partnership entity.

The Incoming Partner's Liability for Existing Partnership Debts

Not Responsible for Partnership Debts Before Becoming Partners

☐ _____ shall not be personally
responsible for, or assume any liability for, any debts of _____
_____ incurred on or before _____, 20___.

Responsible for Partnership Debts From Set Date

☐ _____ hereby
expressly assumes personal liability for debts of _____
_____ incurred on or before _____, 20___, equal
to the amount of his or her contribution to the partnership, totaling $_____ .

Responsible for All Partnership Debts

☐ _____ hereby
expressly assumes full personal liability equal to the personal liability of all other partners in the
partnership of _____
for all partnership debts and obligations whenever incurred.

www.nolo.com

Partnership Agreement

12. GENERAL PROVISIONS

State Law

☐ The partners have formed this general partnership under the laws of the State of _____

_____, intending to be legally bound thereby.

Attached Papers Incorporated

☐ Any attached sheet or document shall be regarded as fully contained in this Partnership Agreement.

Agreement Is All Inclusive

☐ This Agreement contains the entire understanding of the partners regarding their rights and duties in the partnership. Any alleged oral representations of modifications concerning this Agreement shall be of no force or effect unless contained in a subsequent written modification signed by all partners.

Binding on All Successors and Inheritors

☐ This Agreement shall be binding on and for the benefit of the respective successors, inheritors, assigns and personal representatives of the partners, except to the extent of any contrary provision in the Agreement.

Severability

☐ If any term, provision, or condition of this Agreement is held by a court of competent jurisdiction to be invalid, void or unenforceable, the rest of the Agreement shall remain in full force and effect and shall in no way be affected, impaired or invalidated.

13. ADDITIONAL PROVISIONS

_____

_____

_____

_____

_____

_____

_____

_____

_____

Signature: _____ Dated: _____

Signature: _____ Dated: _____

Signature: _____ Dated: _____

Index

Remember:

Little publishers have big ears.
We really listen to you.

Take 2 Minutes & Give Us Your 2 cents

Your comments make a big difference in the development and revision of Nolo books and software. Please take a few minutes and register your Nolo product—and your comments—with us. Not only will your input make a difference, you'll receive special offers available only to registered owners of Nolo products on our newest books and software. Register now by:

PHONE
1-800-728-3555

FAX
1-800-645-0895

EMAIL
cs@nolo.com

or **MAIL** us
this registration card

fold here

Registration Card

NAME _____ DATE _____

ADDRESS _____

_____

CITY _____ STATE _____ ZIP _____

PHONE _____ E-MAIL _____

WHERE DID YOU HEAR ABOUT THIS PRODUCT? _____

WHERE DID YOU PURCHASE THIS PRODUCT? _____

DID YOU CONSULT A LAWYER? (PLEASE CIRCLE ONE)   YES   NO   NOT APPLICABLE

DID YOU FIND THIS BOOK HELPFUL?   (VERY)   5   4   3   2   1   (NOT AT ALL)

COMMENTS _____

_____

_____

WAS IT EASY TO USE?   (VERY EASY)   5   4   3   2   1   (VERY DIFFICULT)

We occasionally make our mailing list available to carefully selected companies whose products may be of interest to you.

❑ If you do not wish to receive mailings from these companies, please check this box.

❑ You can quote me in future Nolo promotional materials.
Daytime phone number _____.

PART 6.3

Nolo
in the
NEWS

"Nolo helps lay people perform legal tasks without the aid—or fees—of lawyers."

—USA TODAY

Nolo books are ... *"written in plain language, free of legal mumbo jumbo, and spiced with witty personal observations."*

—ASSOCIATED PRESS

"...Nolo publications...guide people simply through the how, when, where and why of law."

—WASHINGTON POST

"Increasingly, people who are not lawyers are performing tasks usually regarded as legal work... And consumers, using books like Nolo's, do routine legal work themselves."

—NEW YORK TIMES

"...All of [Nolo's] books are easy-to-understand, are updated regularly, provide pull-out forms...and are often quite moving in their sense of compassion for the struggles of the lay reader."

—SAN FRANCISCO CHRONICLE

fold here

```
┌─────────────┐
│             │
│    Place    │
│  stamp here │
│             │
│             │
└─────────────┘
```

Nolo
950 Parker Street
Berkeley, CA 94710-9867

Attn: **PART 6.3**